Best Irish Walks

Best Irish Walks

THIRD EDITION

EDITOR: JOSS LYNAM

Gill & Macmillan

Gill & Macmillan Ltd
Hume Avenue, Park West, Dublin 12
with associated companies throughout the world
www.gillmacmillan.ie
© Jean Boydell, David Herman, Joss Lynam, Miriam McCarthy,
Sean Ó Súilleabháin, Dick Rogers, The Estate of the late Patrick Simms,
The Estate of the late Tony Whilde, 1998, 2001
0 7171 3065 7
Maps by EastWest Mapping, Clonegal, Enniscorthy, Co. Wexford
Print origination by Carole Lynch
Printed by ColourBooks Ltd, Dublin

This book is typeset in 9½ on 12 point Palatino

The paper used in this book is made from the wood pulp of managed forests. For every tree felled, at least one tree is planted, thereby renewing natural resources.

All rights reserved. No part of this publication may be copied, reproduced or transmitted in any form or by any means, without permission of the publishers.

A CIP catalogue record for this book is available from the British Library.

Maps for Walks 1–68 are based on Ordnance Survey Ireland
by permission of the Government (Permit No. 7273).
© Government of Ireland
Maps for Walks 69–76 are based on the Ordnance Survey of
Northern Ireland with the permission of the Controller of
Her Majesty's Stationery Office
© Crown Copyright (Permit No. 1682).

3 5 4

CONTENTS

Southwest

West

MOUNTAIN SAFETY

The Irish hills are still relatively unfrequented. This is a happy situation for hill-walkers unless they get into serious trouble and need help. As this may well have to come from a considerable distance, it is particularly important to take all reasonable precautions.

1. Wear suitable clothing, and regardless of the weather carry extra warm clothes, wind- and water-proof anorak and overtrousers. Except on short, easy walks it is best to wear walking boots.

2. Plan your walk carefully and be sure you can complete it before dark. To estimate walking times see page 3.

3. Check weather forecasts and keep a look out for weather changes. On high ground, mist and rain can close in with alarming speed.

4. Remember that the temperature drops 2–3°C for each 300m you climb and if, as is frequently the case, there is a strong wind, the temperature drop will be even more marked. It may be a pleasant day at sea level whilst freezing and windy at 800m.

5. Always carry a map and compass, and learn to use them efficiently in good weather so that you will have confidence in your ability to use them in bad. A torch, whistle and small first aid kit should also be taken — remember that the mountain distress signal is six blasts per minute and then a pause.

6. Carry a reserve supply of food including chocolate, glucose tablets, etc., and something warm to drink.

7. Leave word at your hotel, guest house or hostel where you are going, what your route will be and when you intend to get back. If you are parking a car at the beginning of a walk, you can leave a note on the seat.

8. Streams in flood are dangerous and extreme caution is necessary.

9. If your party does have an accident, telephone 999 and ask for the Mountain Rescue or contact the local Garda Station who will organise the rescue.

10. Never walk solo, except in areas where there are other people around.

11. Remember that most accidents happen on the descent, when you are tired, so take special care then.

Some of the precautions listed above are obviously designed for the longer, higher walks but do remember that especially in winter, the Irish hills can be dangerous.

PROTECTING THE COUNTRYSIDE

Ireland has recently introduced a new Occupiers' Liability Act — dealing with the liability of farmers or other landowner for accidents which may happen to a walker or other user crossing their land. The act creates a new category of 'Recreational Users' who, when they enter farmland, are responsible for their own safety and for the safety of any children in their care. This will, it is to be hoped, make farmers, who have been worried about the possibility of claims following accidents to walkers, more willing to permit walkers to cross their land. The Irish Farmers Association, working with the Mountaineering Council of Ireland and other user bodies, has drawn up the following code to which all walkers and other users should adhere:

The Farmland Code of Conduct

- Respect farmland and the rural environment.
- Do not interfere with livestock, crops, machinery or any other property which does not belong to you.
- Guard against all risks of fire.
- Leave all farm gates as you find them.
- Always keep children under close control and supervision.
- Avoid entering farmland containing livestock. Your presence can cause stress to livestock and even endanger your own safety.
- Do not enter farmland if you have dogs with you, even on a leash, unless with the permission of the occupier.
- Always use gates, stiles or other recognised entry points.
- Take all litter home.
- Do not pollute water supplies.
- Take special care on country roads.
- Avoid making unnecessary noise.
- Protect wildlife, plants and trees.
- Take heed of warning signs — they are there for your protection.
- If following a recognised walking route, keep to the way-marked trail.
- Report any damage caused by your actions to the farmer or landowner immediately.
- Do not block farm entrances when parking.

Access

Most land traversed by these walks is private property (even the open hillsides) and generally is the workplace of a farmer. You cross this private property at the discretion of the owner; except on public roads, these walks are *not* 'rights of way'. Some walkers may be confused by the word 'commonage' on the open hillsides. In Ireland, this means private property held in common by a number of joint owners.

The rest of the walks is either on public roads or state property (National Parks or Forestry).

You should be prepared (and allow) for changes, whether temporary/ seasonal (rotation of crops or animals, tree planting or felling), or permanent (re-routing of paths or roads, or change of ownership). If asked to leave, please do so, politely and without argument.

It could be said that the contents of a guidebook are up to date only when last revised. The editor will be happy to hear from readers of any changes in route noted while walking.

Dogs — Warning!

The Farmland Code of Conduct on page 1 points out that walkers should not enter farmland with a dog unless with the permission of the owner. This includes open hillsides where there are often sheep grazing. A dog found attacking sheep may legally be shot by the landowner.

MAPS AND SCALES

For the walker, Ireland used to be one of the worst mapped countries in Europe, but over the last 10–15 years the whole island has been re-surveyed and we have good, up-to-date 1:50,000 coverage of both the Republic (OS) and Northern Ireland (OSNI). I have only one caveat: the survey has generally relied very heavily on air photographs, so that paths and other small features that did not show up in the photography are sometimes misplaced or omitted (especially in woods).

There are also some very useful local maps published commercially, and both the relevant OS 1:50,000 map and any other relevant maps are noted below the sketch map for each walk.

Ordnance Survey and other useful maps

1:250,000 Holiday map in four sheets (OSI and OSNI). This map is useful for general planning.

OS/OSNI 1:50,000 series covering the whole country (see above).

1:25,000. These are few but excellent where they exist: MacGillycuddy's Reeks (reprinting), Killarney National Park (both OS), and Mourne Country (OSNI).

Folding Landscapes: Mountains of Connemara (1:50,000), Connemara (1 inch to 1 mile, 1:63,360), Burren (2 ins to 1 mile, 1:31,680).

Harvey Maps: Connemara Superwalker (1:30,000).

Cork–Kerry Tourism: Dingle Way, Kerry Way (1:50,000 strip maps).

Pat Healy, Curragh: Glendalough–Glenmalure (1:25,000).

Walking Times

Walking times have been calculated on the basis of 4km per hour, and 400m ascent per hour. This is roughly equivalent to 2½ miles per hour, and 1,300ft ascent per hour. These are fairly generous, and should allow you the occasional stop to admire the view, look at the map, take photographs, or recover your breath. They do not allow for protracted lunch stops. Extra time has been allowed if the going is difficult, and vice-versa.

Please note that distances such as 'Walk 300m' are approximate. Since all the maps noted above are metric, all heights and distances are in metric units. However since Irish cars are still using miles, both metric and imperial units are given for motorised approaches, and also for final distance and height calculations.

3

THE WEATHER

The two main factors which shape the weather in Ireland are the Atlantic Ocean and the westerly airflow of the middle latitudes. The westerly airflow brings us a succession of frontal systems, and the ocean ensures that we do not get too cold in winter, or too warm in summer.

The depressions which cross the Atlantic mostly pass north of Ireland, and their associated fronts sweep across the country at a rate of 170 a year, each front bringing its quota of rain. It is no good pretending that Ireland does not get a lot of rain; it does, but because the fronts are generally fairly fast-moving, the rain rarely lasts for very long.

There is a definite seasonal pattern. The early winter (December and January) is characterised by rapidly moving depressions which bring strong winds — often gales — from the west, and heavy rainfall. In late winter and spring (February–May/June) the Continental high-pressure area tends to spread to Ireland and there are occasional visitations from the Greenland high. This produces drier weather, and May is generally the best month in the year. In late June and July the oceanic winds usually re-establish themselves, bringing more rain; and in August the combination of heat and high humidity often produces thunderstorms. In late August and September, cold northerly air masses cause depressions, but often there will be a week or two of fine anticyclonic weather. October and November are characterised by westerlies bringing frontal rain; in November the occasional anticyclone may again produce fine (but often foggy) weather.

Rainfall is perhaps the aspect of the weather that most affects the walker; March, April and May have the most dry days and December and January have the fewest. There is, of course, considerably more rain in the west, where the hills along the west coast force the clouds to rise and discharge their moisture. Most of the western hills have rain on more than 225 days in the average year, while the Mournes, Wicklow Hills and the sandstone mountains of the southeast have less than 200 days with rain. Even in the west there is a substantial difference as you move inland — to take an example in Connemara, when the rain is beating down on the Twelve Bens the hills around Lough Nafooey may be dry.

Apart from wetting the climber as it falls, the rain has the further disadvantage that it causes the Irish hills to be mostly wet underfoot. Many of the valleys are boggy, and while the ridges are usually dry, there are big wet plateaux (such as Maumtrasna) covered in bogland. This is not to say that there are not plenty of good hill walks (quite apart from the 76 mentioned in this book) which are mainly on dry ground, but it is true that, except in a dry summer, it is hard to walk the Irish hills (especially in the west) without a little bit of bog-trotting.

A second important aspect of the weather for the hill-walker is the prevalence of mist and cloud. The clouds will often descend to below 450m in the hills and this poses navigational problems, easily solved by the walker who has a map and compass and knows how to use them, but potentially dangerous for those who are unprepared.

Ireland gets very little snow. The Gulf Stream warms the west coast and so the MacGillycuddy's Reeks, which as the highest mountains in Ireland would be likely to have the greatest snowfall, rarely hold snow for very long. It is the Wicklow Hills, in the colder east, which generally do hold the snow; most years Lugnaquilla may, for a few weeks, be a serious proposition even by the easiest route up Camara Hill. The Mournes also hold snow. There does however seem to be a trend towards milder winters, and Lugnaquilla had very little snow in recent winters. In February, March and April, though, the walker will often have a fine day on the hills with a dusting of snow brought by cold east or northeast winds, not sufficient to provide technical problems, but enough to brighten the sombre colours of the winter or early spring landscape.

The statistics of mist and rain are a little depressing, and perhaps suggest a picture of grey, drab walks in poor visibility. While this may well happen sometimes, a truer picture of Irish hill weather is changeability. There will rarely be a day on the hills when the wind will not blow the mist away and the sun gleam through the clouds to reflect off the streams and pick out the bright greens and russets of the hillsides. Especially in the early summer, there are plenty of days with blue skies and hardly a cloud.

The art of dealing with the weather in the Irish hills is the same as everywhere else — be prepared. Remember always that the temperature drops by anything up to 3°C per 300m of climb, and so a pleasant day at sea-level may be cold on the top of Lugnaquilla. Remember, also, that the wind is often 2½ times as strong at 900m as it is at sea-level, so carry wind-proof clothing and a spare pullover, even if the sky is blue. For that matter, be prepared for the rain even if the sky is blue!

For information about the weather, there are the usual forecasts on radio and television and in the newspapers. As in other countries, these are geared to sea-level activities and need intelligent interpretation for the hills. There are a number of telephone forecasts available including Weathertel live where you can speak to a forecaster (1580–222–221). Other automatic regional forecast numbers can be found in the telephone directory.

ACKNOWLEDGMENTS

This guide is the result of much collaboration, and I am glad to record the names of the collaborators. The walk descriptions have been researched and written by Jean Boydell, David Herman, Miriam McCarthy, Seán Ó Súilleabháin, Dick Rogers, the late Patrick Simms, the late Tony Whilde and occasionally by your Editor. Tony Whilde wrote the Flora and Fauna and Ruth Lynam the Geology, while Bairbre Sheridan prepared the Glossary of Irish terms. I am to blame for the rest! Justin May and the late Nuala Creagh drew the maps for the first two editions, Barry Dalby of EastWest Mapping for this third edition. Fergal Tobin of Gill & Macmillan was patient . . . Thanks to them all and especially to my wife Nora, whose support, helpful criticism and patience through forty-nine years of marriage has always amazed my friends (and even me!). Without that support neither this guide nor many other projects could have been completed.

Patrick Simms
Patrick Simms, contributor to this guidebook, died in November 1997. He had a lifelong love of the hills and a wide experience of the mountains of Northern Ireland. His knowledge and friendship will be sadly missed by the Irish hill-walking community.

Tony Whilde
Tony Whilde, contributor to this guidebook, died from a brain tumour on 8 February 1995. Ecologist, walker, author and lecturer, he devoted much of his life and career to the conservation of the West of Ireland, which he loved. His untimely death is a tragedy for all who knew him and shared his affection for the West.

INTRODUCTION TO THE FIRST EDITION

It is seventeen years since Gill & Macmillan asked me to edit a series of Walking Guides to Ireland. Since then the series has changed shape and had one rebirth. Now we are making a one volume selection of 76 walks out of the 232 walks in the four volumes. It was difficult enough making the original selection, but it has been far worse filleting that selection to one-third its size. The first principle, obviously, was to select the best and most typical in each area, the second was to prefer circular walks, the third was to omit isolated walks (unless they were very important) and concentrate on giving a good selection in the best areas. But please don't forget that for every walk in the guide, there are not just two, but a dozen others waiting, and if you have a map (yes, we begin to have some good maps!) and compass there is nothing to stop you exploring them.

My own first Irish mountain was Knocknarea, all of 327m high in Co. Sligo in 1930 at the age of six, and while there are still quite a few I haven't walked, I suppose I have sampled the hills of most corners of the country and found something worth visiting in all of them.

We do have a great variety of hills. In Wicklow there are rounded domes of granite incised by steep-sided lake-filled valleys like Glendalough and Luggala. The sandstone mountains of the southeast offer their own variety — the dull tableland of the Comeraghs redeemed by the wonderful coums which edge it contrasting with the rolling Galtees, easy underfoot and with well defined tops.

There is more sandstone in the southwest (Kerry and West Cork). Erosion has bitten deeper than in the southeast and the coums have cut back to leave only steep narrow ridges between them. Here are almost all the highest mountains of Ireland — all but two of the '3,000 footers' are in Kerry. Carrauntuohill, the highest, attracts a lot of traffic, but other areas offer you really wild walks on which you are most unlikely to meet a walker or even a shepherd. The contrast between the high peaks and the narrow fjords is another pleasure of the southwest, indeed of the west coast generally.

The quartzite mountains of Connemara, gleaming white in the sun after rain, don't have the narrow arêtes of Kerry, but they offer ridges, peaks and passes that are as rough and challenging as any in the country in the tangled ridges of the Twelve Bens and in the long line of high peaks and deep cols of the Maumturks. In Mayo we are back to sandstone and whole ranges of unfrequented hills (except for quartzite Croagh Patrick, holy mountain of Saint Patrick, and easily the most trodden of Irish hills). In Sligo the limestone of Benbulbin's great prow is unique in Ireland, and it is here you will have your best chance of keeping your feet dry on the Irish hills.

Donegal has everything from granite domes and quartzite cones to magnificent sea cliff walks. Antrim hills don't attract me, but the Antrim and Derry coast are unbeatable for interest, both natural (Giant's

Causeway) and man-made (Dunluce and all the other castles). The Mournes are the most compact group of mountains in the country — you can cross them in half a day, but you can spend years exploring them. They are granite, but much younger, and with their rocky tors, conical summits and deep cols, are in total contrast to Wicklow.

Not so many years ago I pooh-poohed the idea of the Irish hills being crowded, and stressed the need for map and compass because there were no paths. This is no longer true of the Mournes or Wicklow, where you will find paths, not made paths, but paths worn by the passage of boots — and mountain bike wheels. Walking the rest of the country, with some exceptions (Carrauntuohill, Croagh Patrick and a few others) you can still find pathless, unfrequented hills.

The absence of paths and other walkers, to my mind, adds greatly to the enjoyment of the hills. I confess to having gratefully followed paths off Cumbrian and Cambrian mountains in the mist, but how much more satisfying it is to navigate off a mountain with map, compass and watch. Undoubtedly the lack of people and paths necessitates a little more caution on the part of the walker. Crossing deep heather or bogland is slower than striding along a path; you can't rely on getting advice from other walkers on the route, and map and compass are absolutely essential.

One change in recent years is that landowners are less accommodating to walkers. Vandals, thoughtless walkers, sheep-worrying dogs, the upsurge of accident claims, sheer numbers of people have soured many farmers, and even the most accommodating fear that, as the law stands, they are easy targets for unscrupulous claimants. If you keep to the walks in this guide, you shouldn't have too many difficulties, but of course I can't guarantee that the situation won't change, that fences won't be built, 'No Trespassers' signs be erected. Within the last year new legislation has been enacted greatly reducing the duties of landowners and occupiers to 'recreational users'. It is to be hoped that this will reassure farmers who have often discouraged walkers for fear of being held responsible for accidents. Walkers can help by being responsible: close gates, disturb domestic animals as little as possible, don't damage walls or fences, remove litter, keep dogs (and children!) under control, and if in doubt ask permission. Another result of greater numbers has been that theft from car parks in popular areas has increased greatly. Don't leave valuables in cars, do lock them always. I don't want to sound depressing, Ireland has always been a friendly country, and with very few exceptions, walkers will still meet a friendly welcome.

If you enjoy the walks in this book, and want to explore further, there are plenty of more detailed guidebooks. You will find many of them listed in the Bibliography.

The Bibliography also lists many books which will add to your enjoyment of walks, by giving you background information on natural history, folklore, history, etc. in more detail than we can find space for here.

I must draw your attention also to the network of long distance way-marked trails, particularly those which cross the mountain areas. They are hardly mentioned in this guide, because we have preferred to suggest circular walks, but you could make a wonderful walking tour by combining (for instance) the Kerry Way or the Western Way in Connemara with a number of the mountain walks given in this guide. See the Bibliography for sources!

I finish with a plea. As a nation we are not tidy, we are not environmentally conscious — the 'green' vote is only 1–2% at elections. I expect this guide will be bought by many walkers from outside the country. Please don't leave litter, please don't light fires, please keep to paths if they exist — in other words don't follow the bad examples you may see around you!

Joss Lynam
September 1996

INTRODUCTION TO THE THIRD EDITION

Four years on, a third edition... There are changes: a few, sadly, because of access difficulties, more because experience has shown better routes, some of these due to the full coverage of Ireland by up-to-date 1:50,000 maps.

One point in the old Introduction I would like to re-emphasise. Walking numbers are still increasing, and erosion is becoming a greater problem; at some places in the Wicklow and Kerry National Parks, erosion by many feet has made board walks necessary, and thoughtless use of mountain bikes across soft bogland has created wide, churned-up areas. These eroded areas are still small compared with Ireland's untouched mountains and moorlands. I ask you to take care to avoid more erosion.

Litter. I am happy to say that the 'green' vote has doubled to 4%, but on the other hand the litter problem has by no means halved!

Finally, please do read and comply with the two boxes on page 2 on Access and Dogs.

Good walking!

Joss Lynam
December 2000

ACCESS AND ACCOMMODATION
(See Useful Addresses, page 200, for addresses and phone numbers of organisations mentioned.)

Access
There are numerous car-ferry services from Britain:
Cairnryan/Stranraer–Larne
Holyhead–Dublin/Dun Laoghaire

Pembroke/Fishguard–Rosslare
Swansea–Cork
There are also fast catamaran services from Stranraer to Larne, Holyhead to
Dun Laoghaire/Dublin, Liverpool to Dublin, Fishguard to Rosslare.
Ireland is served by almost daily direct car-ferry services from Continental
Europe:
Cherbourg–Rosslare/Cork
Roscoff–Cork

The four major airports in Ireland: Belfast, Dublin, Cork and Shannon.
These are well served by flights from several UK airports and most major
continental airports, as well as from the US and Canada. There are
connections to regional airports of which Kerry (Farranfore, near Killarney),
Galway, Knock (Mayo) and Sligo are the most useful.

Railways are scarce, but where they exist, the services are good. Timetables
from Iarnrod Eireann.

Buses on major routes are frequent, but country buses are rare, and in the
mountain districts almost non-existent. You may find that you can travel to
the start of your walk one day, but have to wait to return at least until the
next day, and perhaps for a week! Timetables are obtainable from Bus
Eireann for the Republic, and Ulsterbus for Northern Ireland. There are also
a few private services.

Accommodation
Bord Fáilte Eireann (Irish Tourist Board) and the Northern Ireland Tourist
Board issue guides listing all registered hotels, guest houses, hostels,
caravan parks and farmhouse accommodation. These are updated each
year, and give detailed information about prices, types of accommodation
etc. The hill-walker who is looking at the cheaper end of the scale will find
in the ubiquitous B & B (bed and breakfast), a friendly welcome and good
value for money. In your travels you will see many B & B signs without the
shamrock of Bord Fáilte registration. Some of these are very good, some
aren't, but one of them might save you a long walk some evening! Some
B & Bs provide an evening meal, others don't, so beware of getting stranded
dinnerless far from any restaurant.
    Information on youth hostels (which are open to all ages) can be
obtained from An Oige in the Republic and YHANI in Northern Ireland. Of
course you have to be a member to use a youth hostel, but joining is pretty
simple, and can generally be done at the hostel. There are also a large
number of independent hostels, similar in style to the youth hostels, though
with fewer rules, and varying from the excellent to the horrible. Most of
them are listed in the Hostel Guide of the Independent Hostels
Organisation (100 hostels). The Independent Holidays Hostels of Ireland

are all Bord Fáilte approved. Irish hostels of all varieties are mostly simple in style and usually self-catering. Especially in the more remote areas they tend to be fairly small and have a relaxed and friendly atmosphere. During the summer, especially at weekends, they soon fill up, and you are advised to book in advance.

There are not many official campsites in Ireland and most of them are geared to caravans rather than tents (some do not accept tents). However 'wild' camping is often possible. Obviously if you are anywhere near a farm, you should ask permission, but this will rarely be refused. Camping in the forests of Coillte, the semi-State forestry company, is forbidden, as is lighting of fires.

Elsewhere we mention the growing network of long distance way-marked trails. Bord Fáilte publishes a list of accommodation suitable for walkers on or close to the trails. This list includes some 'Specialist Walkers Accommodation' not listed in their main guide, and for this reason, and because much of the accommodation listed is in the mountain areas, it is worth getting this list, even if you are not interested in way-marked trails.

A final option, if you are planning a fairly static holiday, is to rent a cottage and look after yourselves. Bord Fáilte issues a guide to self-catering accommodation. Many of these cottages are well-placed for the mountaineer.

GEOLOGY

According to modern geological theory, the earth's crust is made up of many plates which drift independently. When plates collide, one of the results is crumpling and disturbance of the plate margins, in which there is general uplift of the zone, and some material is buried and subjected to heat and pressure. These effects may be so extreme that the buried material melts and rises towards the surface again, forming great blisters of liquid which solidify slowly, becoming coarse-grained, crystalline rocks, such as granite or gabbro. If the blisters break through to the surface, the molten material pours out and quickly cools, to form fine-grained volcanic rocks — basalt for example. The final result of such a collision is a new mountain range.

In time the new range is worn down to a series of rounded stumps, such as we see in the mountains of Ireland, exposing the underlying granites and metamorphic rocks. However, the Irish mountain landscape has been rejuvenated by glaciation, which produced sharp peaks and steep-sided valleys from what would have been a gentle plateau landscape. Remnants of such a plateau can be seen in the flat summits of Devil's Mother and Mweelrea in Connemara, the Comeraghs in Waterford, and some parts of the Wicklow Mountains.

Irish mountain geology is dominated by two main mountain-building episodes, known as the Caledonian and Hercynian. The NE–SW oriented Caledonian episode took place over a long period, ending about 450 million years ago. Sandstones, shales and limestones were metamorphosed to become quartzites, gneisses, schists and marbles, now found in Connemara, Mayo, Donegal, and Tyrone; later granites were found in these areas, and also in East Leinster and near Newry (Knocklayd). Quartzite is an extremely resistant rock and, though it often occurs in thin bands it still tends to form prominent peaks, which are characteristically steep and cone-shaped. There are many examples: Errigal, Muckish, Slieve League, Slieve Snaght (Inishowen) in Donegal; the Twelve Bens and the Maumturks in Connemara; Nephin, Corranabinnia, Croaghaun in Mayo. Granite is also a very hard rock but it is susceptible to chemical attack, and as successive layers are peeled away, rounded, often dome-shaped mountains are formed. Slieve Snaght (Derryveagh) in Donegal, the Wicklow Range, Mount Leinster and Knocklayd are made up of granite intruded at the end of the Caledonian episode. Mount Leinster, Mullaghcleevaun, Tonelagee, Kippure, Lugnaquilla are all characteristic granite mountains, although their flanks have been modified and steepened by glacial action. Lugnaquilla is mainly granite, but the summit rock is the shaly remnant of the original roof over the granite blister. The relatively low rolling Croaghgorms in Donegal are also granite mountains.

While the Caledonian upheaval was still going on, Connemara and South Mayo were covered by the sea, and huge thicknesses of sandstones, conglomerates and shales were laid down. Much of this was folded in the final stages of the Caledonian. Then a general uplift of the area produced a high plateau, which was gradually dissected by rivers and whose relief was much later exaggerated by glaciation. Mweelrea, Devil's Mother, Ben Gorm all have broad flat summits and are separated by deep glacial valleys which often follow weaknesses such as fractures or, as in the case of Glenummera, a soft shale band. Croagh Patrick, made of sediments of the same age, marks the site of an ancient submarine channel where highly quartz-rich sandstones (sedimentary quartzites) were deposited, and shows the characteristic cone-shaped quartzite outline.

Around the same time as the Leinster granite was emplaced, about 400 million years ago when the Caledonian disturbances had finally ended, Ireland became part of a large European land mass with a desert climate, and vast amounts of the reddish-coloured sandstones and shales known as old red sandstone accumulated. Then the sea encroached again, and in the warm shallow waters limestones were laid down on top of the old red sandstone and were followed by a variety of sandstones, shales, and limestones (including coal measures). Limestone can be dissolved by rainwater, and where it is exposed, as in the Burren in Co. Clare, a karst landscape is produced with caves, ephemeral lakes (turloughs), and limestone pavements, and very little surface drainage.

However, about 340 to 280 million years ago the second mountain-building episode, known as the Hercynian, took place. The main zone of deformation lay to the south of Ireland along an approximately E–W line, but the old red sandstone and limestone of Cork and Kerry were compressed and folded. When the folds were subjected to weathering, the limestone was removed from the up-folds (anticlines) exposing the hard sandstone cores which resisted further erosion. The result was a series of parallel high sandstone ridges, such as the peninsulas of Iveragh, Beara and Dingle, including many prominent peaks: Mullaghanattin, Knocknagantee, Coomacarrea, Carrauntuohill and the Reeks, Purple Mountain, Mangerton on the Iveragh Peninsula; Hungry Hill and Eskatarriff on the Beara Peninsula; Brandon and Baurtregaum on the Dingle Peninsula. To the north, further from the main Hercynian zone, the folds are broader and gentler, but have weathered out in a similar way. The Comeraghs, the Galtees, Knockmealdowns, and Keeper Hill are all isolated inliers of upfolded old red sandstone (and older rocks) surrounded by low-lying limestone country.

The last major disturbance to affect Ireland was extensive rifting and associated volcanic activity centred along the Irish Sea about 70 to 50 million years ago. At this time the Mourne Mountains granite was emplaced. These mountains, though generally steeper than those of the Leinster granite, show the same rounded or dome-shaped outlines.

The most recent geological event to have a major effect on Irish mountain landscape was the glaciation of the Pleistocene Ice Ages. During the Pleistocene epoch, starting about 200,000 years ago, periods of general cold known as the Ice Ages, during which Ireland was practically buried under ice, were interspersed with warmer periods when the ice receded. Though a relatively minor event, glaciation had a major impact on the landscape as there have been no great modifying influences since.

In mountain areas the ice had a mainly erosive effect. As the climate deteriorated small patches or lenses of ice built up in hollows, particularly on north- and east-facing slopes sheltered from sun and prevailing winds, and as a lens grew the weight of the ice forced it to creep downhill, becoming a glacier. The small ice patches carved deep, steep-sided corries out of the hillsides, and the corrie glaciers amalgamated to form a valley glacier which exploited any existing valley or weakness, deepening and straightening it to produce a characteristic trough or U-shaped valley, with steep sides and a broad flat floor. Corries and U-shaped valleys are often occupied now by lake or a string of lakes (paternoster lakes), or sometimes by an obviously inadequate stream which meanders across the valley floor. There are numerous examples of corries in Ireland: Coumshingaun in the Comeraghs is a well-known one, and others include the Lough Bray corries below Kippure, Devil's Punch Bowl on the Mangerton, and Coum Gowlaun north of Devil's Mother. The Doolough valley east of Mweelrea is a typical U-shaped glacial valley, as are the Poisoned Glen facing Errigal, Silent Valley in the Mournes, the Gap of Dunloe between Purple Mountain and the Reeks, and Glendalough in Wicklow where the stream still flows through its old valley before dropping steeply into the glacial trough.

In many cases, such as the Wicklow Mountains, the mountain tops protruded through the ice as nunataks, and have been subjected to severe attack by frost. Constant freezing and thawing led to soils becoming so saturated with water that they would creep ('solifluct') downhill, exposing the underlying rock. If this was granite, the surface layers, weakened by chemical action, quickly disintegrated and soliflucted off the sounder layers, leaving a tower-shaped remnant known as a tor. Tors are conspicuous on summits and breaks of slope in the Mournes, and also occur in the Blackstairs and (rarely) in the Dublin and Wicklow Mountains.

When corries were excavated along opposite sides of a narrow ridge, a sharp steep-sided spine or arête was left, jagged and rotten from exposure to frost. Arêtes wind their way between the corries, linking pyramidal-shaped peaks. There are many fine arêtes in the mountains of Cork and Kerry, including that connecting Caher, Carrauntuohill and Beenkeragh.

Spillways are another type of spectacular valley associated with glaciation. When the ice began to melt, the meltwater was sometimes impounded between unmelted ice and surrounding hills, until it poured through a gap in the hills scouring a deep gorge-like spillway.

Glacial deposits are a smaller-scale feature of mountainous areas. Moving ice carries large amounts of material on the surface of, below, and within, the ice. Debris carried on top of the glacier was sloughed off along the valley sides as lateral moraine, and when the ice melted the terrace thus formed indicates the depth of ice that once filled the valley. Other debris was dumped at the front of the glacier as terminal moraine. Where the front was stationary for a time a ridge of moraine built up across the valley, often forming a dam containing a present-day lake. A series of terminal moraines may mark the final retreat of the glacier.

Material transported by ice has also helped to determine the larger-scale pattern of movement — boulders originating in Connemara have been found in Kerry, for example. It is now known that during glaciations the ice advanced initially from Scotland, proceeded down the Irish Sea, then spread out over Ireland, avoiding such barriers as the Wicklow Mountains. Later local ice centres developed in Ireland. The ice receded about 10,000 years ago, though the climate has continued to fluctuate.

FLORA AND FAUNA

Ireland's mountains are low and small in extent compared with many ranges in Britain and on the Continent. And, in common with offshore islands elsewhere, the number of species of plants and animals which can be found here is smaller than on mainland Europe. But this is not to say that Ireland's mountains are uninteresting places for the naturalist.

We are lucky in Ireland, because our strongly maritime climate provides

14

favourable conditions at low altitudes for many plants which elsewhere, can be found only at considerable elevations or at high latitudes. The diminutive least willow (*Salix herbacea*), an Ice Age relic forced to retreat by an improving climate, still occurs on the high rocky ridges of most of our mountain ranges. But in the west, it can be found occasionally at elevations of less than 300m. Another interesting mountain plant, this time with its origins in the Pyrenees, is St Patrick's Cabbage (*Saxifraga spathularis*), a native of Ireland, but absent from Britain. It occurs from sea-level to the top of Carrauntuohill in its Kerry headquarters and on the high ridges of the Connemara and Donegal mountains, where it adds welcome colour to the bleak quartzites. It also occurs on the Galty mountains (generally known as the Galtees), the Knockmealdowns, the Comeraghs and at two isolated sites in the Wicklow Hills.

Looking briefly at each range in turn, we find that the Mourne Mountains, with their impressive granite peaks, are perhaps the least interesting for the botanist. Generally speaking they support few alpine plants and not many other plants worthy of special note. On the high ground the following species have been recorded: starry saxifrage (*Saxifraga stellaris*); roseroot (*Sedum rosea*); alpine saw-wort (*Saussurea alpina*); water lobelia (*Lobelia dortmanna*) a species more common in the west; cowberry (*Vaccinium vitisidaea*); least willow (*Salix herbacea*); a prostrate form of juniper (*Juniperus communis nana = J. sibirica*) generally restricted to the north and west; parsley fern (*Cryptogramma crispa*) a rare plant of the north and east; alpine clubmoss (*Diphasiastrum alpinum*); and the quillwort (*Isoetes laustris*) which typically fringes mountain loughs in the north and west. The Welsh poppy (*Meconopsis cambrica*) occurs on the lower ground and the rare rosebay willow herb (*Epilobium angustifolium*) grows on the highest cliffs of Slieve Binnian and Eagle Mountains.

The Dublin and Wicklow mountains present the largest expanse of high ground in Ireland, some 500 sq km being above 300m; but, as with the Mournes, the heather-clad granite domes offer little of excitement to the botanist. Farmland predominates to about 270m where it gives way to heather moor (*Calluna vulgaris*) on the gentle slopes as they rise to the summits, which are carpeted with deergrass (*Trichophorum cespitosum*), cotton grass (*Eriophorum angustifolium*), woolly hair-moss (*Racomitrium lanuginosum*) and peat mosses (*Sphagnum*). On the highest peak in the east of Ireland, Lugnaquilla, there have been recorded, in addition to the species already mentioned, such plants as bilberry (*Vaccinium myrtillus*), heath bedstraw (*Galium saxatile*), common mouse-ear checkweed (*Cerastium fontanum*) and alpine clubmoss (*Diphasiastrum alpinum*) as well as several more common grasses, sedges, rushes and mosses.

The Galtees are the most inland range in the country and therefore the most remote from maritime influences, and their flora generally reflects their location. Even the highest peak, Galtymore, has only a small flora, almost devoid of alpine plants. According to Praeger in *The Botanist in Ireland* the 'best plant of the Galtees is *Arabis (Cardaminopsis) petrara'*, the northern rock-cress, which has only been recorded at two other sites in the British Isles, one in Leitrim, the other in the Cuillins of Skye. The cliff flora of the Galtees, the Knockmealdowns and the Comeraghs, unaffected as it is by man or his grazing animals, will prove more interesting to the botanist than that of the hillsides. Lesser meadow rue (*Thalictrum minus*) more common near the coast, has been recorded in the Galtees, as have scurvy grass (*Cochleria alpina*), roseroot, starry saxifrage, St Patrick's Cabbage, cowberry, mountain sorrel (*Oxyria digyna*), and least willow. Green spleenwort (*Asplenium viride*), another rarity which is mainly restricted to the western mountains, finds refuge on the cliffs of the Galtees and around the great coums of the Comeraghs.

Moving west to the Cork and Kerry mountains we enter a harsher environment, but one which will offer more interesting rewards in return for modest exertion. Carrauntuohill, the highest peak in the land, supports a varied alpine flora and even on its exposed summit about twenty species have been recorded. In addition to some of the species already mentioned (such as the saxifrages, bedstraw, bilberry and heather) one can find tormentil (*Potentilla erecta*); thrift (*Armeria maritima*) a plant more familiar on the coast; wild thyme (*Thymus drucei*); sorrel (*Rumex acetosa*); sheep's sorrel (*Rumex acetosella*); rushes (*Juncus*); greater wood-rush (*Luzula sylvantica*); fir clubmoss (*Harperzia selago*); and several species of grasses.

To the northwest, Mount Brandon offers some of the richest alpine grounds in the country in and around its large eastern coum. Here alpine lady's mantle (*Alchemilla alpina*) may be found at one of only three reported sites in the country. Alpine meadow-grass (*Poa alpina*) is another rarity which graces this fine mountain.

The lower, more barren, summits of the Connemara mountains are devoid of all but the toughest plants such as St Patrick's Cabbage, the lichen Cladonia and some primitive club-mosses. In the Twelve Bens it is only on Muckanaght, where the more fertile schists rise to the summit, that a continuous carpet of vegetation can be found above 600m. Here, there are several rare alpine plants such as alpine meadow-rue (*Thalictrum alpinum*), purple saxifrage (*Saxifraga oppositifolia*), mountain sorrel, saw-wort, least willow and holly fern (*Polystichum longchitis*). The mountains of Mayo are less harsh than the Bens or the Maumturks and support a summit flora somewhat similar to that of Carrauntuohill.

The limestone hills of Sligo provide a sharp contrast in both form and flora. The flat-topped, cliff-girt plateau of Benbulbin and its associated peaks offer a wealth of material for the botanist. The plateau is covered with thick peat and the flora is typical of such an acid soil. But where the limestone projects, as on Truskmore, a variety of interesting species appear including tormentil, heath bedstraw, golden rod (*Solidago virgaurea*), bilberry, heather, common cow-wheat (*Melampyrum pratense*), crowberry (*Empetrum nigrum*) and the orchid *Dactylorhiza maculata*. However, the cliffs offer the most interesting, if most inaccessible, species in the forms of sandwort (*Arenaria ciliata*), alpine saxifrage (*Saxifraga nivalis*) and chickweed willowherb (*Epilobium alsinifolium*). The former is a particularly rare plant, occurring nowhere else in the British Isles, and the others occupy their only Irish station. Several other arctic/alpine and Lusitanian species are to be found on Benbulbin, as well as such relatively uncommon plants as the strawberry tree (*Arbutus unedo*) better known in the south; blue-eyed grass (*Sisyrinchium bermudiana*); and the pink butterwort (*Pinguicula lusitanica*).

Across Donegal Bay, the landward slopes of Slieve League are an important resort for many of the alpine plants already mentioned. Surprisingly, the distinctive mountain avens (*Dryas octopetala*), familiar to the Burren visitors, have been recorded here, many miles from their best known and major haunt. There are also some interesting non-alpine plants on the rich swards of Slieve League, including several uncommon hawkweeds (*Hieracium*).

Donegal is dominated by mountains linked by extensive bogs. It is washed on three sides by the Atlantic and its continuous exposure to harsh, wet winds has enabled (or forced) many alpine plants to descend to lower altitudes than elsewhere in the country. For example, hoary whitlow grass (*Draba incana*) occurs only from sea-level to a few hundred feet here, whereas it can be found at over 750m to the south. Purple saxifrage occurs from sea-level to nearly 600m, and summit species such as alpine meadow-rue and alpine saw-wort can be found below the 300m contour.

However, the warming influence of the Atlantic has also left its mark by allowing plants such as the Killarney fern (*Trichomanes speciosum*) and the maidenhair fern (*Adiantum capillus-veneris*) to thrive outside their more usual southwestern haunts.

The animals of the Irish mountains are generally few in number, small in size, and secretive in their habits, so the walker must be ever watchful and, above all, patient if he/she wishes to study our native fauna. Birds will be the walker's most obvious companions and the ubiquitous meadow pipit (*Anthus pratensis*) will never be far away, flitting from rock to rock uttering its piping call. The skylark (*Alauda avensis*) will fill the spring air with its familiar song as it hovers overhead. But, to me, the return of the 'chack-chack-chacking' wheatear (*Oenanthe oenanthe*) in March or early April heralds the approach of spring and, hopefully, good weather in the mountains. The shrill call of the common sandpiper (*Tringa hypoleucos*) will greet the walker as he/she approaches many a mountain lough between April and June. The attractive dipper (*Cinclus cinclus*), a bird of the fast-flowing streams, dives to collect its animal food from the streambeds. But the monarch of the hills is the dark and husky raven (*Corvus corax*) flying easily along the glens and over the ridges of all our mountain ranges. Its smaller relation the chough (*Pyrrhocorax pyrrhocorax*) with its bright red legs and bill, is more restricted in its range, but can be seen in the mountains of Cork, Kerry and Connemara. The red grouse (*Lagopus lagopus*) is at home on the heather slopes of the Wicklow Mountains, but is less common in the west where the climate and heather are generally poorer. Winter visitors, such as the woodcock (*Scolopax rusticola*) and snipe (*Gallinago gallinago*) may startle the walker when they rise suddenly from under his feet, but skeins of white-footed geese (*Anser albifrons*) flying silently to and from their secure mountain lough roosts, will restore a feeling of peace and tranquillity. The kestrel (*Falco tinnunculus*), hovering in search of food, is a common sight in the hills and the smaller merlin (*Falco columbarius*) is often seen in the western mountains. But of the birds of prey, pride of place must go to the peregrine (*Falco peregrinus*), screaming fearsomely as it soars high over precipitous cliffs in remote glens.

Red deer (*Cervus elaphus*) once roamed freely through most of Ireland's mountains, but today, alas, wild herds occur only at Glenveagh in Donegal and in the Kerry and Wicklow Mountains. In the latter two ranges the introduced sika deer (*Cervus nippon*) is also common. But the commonest large mammals in the mountains are the fox (*Vulpes vulpes*) and the badger (*Meles meles*). Neither is seen frequently, but their regular paths are easily recognised. The Irish hare (*Lepus timidus*) is often seen in silhouette as it lopes over the horizon to safety. But the rabbit (*Oryctolagus cuniculus*), which is abundant on some fertile hillsides, is not easy-going and scampers quickly to its burrow when disturbed. The red squirrel (*Sciurus vulgaris*) is a woodland species which is rare in the west but quite common on the wooded lower slopes of the mountains to the east. One of the smaller animals, the long-tailed mouse (*Apodemus sylvaticus*) is probably Ireland's commonest mammal, according to Dr James Fairley, who has even found it at the top of Carrauntuohill.

One of the most interesting fish in Ireland is the char (*Salvelinus alpinus*), an Arctic relic which inhabits some of the deep, cold loughs in and around the western mountains. Then come the 'mountainy' brown trout (*Salmo trutta*) which can provide fine sport in spite of their small size.

The invertebrate animals of the mountains have been little studied and offer a fertile field of investigation for the hill-walking naturalist. Butterflies can be seen occasionally at considerable heights in the mountains, but only one species could be said to be a truly mountain species. This is the elusive mountain ringlet (*Erebia epiphron*), a butterfly of arctic/alpine origin which has only been recorded on a few occasions in the west. A variety of other insects — biting and non-biting — make themselves evident on the hills, particularly during the summer months. Finally, an animal of some renown is the Kerry spotted slug (*Geomalacus maculosus*) which I have had the fortune to see on the Reeks. It is widely distributed throughout Kerry and west Cork, but is found nowhere else in the British Isles.

KEY MAP

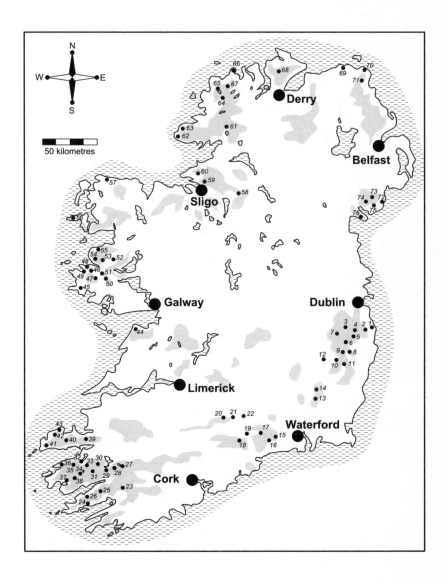

N
W ●—✦—● E
S

50 kilometres

66
65 67
68
69 70
71
64
63
62
61
Derry

Belfast

57
60
59
58
73
74 72
76 75
Sligo

55
54 53 52
48 46 51
49 47 50
45
Galway

Dublin

3 4 2 1
7 5
6
12 9 8
10 11

44

14
13

Limerick

20 21 22
19 17
18 16 15
Waterford

43
42 39
41 40
36 33 30
35 34 31 28 27
37 38 29
Cork
23
26 25
24

19

1. BRAY HEAD

It is probably not fully appreciated that height is not a prerequisite for an excellent mountain viewpoint. A low but well-placed vantage point can offer better views than a high summit hemmed in by dull shoulders. Bray Head is an example: it offers a varied and scenic panorama of indented coast, nearby shapely rocky hills and further away rolling domes of the whole northeast of the range, all from a mere 200m high. If you want to spend a half-day you could do a lot worse than sample the scenic and varied walking on lowly Bray Head.

Bray is well served by DART and buses. Travellers by car can drive along the Strand Road (seafront) and park at the southern end or in the car park at the end of Raheen Park, near the Pitch-and-Putt course.

From the start of the Cliff Walk climb by any convenient path to the Cross on the hummock which dominates the northern top. This is a rather unkempt and eroded stretch but do not be discouraged; better terrain awaits. At the Cross walk to a track running close to the next rocky hummock. And here I can reveal the great navigational simplicity of this walk; *all* turns from here on are left! So turn left onto the track and walk along a tiny plateau towards the South Top — an upland world of tiny rocky 'haystacks', rough gorse and bracken, the swelling ocean on one side, the small but impressive Sugarloafs on the other. You might even be lucky enough to see the herd of feral goats whose stamping ground this is. All in all, quite a contrast to busy Bray so close at hand.

The South Top is out of bounds, so you must walk west down the track to a bypassed stretch of road, turn left here and turn left again onto the Bray–Greystones road. Keep on the main road through the hamlet of Windgates, turning left on its far side onto a minor road. Walk to the end of this road. Going left in front of a large apartment block, pass through a gate and take the path beyond it, which ends at a stile on the Cliff Walk. Turn left here.

The 2.5km back to Bray are dominated by the wrinkled waters of the ocean stretching away seemingly to infinity: its littoral of ancient rock; the myriads of kittiwakes, gulls, guillemots and shags which depend on it; its erosive power as evidenced by the abandoned railway tunnels. Man, perhaps mercifully, is not yet quite the measure of all things!

Distance: 8km/5miles. Ascent: 240m/800ft. Walking time: 2½ hours.

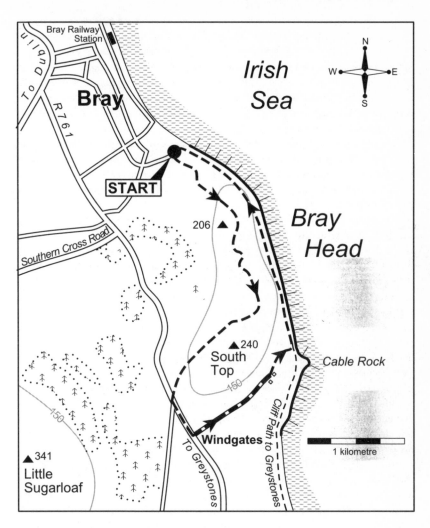

Reference OS Map: Sheet 56 (1:50,000).

2. GREAT SUGARLOAF

The Great Sugarloaf is a must. If you head south from Dublin by either the Bray or Enniskerry roads, its symmetrical cone dominates the landscape. A big heather fire a few years ago exposed the white quartzite rocks and scree so that from a distance it appeared that the mountain was snow covered; now the vegetation is gradually recovering. I have to say that although I have seen three-year-olds and eighty-year-olds climb it, it is not easy: the summit is a real scramble over scree and broken rock.

Go by car or bus to Kilmacanogue, 5km/3miles south of Bray on the N11. You can walk or drive the next bit. Turn up the R755 and almost immediately, just after a shop, turn left up a narrow road signposted to the John Fitzsimons GAA Club. Just before the GAA Club park on the verge — plenty of room.

Go along a path between the fences of the GAA and a private house to reach the open hillside. Straight ahead is a broad, shallow re-entrant leading up to the long, almost level shoulder which the Sugarloaf throws out to the north. There are many small paths; take advantage of them to ease your upward journey to the shoulder. On arrival there you will find a broad path which slants left and curves round a rocky hump before passing along the right (west side) of the summit cone.

Soon you will see a network of heavily eroded tracks leading up the cone. Pick one without too much scree and climb to the summit, which commands a full circle view: Bray in the northeast, backed by the Irish Sea (and Wales if you are lucky); then the Little Sugarloaf, the gash of the Glen of the Downs, a glacial overflow channel; far to the southwest Lugnaquilla should be visible. Then, running northwards, the backbone of Wicklow — Tonelagee, Mullaghcleevaun, Djouce, Maulin, and Kippure with its television mast. North is another glacial overflow channel, the Scalp, flanked by Carrigollogan's attractive domed summit.

Retrace your steps down the scree to the main track and turn left along it. When you come to an earth bank, follow it to the left and where it dies out, head for the entrance to the Glen of the Downs till you meet a track heading north, which with some meanderings will take you past a wood. Just beyond the wood fork right onto a paved road that leads to the GAA Club.

The route described is the most satisfying one; the shortest (if you have private transport) is to continue along the R755 to the top of the Long Hill, turn left onto the by-road over Callary Bog and stop at the car park (235 119). A broad network of tracks leads you easily to the foot of the final cone, which is climbed as before. Return by the same way.

Long Route

Distance: 5.5km/3.4miles. Ascent: 380m/1,250ft. Walking time: 2½ hours (Allow an extra 10–15 minutes each way if starting from Kilmacanogue.)

Short Route

Distance: 2.4km/1.5miles. Ascent: 200m/650ft. Walking time: 1 hour.

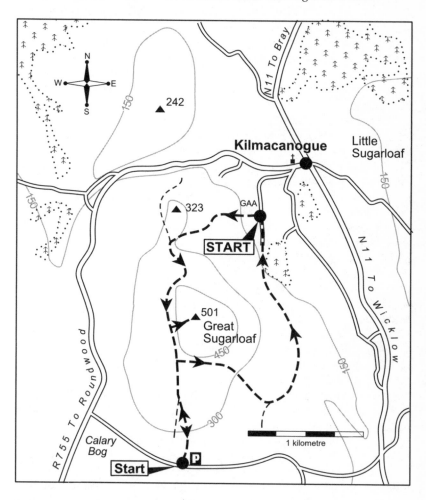

Reference OS Map: Sheet 56 (1:50,000)

3. SEEFINGAN, KIPPURE AND CORONATION PLANTATION

This route combines some bleak, austere and gently-rolling mountain-side with the more intimate secluded river bank of the youthful River Liffey. The megalithic tombs on Seefin and Seefingan and the TV mast on Kippure exemplify ancient and modern worship customs, and on a severely practical note they are useful landmarks in a fairly blank terrain.

Take the N81 for 2.7km/1.7miles beyond Brittas, turning left here onto the R759. Drive onward on the R759 for 8.8km/5.5miles (after 1.5km/1mile approx. the R759 turns left, signposted Sally Gap) and park in Kippure Wood car park on the left at 080 145. This route is also suitable for cyclists from Dublin.

From the car park follow the track upstream. Do not cross the river where this track descends to a small ford. Veer right and follow a faint path, keeping the forest on your right, and carry on resolutely over fallen trees where the track succumbs. Crossing a fence (carefully) at the edge of mature forest which meets the stream, continue upwards between the stream on the left and young trees on the right. When this is not possible, head into the forest to avoid impediments. Head back to the stream when appropriate. The valley is particularly beautiful. Follow the fence on the left uphill, after the stream has become insignificant, to the corner of the fence. Head directly west, along the ridge on a rough track, to Seefin (*Sui Finn*, Seat of Finn, 621m).

Only at the enormous prehistoric burial chamber on the summit will you fully appreciate your position. West lie the plains of Kildare, while north and south the mountains of the northwest of the range peter out in the low hills on the Kildare border.

Seefingan, 724m, a loftier version of Seefin and like it crowned by a prehistoric grave, is the next target. After it there is a long featureless stretch terminating in Kippure, along the unfortunately unmarked county boundary. Along this stretch you have a choice of views towards Glenasmole to the north or over the Mullaghcleevaun range to the south, though neither direction is particularly exciting.

A soggy mound, unnamed on the maps, followed by a rise through black mud interspersed with startlingly green wedges leads to Kippure (*Cip Iúr*, Yew Mountain, 757m) the highest point in County Dublin. Its TV transmitter is evident, all too evident, for miles around so you will have no difficulty finding the peak, though the surrounding terrain, an inverted pudding bowl, precludes good scenery except in the middle distance and beyond, and even there it is none too inspiring.

The next stage requires careful navigation. Take a compass bearing of about 220° to reach a bridge on the R759 (as you descend, aim for the scattered dark green trees at the eastern extremity of Coronation Plantation). Cross the road and walk down to the River Liffey, here a clear vibrant brook and a far cry from the sluggish, mature river it becomes in the more familiar environment of Dublin.

The homeward stretch starts with a scenic, sometimes marshy walk, keeping close to the right bank of the river. Going downstream, you pass an old house and a bridge and meet a green road which brings you back to the main road about 2km from the start.

Distance: 14.5km/9miles. Ascent: 580m/1,900ft. Walking time: 5 hours.

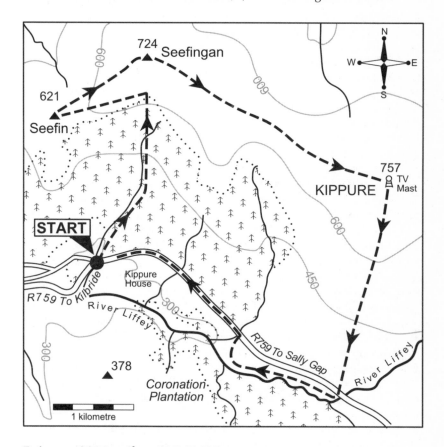

Reference OS Map: Sheet 56 (1:50,000).

4. THE TONDUFFS AND MAULIN FROM CRONE

The south side of Glencree is dominated by Maulin. Although, at 570m, not the highest peak around Glencree, it is the most distinctive with its neat cone. To the west, higher and more sprawling, lie Tonduffs North and South, close together in rolling moorland. Then there are the valleys: the rocky slabs of the Raven's Glen, lonely Glensoulan and the Deerpark with the Dargle River falling as the dramatic Powerscourt Waterfall. Although short, the walk offers variety.

Transport must be by car or bicycle. From Enniskerry take the road south, passing Powerscourt Estate on the right and turning right at the T-junction 3.4km/2.1miles from Enniskerry. Park in Crone car park (193 142) on the left 3.9km/2.4miles from this T-junction.

From the car park take the main track. Continue straight at the first junction, passing a marker — the Wicklow Way goes left. Walking west and parallel to Glencree views open up with Knockree in the foreground and the mountains along the Dublin/Wicklow county boundary forming the northern skyline.

At the next junction go right and over a bridge. Cross the stile beside the wooden gate on the left onto a path heading towards the wall on your right. This is the impressive Raven's Glen with its rocky slabs. The path rises alongside the wall, weaving between rocks, heather and gorse.

Approaching the highest point in the wall with a lone bush on a rock about 50m out from it, turn onto a path branching left. It parallels the wall for a short distance and then turns uphill between rocks and heather, easing a little the climb up the rough, lower, steeper slopes of Tonduff North. By the time the path peters out the slope has relented and vegetation become shorter for the long steady pull over easier ground to the top.

A cairn on a peat hag in a desolate lunar-like landscape marks the summit of Tonduff North. Five minutes' walking across almost level ground to the south is Tonduff South (not shown separately on OS Sheet 56), marked by a large rock with a hollow in it — a convenient 'chair' if sometimes damp. Leave Tonduff South, heading southeast, on a path starting very near the summit. This path is clearly defined, veering east, winding amongst peat hags, going over 593m, descending to the col, before reaching firmer ground and finally the top of Maulin. As you walk, the mass of War Hill is on the right across the source of the Dargle River and Glensoulan.

Ascending Maulin (*Malainn*, Hill Brow, 570m) is quite steep on this approach, with the path negotiating a rocky step before the last run up to the summit — an impressive viewpoint.

From here most of the way is downhill. A wide track runs along the eastern shoulder gradually dropping to a wall. Turning right and walking alongside the wall descend into Glensoulan until the Dargle River comes into view below, trees now behind the wall on your left. Watch for a black marker post across the wall — on its other side a yellow arrow directs to a path in the trees and the Wicklow Way back to Crone.

Walking through these trees we have a last short, sharp climb before suddenly exiting onto a high level path along the rim of the Deerpark spread below our feet, pointed Great Sugarloaf beyond and the Dargle River cascading down the valley head as Powerscourt Waterfall. Deer are sometimes in the mixed woodland bordering the path. The view of the waterfall changes as we progress and it is worth stopping for a final look before the path heads left into the trees. Further down the forest track large, old deciduous trees still stand amongst the recently planted conifers. Eventually, at a T-junction the Wicklow Way and our route turn right, curve and turn right again to quickly reach the car park.

Distance: 14.2km / 8.8miles. Ascent: 610m / 2,000ft. Walking time: 4½ hours.

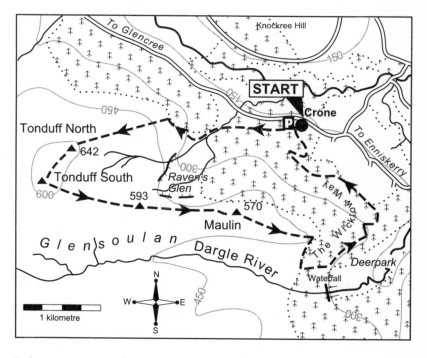

Reference OS Map: Sheet 56 (1:50,000).

5. FANCY, COFFIN STONE AND DJOUCE

This walk might be fancifully described as a 'reverse' sandwich: the tasty meat on the outside with a slice of rather stodgy bread within. The scenic delights of the climb to Fancy yield to the boggy slog to the Coffin Stone. From Djouce on, however, the views are excellent.

Go by car or bus on the N11 to Kilmacanoge, 5km/3miles south of Bray. Turn right onto the R755 here and turn right again onto the R759 after a further 11.3km/7miles. Drive uphill for 3.2km/2miles and park near the large set of gate pillars on the left at 172 064. This is Pier Gates. This walk may also be done using the St Kevin's bus to Roundwood.

From the pillars, walk the tarmacadam road down towards the valley floor along what must be one of the most spectacular motorable roads in the country: the great cliffs under Fancy directly ahead, bumpy Knocknacloghoge to its left and a whole array of lovely mountains around with the purple heathery slopes of the Cloghoge valley close at hand.

At the valley floor cross the first bridge and then, just before a second, turn right up a side track, beside a high wall. Walk a few hundred metres along this track after which you can tackle Fancy (*Fuinnse*, Ash Tree, 595m).

The cliffs of Fancy belie its rather dull top, a heather plateau stretching away to the northwest, but commanding magnificent middle-distance views, prominent among which is the great bulk of Djouce, now to be tackled. To do so head east to a path running parallel and close above the cliffs, turn north onto it and follow it to its end in pathless and very rough country. Continue north through high bracken (in summer), aiming for the stone-cut bridge (Sheepbanks Bridge) over the R759 at 154 095. On the way you will cross the delightful upper Cloghoge River where there are excellent spots for a leisurely lunch.

Cross the R759 at the bridge and walk upstream along the river which the bridge spans, through a desolate, wet moorland towards the Coffin Stone, a prominent heap of stones crowned by a massive boulder which gives the whole assembly its highly appropriate name. On the new OS map, sadly, it is simply called a standing stone.

From the Coffin Stone the ascent to Djouce is easy navigationally, whatever about corporeally; a rather boggy path leads to the semi-plateau on which Djouce, 725m, stands. The summit is marked by three large outcrops of schist and a trig. point so it is unmistakable and the views predictably magnificent.

The descent is along its southern spur towards White Hill, from which elevated route the Barnacullian ridge to the west, linking the second and third highest peaks in Wicklow (Mullaghcleevaun and Tonelagee), may be seen to perfection.

On this descent you will pick up the Wicklow Way, which you follow going south for the rest of the route. Following a sleeper boardwalk from the top of

White Hill the route offers excellent views, best of all when Luggala cliff below Fancy, with Lough Tay tucked in beneath it, is revealed suddenly and dramatically. Hereabouts you will find a memorial stone to J. B. Malone, whose dream of a 'Wicklow Way' eventually came to fruition after nearly twenty years. 'J. B.' was also notable for his weekly articles in the *Evening Herald* which did much to popularise walking in Ireland.

The last stretch is through forest. This would involve complicated directions were it not for the necessarily frequent Wicklow Way markers. Once on the road, the R759 again, turn left and walk first up, then downhill for about 1km to the start.

Distance: 13.7km/8.5miles. Ascent: 730m/2,400ft. Walking time: 5½ hours.

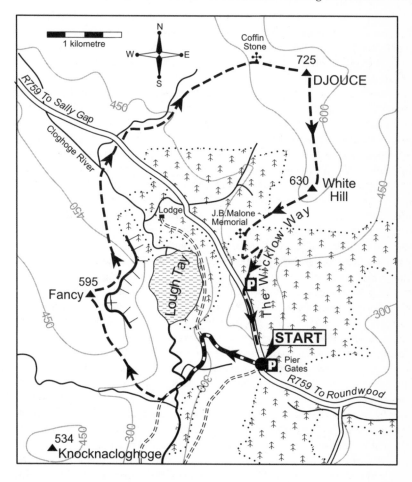

Reference OS Map: Sheet 56 (1:50,000).

6. SCARR AND KNOCKNACLOGHOGE FROM OLDBRIDGE

Scarr is at the centre of one of the most shapely mountain areas in Wicklow. Itself a grassy up-and-down ridge running north and south, it sends three broad, grassy spurs out towards the east and a delightful rocky, hummocky ridge, Kanturk Mountain, running in a wide crescent towards the north. North of Kanturk is the narrow, flat trough of the Inchavore River and northwards again looms rocky Knocknacloghoge, somewhat overshadowed by its higher southern neighbour. Add to this the sylvan valley of the Cloghoge River and the result is one of the most delightful walking areas in the Wicklow Mountains. After heavy rain the rivers on this walk may be difficult to cross.

This is a route which may be conveniently undertaken by St Kevin's bus to Roundwood. Check times for the return before you start! By car drive to Roundwood on the R755, follow signs here toward Lough Dan, turn right at the junction at Oldbridge, 3.8km/2.3miles from Roundwood, and park about 200m up the road on the left hand side.

Take the boreen just beyond the parking spot (158 019) and follow its twisty course uphill and across a cattle grid to a sharp bend about 1.25km from the road. Looking straight ahead there are two houses on the left (only one marked on the 1:50,000 map); the track looks as though it is going into the farmyard, but in fact it continues between the houses and the wood to the open mountain. Bear a little right and you will find yourself on the northmost of the three spurs leading to the summit of Scarr. The climb is straightforward and steady — keeping slightly to the right gives a better view of Lough Dan. The summit of Scarr (*Sceir* or *Scor*, Sharp Rock, 641m) is uncairned but the series of little grassy mounds forming the top is unmistakable. The views of the Barnacullian ridge to the west are particularly fine, especially after rain when the tributaries of the Glenmacnass River cascade down the steep-sided slopes into the glen below.

From the top of Scarr, walk northwest on a distinct path to cross a rickety fence leading to a broad ridge. Descending along this ridge Glenmacnass Waterfall comes into view on your left. If you need reassurance that you are on course you may come across a roughly hewn pillar about 200m beyond the descent. Continue northwards to the area of hummocks, Kanturk (523m), already described. The problem now is to find the firebreak which runs directly down to the copse on the Inchavore River at 133 047. Descend north through high heather and over rough ground to meet a rough track bounding forestry, turn right onto it and within a few metres of its end take the firebreak directly downhill to near the copse. Take great care on this section as there are numerous deep holes concealed in the long grass and heather.

The copse is a delightful spot. The shady oaks and the deep pools of the stream make an ideal place for a well-deserved rest. After that let's hope you have sufficient energy to tackle Knocknacloghoge. Cross the river at the copse and, keeping the forest fence on the left, head towards the summit. Knocknacloghoge (*Cloghog*, Stony Land, 534m) has a small neat cairn set on a jagged rocky summit. The views of Lough Dan and back to Scarr are particularly fine.

North of Knocknacloghoge, head directly and steeply over rough heather to the Cloghoge Brook, ignoring tempting paths. Once on the far side walk downstream. If the weather is hot, leave time to bathe at a delectable spot further down the brook. A little below this pool and still on the left bank pick up a track, take it to the main track, turn left and head up to the R759 at Pier Gates. This involves a punishing 180m climb, not exactly an inviting prospect towards the end of the day.

From Pier Gates follow the Wicklow Way through the woods and along the road back to Oldbridge or Roundwood.

Distance: 19.3km / 12miles. Ascent: 970m / 3,200ft. Walking time: 7½ hours.

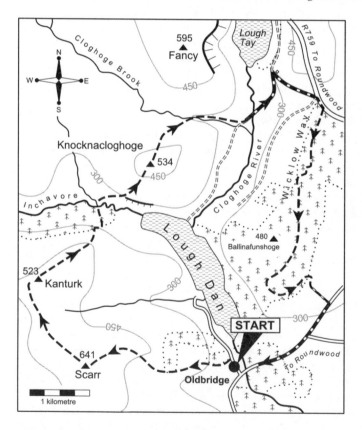

Reference OS Map: Sheet 56 (1:50,000).

7. MULLAGHCLEEVAUN AND TONELAGEE

The second and third highest mountains in Wicklow, Mullaghcleevaun and Tonelagee, are linked by a broad undulating ridge never dipping below 600m, riven in some parts by deeply fissured bogland and covered in other parts by flat areas of sticky, black mud. Indeed the only really firm terrain on this walk is the short grass north and east of Tonelagee. The panorama around it and particularly down onto the steep corrie of heart-shaped Lough Ouler is magnificent and forms a fitting climax to the day's walk.

Park in the small car park on the right (west) of the Military Road R115 at 101 050 about 9km / 5.6 miles south of Sally Gap. There is space for only a few cars here but more can be parked in the forest entrance on the left (east), a few hundred metres north. If you have two cars, one may be parked in Glenmacnass car park on the right, nearly 3.2km / 2miles south along the Military Road, thus avoiding a road walk at the end of the day.

From the car park climb the right side of Carrigshouk, 571m, on an intermittent path, avoiding the steep slabs of the direct approach. The summit of Carrigshouk may be bypassed and Mullaghcleevaun East Top tackled directly over featureless terrain. East Top, 795m, has a small cairn and a more impressive heap of boulders which looks as though it is artfully arranged to form a modern sculpture. Beyond the East Top a sea of oozy bog confronts the walker intent on a direct approach; a prudent tack to starboard (right) is advisable.

Mullaghcleevaun (*Mullach Cliabháin*, Summit of the Basket i.e. corrie: 849m) stands at the centre of many peaks and offers good views but, mainly because of the gentle slopes around, not as good as its height would suggest. Near the summit cairn and close to the steep dip sweeping down to Cleevaun Lough is a memorial to three An Oige members who perished in a boating tragedy off Port Oriel in the fifties. Take the ridge southwards (with the slightest hint of east) along the Barnacullian ridge here, at the headwaters of the Glenmacnass River, rent by deep fissures which make for tortuous progress. If you wish to avoid sticky mud further on keep to the east of the ridge.

South of Barnacullian the ground is better — rough grass and moorland. A gentle drop is followed by a distinct rise to Stoney Top. Head south from Stoney Top to confront the steep rise to Tonelagee close by, watching out, in cloud, for the grassy cliffs above Lough Ouler to the east. Tonelagee (*Toin le gaoth*, Backside to the Wind, 817m) is an impressive viewpoint, far more commanding than the somewhat higher Mullaghcleevaun. Lough Nahanagan and the flat top of Turlough Hill reservoir are visible to the south with the entire Lugnaquilla massif to the right. Scarr and the other mountains around Lough Dan dominate the east with a bumpy skyline. Add to this the great corrie of Lough Ouler, soon to be encountered on the descent, and the remaining pains of the ascent will soon be forgotten.

The rock-strewn descent along the south side of Lough Ouler is navigationally straightforward. Beyond the lake featureless moorland warrants a compass bearing directly to Glenmacnass car park. To avoid wet feet it may be worthwhile diverting about 70m upstream of the car park where there are natural stepping stones. Turn left and walk left along the road to the start unless you have a car here. A footbridge was erected about 800m upstream of the car park but washed away by floods. It may be replaced sometime.

Assuming two cars
Distance: 13.7km/8.5miles. Ascent: 700m/2,300ft. Walking time: 5½ hours.

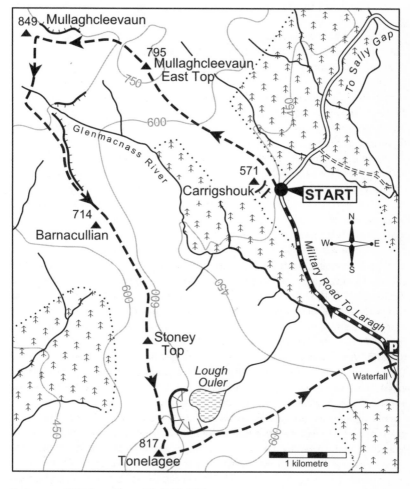

Reference OS Map: Sheet 56 (1:50,000).

8. GLENEALO, TURLOUGH HILL AND CAMADERRY

The view west up the Upper Lake in Glendalough towards Glenealo is magnificent, seen by countless thousands of day-trippers annually and captured on hundreds of photos and drawings. But what about the view from Glenealo east towards Glendalough? It is equally good (probably better) but is seen and enjoyed only by the hardy souls who ascend the zig-zags terminating the western end of Glendalough. Add to this Camaderry, the great wedge of mountain lying between Glendalough and Glendasan, and the ingredients are those of a most enjoyable walk.

Start at the upper car park, Glendalough (111 964). Directions are given under Walk 9.

From the car park join the throngs (on Sundays anyway) strolling along the shores of the Upper Lake. Beyond its end, thread a way through the old lead mine workings. While these are not a thing of beauty and certainly promise to be an eyesore forever, they are interesting geologically. They stand on a metamorphic zone between the granite further west and the ancient Ordovician strata to the east which were thrust aside by the up-swelling granite. Similar workings occur in Glendasan and Glenmalure, all three along this zone.

Ascending the zig-zags you will find some excellent resting and swimming places along the river on the left; they are especially good higher up. (On hot days better take a solemn vow before you stop that you won't abort the walk!) The scenery is not quite so good on the fairly level ground in Glenealo and you can concentrate on pleasant, though wet, walking along the left (true) bank of the river.

Continue up the valley taking the main stream rather than tributaries and at the soggy headwaters climb the remaining distance to the level ground between tiny Lough Firrib and the gigantic sloping sides of Turlough Hill Reservoir. Thanking your lucky stars that you have to find the latter rather than the former, walk round the southern perimeter fence of the reservoir, negotiate the peat hags beyond and ascend Camaderry (*Ceim a' doire*, Pass of the Oakwood, 698m) which has a rather flat top thus making the cairn particularly useful. There is a lower second peak of Camaderry to the southeast, after which a good path gives easy walking right down the spur between Glendasan on the left and Glendalough on the right, a long easy descent with lovely views.

You can cut the walk short by descending a steep path right to the upper car park, but if you have the time why should you? Instead continue down the spur, keeping on top rather than being tempted down to the right, pick up a forest track near the end and turn left onto it. It will guide you back on a boomerang's progress high above the shore of the Lower Lake and then gently to earth near the eastern shore of the Upper Lake, crossing the direct descent via the steep path, to end what should have been an enjoyable day.

Distance: 14.5km/9miles. Ascent: 610m/2,000ft. Walking time: 5 hours.

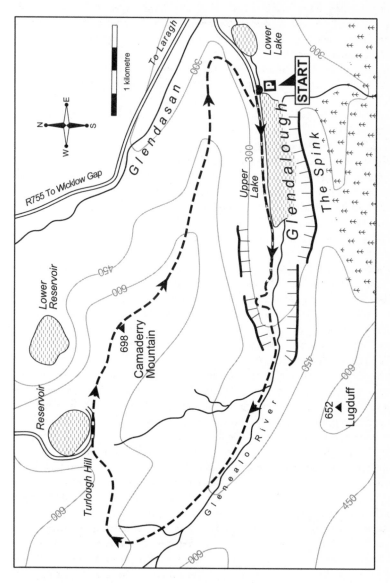

Reference Maps: OS Sheet 56 (1:50,000);
Healy Map Glendalough–Glenmalure (1:25,000).

9. THE SPINK AND THE DERRYBAWN RIDGE

The wooded Spink rears impressively over the eastern end of the Upper Lake at Glendalough and runs from there along its southern shore in a line of sheer cliffs occasionally indented by rocky bluffs. After an impressive start along the Spink the route takes us to grassy, gently sloped Mullacor and down narrow Derrybawn, a rib of metamorphic rock and the finest ridge in Wicklow. A short but memorable walk.

Drive to the upper car park, Glendalough (111 964) about 1.5km/1mile beyond the Royal Hotel Glendalough. Or take St Kevin's bus to the Glendalough terminus. Travellers by bus should walk into the cemetery containing the Round Tower, cross the bridge at the far end, turn right and walk the 1.5km or so to the start proper.

Leave the car park at the southwestern corner and walk south to the small information office (open during the summer months only). Turn right joining the Wicklow Way, cross the bridge and climb up the steps by the foaming Pollanass Waterfall to the forest track above and at the multiple junction leave the Wicklow Way and turn sharply right uphill.

Just after the first (left) bend, cross a stile and climb steeply up a boardwalk to the top of the Spink. The first sight from the crest of the Spink is breathtaking — the Upper Lake seemingly at your feet, the great cliffs of Camaderry half-left, and the undulating crest of the Spink reaching towards the high hills to the west. It is a marvellous panorama.

Now follow the crest of the Spink parallel to the Upper Lake along a fine boardwalk. It certainly makes for easy walking compared with the muddy ups-and-downs it replaced, but do we really want this intrusion of civilisation? To be fair to the National Park, both here and on White Hill (Walk 5) conditions underfoot were so bad that they really had little choice but to lay the boardwalk. Anyway, enjoy it while you can, for it eventually descends into Upper Glenealo — not the way you want to go at all! When the forest bears away to the left, you must leave the boardwalk and follow the fence and a vague track leading southeast and then south until near the pass between Lugduff and Mullacor. Cross the fence line and lose a little height to the pass itself. It is horribly boggy, but with foresight and intelligent use of the stretch of boardwalk that crosses the pass from Glendalough to Glenmalure at an angle, some bog at least can be avoided. Now climb steeply up to Mullacor (*Mullach mhór*, Great Summit: 657m), a summit which commands fine views especially towards the Lugnaquilla massif.

On the descent east a boggy path follows the centre of the ridge, trees coming into view on the left as you approach a fence and the corner of the forest. Cross a stile at the southern corner of the fence and head northeast for the start of the bumpy Derrybawn ridge. The views along here, especially towards the Upper Lake, are excellent and a path, much of it on rock, leads you out along the ridge which slopes sharply away on both sides. From the cairn on Derrybawn Mountain continue straight ahead for a short distance down to a small saddle from which a path drops steeply to the left, heading towards a vee at the lowest point of the forest edge below. (Here we might note that though the remainder of the walk is in forest, the trees are mature and well spaced and the views through them excellent.) Cross the stile at this vee and continue on the path to turn right onto the first forest track, the Wicklow Way. Keeping on the Way take the first turn left and then, to provide a slightly different perspective from the outward journey, take the first right (it is just before the first of two bridges). This track zig-zags downhill to the valley floor with Pollanass Waterfall on the left. Here a left takes you back to the small information office and the car park, while the bus is to the right.

While you are at Glendalough, it would be a pity (if you don't already know them) not to visit the monastic ruins below the Lower Lake. The Visitor Centre at the lower car park is also well worth a visit.

Distance: 12km/7.5miles. Ascent: 630m/2,080ft. Walking time: 4½ hours.

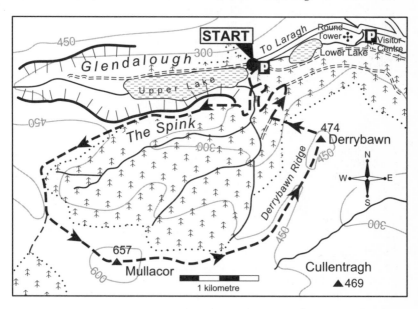

Reference Maps: OS Sheet 56 (1:50,000);
Healy Map Glendalough–Glenmalure (1:25,000).

10. GLENMALURE, THE FRAUGHAN ROCK GLEN AND LUGNAQUILLA

Probably the most rewarding approach to Lugnaquilla is from Baravore at the head of Glenmalure. A short but steep ascent via a series of tiny valleys culminates in Wicklow's only 900m summit, and is followed by a high-level, easy stroll with stunning views in all directions. A lovely walk.

Car only, though this walk may also be done from Glenmalure Youth Hostel. Take the R755 for 1.4km/0.9mile south of Laragh turning right here steeply uphill towards Glenmalure. Drive for a further 7.5km/4.7miles and turn right at the Drumgoff crossroads. Park in the large car park at the head of the valley (066 941) a further 5km/3miles on.

Cross the river by the footbridge and walk on tarmac upstream to just past the youth hostel. Fork left uphill here and walk steadily upwards along a track through forest until it comes close to the river in the Fraughan Rock Glen on the left and a forest track comes in from the right. Continue straight on the forest track, which gradually deteriorates as it climbs up beside the rapids and small waterfalls at the head of the Glen. You emerge from the trees into a second, higher coum, which itself is rather dull and boggy but is surrounded by magnificent scenery. Behind you is the far wall of Glenmalure, in front the rocks closing the heads of the coum, to the left the rugged shoulder of Clohernagh, to the right the great crags below Benleagh.

Bear a little right, crossing the stream to find the best route to climb the coum headwall, behind which you find yet a third valley, and when you climb the steep grassy slope behind this, the gently sloped terrain above heralds the summit plateau of Lugnaquilla itself.

The view from the immediate area of the great cairn on Lugnaquilla (*Log na Coille*, Hollow of the Copse, 925m) is dull, a grassy plateau whose pastoral atmosphere is accentuated by grazing sheep. But walk a few yards in any direction and a great panorama is suddenly revealed. The high hills of the range crowd in from all directions: whale-backed Tonelagee and Mullaghcleevaun to the north, Keadeen to the west, the long spur of Clohernagh reaching out to the east, to the southeast the graceful cone of Croaghanmoira, and Mount Leinster, topped by its TV aerial, to the south. A wonderful series of views.

From Lugnaquilla descend a gentle slope to Clohernagh (*Clocharnach*, Stony Place, 800m), a long stretch with wide spectacular views and excellent underfoot conditions. Just two points about the otherwise easy navigation: firstly if you take a direct bearing from the top of Lug to Clohernagh, be prepared at the start to swerve prudently left to avoid the cliffs of the South Prison, and secondly take care to choose the Clohernagh spur (left) rather than the Carrawaystick spur at the one distinct junction.

The summit of Clohernagh barely rises from the general level, so its large cairn is an important landmark, especially as the next stretch to Art's Lough is a little difficult navigationally. To avoid cliffs on the direct route from the summit, walk about north/northeast for approx. 500m, then swing north and finally northwest to descend on a grassy ramp to the lake.

Art's Lough has a lovely setting: rocky cliffs bounding it on its southwest side, and if you care to walk a little further northwest, giving a lovely view over the Fraughan Rock Glen, up which you toiled earlier.

But alas, back to navigation. The idea now is to reach the high end of the track which reaches tarmac at 079 928 and which extends much further than is shown on the OS map. To do this, cross a fence running into the lake roughly halfway along the northeast shore and follow it to another fence a few metres away and parallel to the lake. Walking left inside the second fence leads to a stile a short distance away. Cross the stile and turn left immediately onto a rough path through heather. (There are two more fences running out of the northwestern end of the lake which should *not* be followed.) This path initially runs parallel to the fence, but then swings away from it to reach the indistinct end of the track (if you lose the path simply head northeast to pick up the track).

Once on the track you can breathe easily. Turning left at the T-junction and ignoring what are obviously minor tracks, follow it down through forest in various stages of growth, which allows glimpses down into Glenmalure and across to the mountains to its north. At length you should cross a forest bridge, beyond which is tarmac. Turn left here to reach the car park less than 2km away.

Distance: 15.3km/9.5miles. Ascent: 800m/2,600ft. Walking time: 5¾ hours.

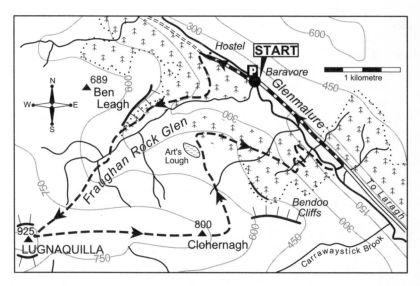

Reference Maps: OS Sheet 56 (1:50,000);
Healy Map Glendalough–Glenmalure (1:25,000).

11. CARRAWAYSTICK AND CROAGHANMOIRA

Croaghanmoira, with Great Sugarloaf, is the nearest approach to the classical pyramid-shaped mountain in Wicklow and though Carrawaystick is merely a spur of Lugnaquilla and not really a distinct peak, under it nestles the delectable Kelly's Lough. It is a pity that a rising tide of monotonous conifers swathes the valleys and threatens the solitude of Kelly's Lough itself. Come before it rises even higher!

By car drive to Drumgoff crossroads (107 909) as described under Walk 10.

Walk south past the ruins of the military barracks, turning right after about 300m, thus following the Wicklow Way. Continue on the Way uphill but where it branches left downhill continue straight ahead. Turn first right onto another track and continue steadily upwards to pass between the pillars normally found with a bar at a forest entrance. Just beyond these pillars turn right onto another track and continue, going right at the fork. Where the track reaches a fence and bends sharply right downhill, leave it to walk uphill inside the fence, past a bend left and to a stile. Cross the stile and walk southwest to the corner of Kelly's Lough, an unusually large corrie lake at a high altitude, and a delightful spot for a rest.

From the eastern end of Kelly's Lough climb the steep slope to its south (care should be taken here as in places only a thin coating of vegetation covers very steep rock slabs) to Carrawaystick Mountain (*Ceathramhadh istigh*, Inner Quarter, 676m). Returning to the fence and continuing up along it, although still steep, gives easier walking. No need to find its exact top, though if you do find the small cairn perched precariously on a peat hag, count it a bonus. Another stile on top of the ridge takes you over the fence as the next target you really must find is an angle in a forest fence southeast of Carrawaystick and about 1.5km away, an absolute necessity given the wide tracts of forestry all around. This is easier said than done since the forest has been extended upwards. A compass bearing of 130° will take you to the edge of younger trees. Walk one of the trenches between them down to a forest track. To reach the angle in the fence leave the track at a small cairn at roughly the highest point on the track and at a corner in the forest on the southeastern side of the track. Walk along the edge of the trees, keeping them on your right, to reach the stile and angle in the fence and the wide firebreak which will take you along the northwestern side of Slievemaan.

About 15 minutes walking from the fence and stile take a wide well-defined firebreak on the left, opposite a point on the right where the fence posts change direction slightly rightwards. At the end of this firebreak, turn right onto the forest track, the Wicklow Way, and take it around a sharp bend to the left, leaving it where it turns right onto another forest track. Continue straight until you reach tarmac at the top of the pass between Drumgoff and Aghavannagh.

Most navigational difficulties now behind, you can face the climb to Croaghanmoira with equanimity. Cross the road and follow the path on the opposite side which leads to the obvious forest corner. Once here, cross the fence (with care not to damage it) and continue with forest on your right for a few hundred metres until the path turns sharply left. Follow this path steeply to the summit of Croaghanmoira (*Cruachan maoir*, Hill of the Steward or Overseer, 664m) which commands excellent views stretching all the way from Great Sugarloaf to the Blackstairs. Small wonder then that it was a pivotal point for the triangulation of the country in the original survey in the nineteenth century.

From Croaghanmoira retrace your steps to the forest corner and then walk northeast along the Fananierin ridge, a rocky, narrow rib and one of the best such in the range. Fananierin (*Fana an iarainn*, Iron Slope, 426m) at the end of the ridge is not strictly necessary to the route but the views it offers along Glenmalure make it worth the effort.

From here retrace your steps to the lateral stone wall encountered along the ridge and descend half-right to a gate at a break in the forest that stretches along the Military Road. Cross the bridge here, walk through the forest to tarmac, turn right and walk the 2km to Drumgoff.

Distance: 20.5km / 12.8miles. Ascent: 940m / 3,100ft. Walking time: 7½ hours.

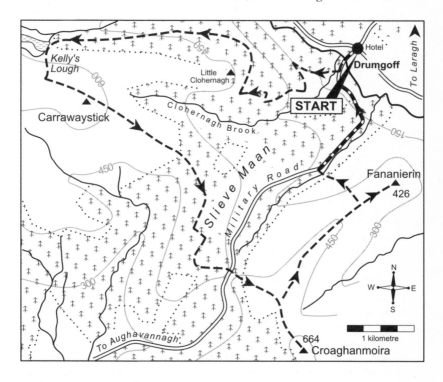

Reference OS Maps: Sheets 56 and 62 (1:50,000);
Healy Map Glendalough–Glenmalure (1:25,000).

41

12. CIRCUIT OF IMAAL

The circuit of Imaal makes a long and rewarding walk taking in a wide array of high mountain scenery and culminating in Lugnaquilla itself. Whether it is better to do it clockwise or anti-clockwise is a toss-up, but anti-clockwise as described below has the advantage of a long scenic descent through magnificent country ahead so that the need to emulate Lot's wife is avoided.

Most of this walk lies within or along the boundary of an artillery range. At weekends there is usually no artillery practice, but phone 045–404653 or 045–404626 (open 24 hours) for information. If red flags or lanterns are raised, do not attempt this walk.

Car only. Take the N81 for about 17.7km/11miles south of Blessington turning left at The Olde Tollhouse for Donard. In Donard take the road east towards the youth hostel (this is straight ahead but the offset crossroads in Donard may cause brief mystification). Shortly after passing the hostel turn right and follow the road to Knockanarrigan crossroads. Turn left here and drive 2km/1.2miles to the pub at Seskin. The trek from here to Lugnaquilla passes through military lands and walkers should not stray off the route.

Walk back a few metres beyond the pub and up the road behind it to the T-junction at the base of Camarahill. This road, on which private vehicular traffic is not allowed, is in a very poor state of repair with crater-like pot-holes. Continue straight ahead through a gate to follow a way-marked track, which soon peters out to become an intermittent path. This is the start of the climb to Lugnaquilla.

On this ascent Camarahill (*Caméirí*, Curving Hill, 480m) is followed by a slight dip, otherwise it is a continuous uphill all the way to the summit of Lugnaquilla. But be not faint-hearted; magnificent views unfold as you ascend, while ahead the huge block of Lugnaquilla beckons, the focus of the day's walk. The last part of this ascent is through a rock-strewn, steeply rising area. Keep left here to view the great cliffs of the North Prison.

The summit of Lug is described in Walk 10. For navigational purposes we need only note here that the top is a virtual plateau of short grass topped by a mighty cairn.

The descent is tricky in mist and, at least initially, requires careful navigation to avoid the cliffs of the North and South Prisons. Descend very gradually northeast for about 300m before turning northwest to follow the high ground downwards for about 2km to the col facing Camenabologue. Take care on this descent to avoid the long west-running spur of Cannow and two rounded mounds of high ground to the east of the route. As already said this is a marvellous stretch with a lovely panorama of peaks, prominent among which is the great whale-backed ridge of Tonelagee. Watch out along here for Art's Lough tucked in below the cliffs north of Clohernagh. Watch out even more to avoid two spurs heading northeast of the correct route which would terminate in grief and painful backtracking above Glenmalure.

The descent over firm ground comes to a sticky end in the peat hags and soggy ground south of Camenabologue (*Ceim na mbulog*, Pass of the Bullocks, 758m) and is followed by a sharp pull-up to its summit, crowned by a large reassuring cairn — reassuring because its magnitude is unique in this area.

Descending north from Camenabologue the next landmark is between it and Table Mountain where an ancient track from Glenmalure crosses west into Imaal. Turn left (west) here and almost immediately take the left fork downhill, following a track, until a forest and metal gate are reached after 2km. Here an Army way-mark, reinforced by a stern Army notice, directs the cowed traveller right downhill, forest on the left. Cross two footbridges further down and pick up a forest track beyond them. (Note that recent felling means that the maps give an impression of much more forest than actually exists.) Follow this track until you come to a forest entrance with a gate and stile and a track heading diagonally away southwest. Cross the stile and a short pleasant walk brings you to a tarmac road where you will notice another road directly opposite. Follow this road southwest for about 2km back to the pub at Seskin and perhaps some well-earned refreshments.

Distance: 18.5km/11.5miles. Ascent: 850m/2,800ft. Walking time: 6¾ hours.

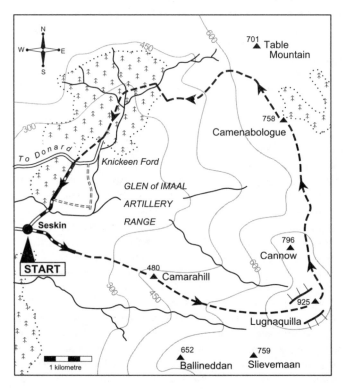

Reference OS Map: Sheet 56 (1:50,000).

43

13. BLACKSTAIRS MOUNTAIN

The 'tail' of the Blackstairs from its southern tip to the Scullogue Gap is just one ridge wide. This ridge falls gradually to east and west into the rich pastures of Wexford and Carlow. The walk described here covers the northern end of the 'tail', that is the central section of the entire range, taking in the granite tors around Caher Roe's Den and Blackstairs Mountain itself. It ends with a pleasant stroll through country lanes.

Drive to Ballymurphy, a village situated 5.5km/3.5miles west of the Scullogue Gap on the R702. From here take the road signposted St Mullins and Glynn, turn left off it after 1.3km/0.8mile and continue straight on for about another 2km/1.2miles to where the road swings sharply right (792 451).

Park just beyond the bend. On the left, before the farm, a gate opens onto open land. Up on the hillside you can see a green road slanting up to the right (south) to the saddle between Carrigalachan, 463m, and the main mass of Blackstairs Mountain. Go through the gate (you can actually see some remains of green road a few metres inside) and walk diagonally up the hill, passing successive walled corners of pastures to the green road, which is followed to the saddle.

At the saddle turn northeast onto the main ridge to climb the rock-strewn shoulder, marked by a massive tor. Descend the small drop beyond and then resume the upward and fairly steep climb to Blackstairs Mountain, a climb enlivened by the spectacle of the rocky teeth of granite protruding from its western flank (one of these is Caher Roe's Den).

The summit of Blackstairs Mountain, 735m, is a slight disappointment: a small cairn set on a flat area of scattered peat hags. Beyond it Mount Leinster, topped by its TV transmitter, dominates the view ahead with Knockroe a nearer and lower rounded peak across Scullogue Gap. From the summit continue more or less north (it is important not to bear too far to west or east) along the broad ridge until the road from the Scullogue Gap to Ballymurphy comes in sight. Aim 200–300m to the left (west) of the woods, cross a vague track running diagonally down to the west, and you will find a grassy track between high stone walls barring your way. At the east end where it turns downhill there is a gate. This track has become very overgrown so it is better to hop into one of the adjoining fields and head straight down to the road, rather than to try to follow the track down.

On the road turn left and walk west along it for about 2.5km to the crest of a low hill. The road swings sharply left here and as it resumes its original direction, take a left turn onto a narrow road. This road, in parts scarcely more than a lane, runs in a meandering course between high hedges and stone walls and in its course passes through the tiny hamlet of Walshstown nestling in a pronounced dip in otherwise undulating terrain. Directions along here need be minimal only: continue straight ahead to the T-junction and turn left here within a few hundred metres of the car.

Distance: 13km/8miles. Ascent: 640m/2,100ft. Walking time: 5 hours.

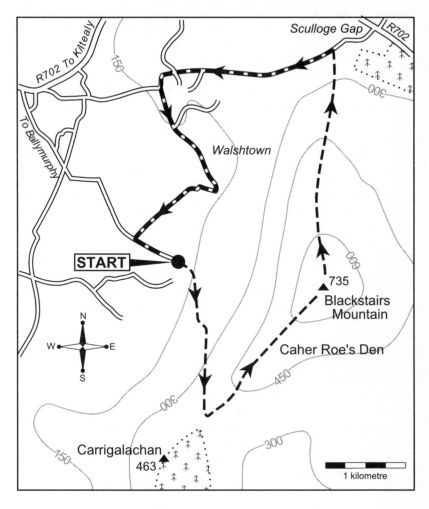

Reference OS Map: Sheet 68 (1:50,000).

14. MOUNT LEINSTER AND BALLYCRYSTAL

The major exception to the general north–south trend of the Blackstairs is provided by the undulating spur reaching out east to Black Rock Mountain. This is probably the most interesting approach to Mount Leinster; the spur makes for a varied and scenic walk, and after the slog south beyond it, the remote basin of Ballycrystal forms a leisurely end to an easy day.

When you have found the start of this walk, relax — most of your navigational problems are behind! From the village of Kiltealy take the R702 towards Enniscorthy, branching left onto the R746 towards Bunclody after just over 1.5km/1mile. Turn left at the multiple junction 2.6km/1.6miles further on and left again a few hundred yards on. Drive straight on for 2.6km/1.6miles and park at a forest entrance on the right just before a bungalow at about 852 512.

Walk past the bungalow and the narrow strip of mature forest beyond it and turn right through a gate between the forest and a field. Walk to the top of the forest, pass through another gate and continue directly upwards to the crest of the ridge, picking up a useful track (but useful for a short time only) near the crest. The large flat-roofed, stone building at the crest is worth inspecting. The summit of Black Rock lies a few hundred yards further east and is a there-and-back which may be visited by purists or those who do not intend to tell even little fibs about the mountains they climbed.

The rest of us will head directly west to Mount Leinster, climbing on the way a couple of rocky protuberances. Beyond them, cross an area of strewn boulders as you approach the summit plateau. Mount Leinster stands at the centre of four distinct spurs and, as is appropriate to its height, commands good views over most of the Blackstairs, the southern Wicklow Mountains, including pre-eminently Lugnaquilla, and a wide variety of low hill and agricultural country. Its attraction is severely diminished by the sore thumb of the TV transmitter. Injury has recently been added to insult by the erection of a solid fence round the whole area, so that one can no longer eat one's sandwiches in the warm air from the extraction fans!

From the summit head south along the spur ending in Knockroe keeping to the east side of it. Here you may recoup the cost of this book by betting (but not too insistently, mind) that the track to which you are heading is not rising, though to the naked eye it certainly appears as if it is.

Take this track (and it is level!) to the south and then southeast and when it disappears collect your winnings and head down to the ruin with the two beautiful beech trees at the southwest corner of Ballycrystal (at this point the track has re-emerged and can be seen sneaking round to the ruin).

Take this track north (it shortly graduates to a narrow road) which a little way down passes through a region of pleasant forest. From here it is but a short walk through mixed farmland and forest back to the car.

Distance: 10km/6miles. Ascent: 580m/1,900ft. Walking time: 4 hours.

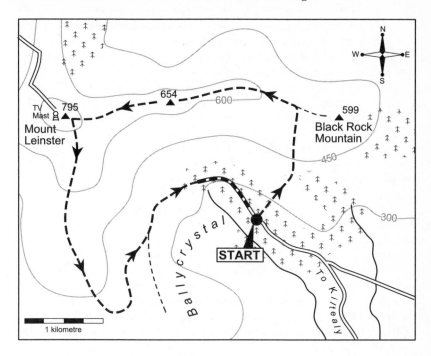

Reference OS Map: Sheet 68 (1:50,000).

15. THE CIRCUIT OF COUMSHINGAUN

The gigantic glacial amphitheatre of Coumshingaun (Hollow of the Ants) is claimed to be the finest example of a corrie in these islands. Situated very close to the main road, it is a perfect place to experience a mountain environment with very little effort.

The lake itself, the largest in the Comeraghs, is said to be 'bottomless and containing evil spirits'! Less than one hour's walk from the road, it is a popular location for family picnics. The towering cliffs rising above the lake have many rock-climbing routes.

The route around the encircling coum is perhaps the finest and most invigorating walk in the Comeragh Mountains. The southern ridge offers some enjoyable but easy scrambling, the nearest thing to the Kerry Reeks in this part of the country.

There are two starting points for this walk, both of which I will describe. The first starting point is at 349 116 close to a bridge on the R676 about 14km/9miles south of Carrick-on-Suir. The bridge is over the stream that flows down from the lake. Park close to the junction of a minor road.

Enter by a gate across the main road and follow a track down to the steam and across a grassy field. **This field and entrance area is often occupied by a large herd of cattle and can be very muddy in winter.** Cross the style out onto the open mountain and follow a clear path in the direction of the corrie lake. Approaching the lake, head for the southern spur of the corrie.

A more popular starting point is now at Kilclooney Wood car park (341 103), 1.5km/1mile further south along the R676. Follow a short well-worn path through the wood westwards until it joins a forest road. Take a right turn along the road until it runs out, then along a narrow path through the trees as far as the northern edge of the wood. Cross a fence and follow a stone wall uphill to the northwest edge of the wood.

Take a line north of west towards the southern spur of the corrie where both routes join up. As you move along, doing some mild scrambling, you will be rewarded by spectacular and plunging views down both sides — glimpses of the lake beneath you to your right as you move around the rocks and views into a deep narrow valley on the opposite side.

These rocks lead to a grassy section with a sheep track to the left of the crest. The last scramble up to the plateau must be taken with great care and is not at all suitable for inexperienced walkers. Once on the plateau you will be able — on a clear day — to see the Waterford and Wexford coastlines.

You may wish to detour towards Fauscoum, 792m, the small cairn which represents the highest point in the Comeraghs. Fauscoum rises only a few metres above the surrounding boggy plateau and may be difficult to locate.

Back to the cliff edge again — head around the rim of the corrie toward the grassy cone of Stookanmeen (Smooth Peak, 704m). Proceed along the northern spur keeping the stream Iske Sullas (Water of Light) on your left.

Descend carefully over rough terrain, taking care not to leave the spur too early and end up on steep ground over the lake.

When you finally reach the vicinity of the lake you deserve a rest and an opportunity to admire the splendour of Coumshingaun, and retrace with your eyes the route you have just taken. You must eventually drag yourself away from the serenity of this place and head back to the hustle and bustle of civilisation.

Return to your car by heading towards the southern spur again. If you are lucky you will pick up a narrow path going in the same direction. This will take you within sight of the wood and the main road (R676) below.

Distance: 8km/5miles. Ascent: 700m/2,300ft. Walking time: 4 hours.

To the lake and back
Distance: 4km/2.5miles. Ascent: 240m/800ft. Walking time: 1¾ hours.

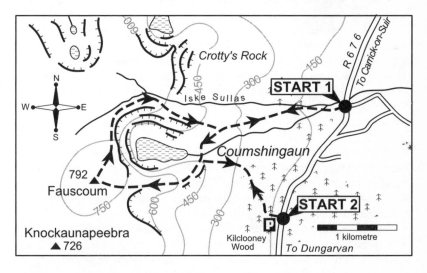

Reference OS Map: Sheet 75 (1:50,000).

16. THE MAHON FALLS AND COUMTAY

The upper section of the Mahon River is a rugged and beautiful place, one of the finest in the Comeragh Mountains. This broad, glaciated valley has a large stream, the sources of which rise in the desolate plateau above, before converging and tumbling down in a series of spectacular cascades with precipitous walls. In summer it forms rock pools with just a trickle of water flowing over the boulders but in winter it falls in a really impressive drop of around 150m.

It can be reached by turning west off the R676 (north of Dungarvan) at Mahon Bridge (Furraleigh, 343 060). Turn right immediately by a shop following the signs for 'Comeragh Drive'. In a little over 1.5km/1mile turn right along a road with the Mahon River on your right. Park in the car park where the road turns south at 314 078.

Two large boulders mark the footpath which leads directly to the bottom of the falls. Cross the stream over the stepping stones where the footpath meets the stream. (N.B. It is sometimes impassable in wet winter conditions and climbing to the left of the falls is not advisable.) Climb steeply along faint tracks with the falls on your left.

Cross the river above the falls and head uphill in a south-westerly direction over a wide plateau with the infant Mahon tributaries draining down from the marshes and peat hags. The area, however, offers some of the finest views in the southeast. The majestic cone of Knockaunapeebra, 726m is behind you, while southwards you have fine views of the Waterford coastline and Dungarvan Bay — if the day is good! You can also see Seefin, 726m, the highest point of the Monavullaghs with its ugly building spoiling this wilderness area.

Further along the route you will approach the narrow neck where the cliffs of Coumfea to the north and Coumtay to the south are only a few hundred metres apart. On your way you will catch glimpses of Slievenamon, Knockanaffrin and, in the distance, the Galtees and Knockmealdowns.

Turn in the direction of Coumtay. Circle around the edge of the cliffs and only begin to lose height when you reach the far end of the southern encircling spur. When you drop down to the end of the spur turn left and cross the valley by the ruins of an isolated house.

Walk uphill along the forest edge and back along the road to rejoin your car.

Distance: 10.5km/6.5miles. Ascent: 400m/1,300ft. Walking time: 4 hours.

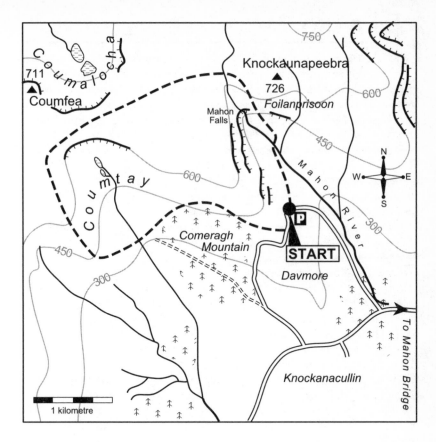

Reference OS Map: Sheet 75 (1:50,000).

17. CIRCUIT OF THE NIRE VALLEY

The word Comeragh comes from 'Cumarach' which means full of hollows, glacial in origin. Indeed the majority of Comeragh names incorporate coum (hollow or valley) in some form. The main tributary of the Nire (Nier) rises from the most easterly of them — the Sgilloge Loughs and is joined by other streams. The Nire itself rises from the central group, the Coumalochas, and to the west is one more, the highest, the deepest and the largest, Coumfea.

From Clonmel take the R671 south to Ballymacarbry. Drive eastwards along the valley of the Nire River towards the Nire church. Pass the church and carry on to the large lay-by above the river (276 129). The lay-by is a very popular place in summer. It overlooks the Nire Valley and is an ideal spot from which to explore these mountains.

From your starting point you can see clearly (on a fine day) the outline of your day's walk — Coumfea the westernmost coum, the Coumalochas, the Sgilloge Loughs and Coumlara, all north-facing coums and all except the last one containing attractive little lakes.

From the car park walk down the road for 500m to a gate on the left. Follow a track down to the river observing a number of small sheltered green fields around Lyre. Cross on a wooden bridge (which you may notice has not been grant-aided by the EU structural funds!).

N.B. This river is prone to flash floods and the water level may rise well above the bridge after a spell of heavy rain.

Continue along the track which will join an old track coming from Lyre. Cross over to this track by the stepping stones. Go up the track to a gate and out onto the open mountain where you veer right towards a fence. Follow the fence which leads roughly southeastwards in the direction of the western shoulder of Coumfea. You will be rewarded by spectacular views of the coums on your left with their sheer precipices dropping down to the lakes which are the special splendour of the Comeraghs.

Having reached the spur the route continues uphill in a southeast direction along a gentle grassy slope. The cliffs of Coumfea are just below you on the left. A tiny cairn marks the summit of Coumfea, 711m.

You are now on the relatively featureless plateau of the Comeraghs, which in these parts offers some pleasant walking and fine views — the lakes nearly 300m below, the Gap, the Knockanaffrin ridge, the valleys of Nire and Lyre and, in the distance, other mountains.

Soon, you will be just above the coum containing the Sgilloge Loughs, beside a little stream which plunges steeply over rocks to the inner lake below. The northwest winds blow the spray back upwards along cliffs (known as *Sean Bhean ag caitheamh tobac*, Old Woman Smoking a Pipe) which in winter freezes into weirdly shaped icicles on the vegetation and rocks.

About 500m of uphill walking will take you to Point 751m and the head of Coumlara. This valley is narrow and, on its western side, steep. It contains a sparkling stream which runs busily down the first few hundred metres and then meanders gently as the valley floor levels out towards the Gap.

Descend by the middle of the valley over ferns and mosses, keeping the river on your left. If you are fortunate you will pick up a contouring sheep track on the eastern slope which will take you all the way to the Gap.

At the Gap you now have a choice — of continuing the circuit by taking in Knockanaffrin or returning directly to the lay-by. If you decide on the latter, follow the white stakes out to the lay-by in order to avoid the marshy ground lower down.

If you decide on taking in Knockanaffrin you can look forward to enjoying some very pleasant, easy walking up along the ridge. You will be surprised how quickly you will gain height. After approx. 45 minutes and about 300m of ascent you will be on top at 755m.

Descend by retracing your steps to the cliffs above Lough Coumduala. From here walk in a southwest direction along the spur which drops down directly to the lay-by.

Distance: 17.7km/11miles. Ascent: 820m/2,700ft. Walking time: 6½ hours.

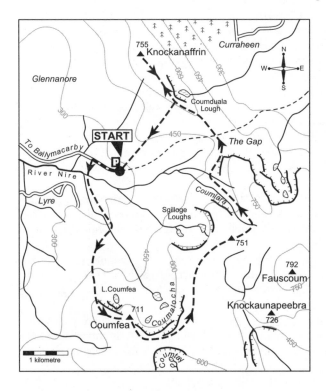

Reference OS Map: Sheet 75 (1:50,000).

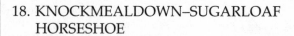

18. KNOCKMEALDOWN–SUGARLOAF HORSESHOE

The Clogheen–Lismore road, R668, is one of the most scenic drives in the southeast. From Clogheen the road winds up through steep woods as far as the Vee Gap and continues southwards across moorland with superb views. The Grubb monument is about 150m beyond the hairpin bend opposite the sign for 'Premier Drive'. This tombstone marks the grave of Samuel Grubb who had lived and owned property in the Golden Vale and wished to be buried in sight of his paradise. According to a local tale, he gave orders to be buried on the very top of the hills but six strong bearers could go no further — he would see no better on top!

Continuing along the road you come to Bay Lough on your right. It is a corrie lake, dammed by morainic deposits. It is reputed to be bottomless and inhabited by the ghost of 'Petticoat Loose'. In summer it is surrounded by a magnificent display of rhododendrons. The old road used to go straight up the valley past the Bay Lough. It is still walkable. The Sugarloaf and Knockmealdowns are on your left.

Just before the junction with the Cappoquin road (R669) you can park your car in the car park on the right, across the road from some trees which hide a derelict house (039 078).

Proceed uphill along a gentle slope with patches of short heather until you reach the summit of *Cnoc Maol Donn* (Bare Brown Mountain, 794m).

For those walkers who do not have time to continue the route you may now retrace your steps to your car.

Lismore and Cappoquin lie at the foot of the ridge while the south coast can be made out in the distance. On very clear winter days sightings of the Kerry mountains have been reported.

It is said that this was the spot chosen for burial by Major Eeles of Lismore who wrote extensively in the eighteenth century on the use of electricity as a cure for mental illness. There are no traces of his grave, however.

Descend in a northwesterly direction over short springy heather, again along the wall to a col. Ascend the final 90m of the day to the summit of Sugarloaf, 663m, a double-cairned peak overlooking the broad plains of Tipperary.

This section from Knockmealdown to Sugarloaf is the most spectacular part of the walk. The ridge is at its narrowest and the views are superb.

From Sugarloaf descend steeply, following a low wall to the large lay-by at the highest point of the Vee Gap.

The shelter at the top of the road marks the spot where Bianconi's tired stagecoach horses were changed after the long haul up from the valley below. At the lay-by also, there is an altar where Mass is celebrated every year.

Return to the car by walking along the road.

Knockmealdown Mountain
Distance: 5km/3miles. Ascent: 520m/1,700ft. Walking time: 2½ hours.

Horseshoe
Distance: 9.6km/6miles. Ascent: 610m/2,000ft. Walking time: 3½–4 hours.

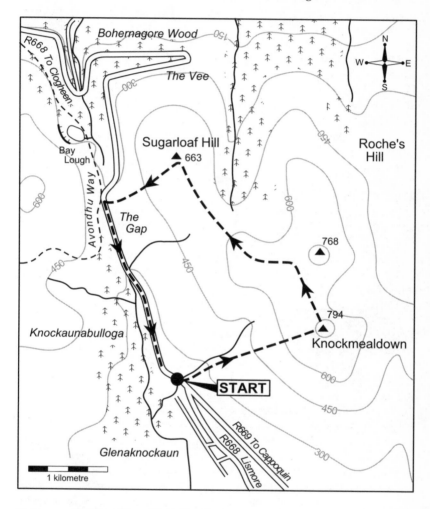

Reference OS Map: Sheet 74 (1:50,000).

19. THE EASTERN KNOCKMEALDOWNS

(From the Liam Lynch Monument to the Vee Gap)

This traverse over easy terrain takes in most of the major peaks of the range and is an exhilarating walk. The ridge forms part of the boundary between Counties Tipperary and Waterford and contrasts dramatically with the lush farms of the lowlands.

Drive to Goat's Bridge (*Goatenbridge*, 087 136) on the Clogheen to Newcastle road and turn south along a narrow road signposted to the Liam Lynch Monument. This road leads onto a forest road with several junctions all of which have signposts to the monument. Park just before the entrance to the monument at 097 110.

This monument, a small round tower for which the stone was gathered off the surrounding mountains, commemorates Liam Lynch who was commanding officer of the First Southern Division of the IRA during the Civil War. He was shot down on the mountainside near Goatenbridge in April 1923 shortly before the ceasefire.

From the ornate entrance to the monument, follow a forest road east for 100m. Climb over a new wire fence and follow it to the open mountain. Proceed out on to open moorland towards the top of Crohan West, 521m. Pause, now and then, to absorb the fine views unfolding all around you. (Because of the rough nature of the terrain, this route is easier to ascend than descend.)

Drop down along a wall to a col and ascend gradually over grassy terrain to Knockmeal, 560m. Descend to the southwest along a wall after Knockmeal towards the corner of a new wood. Here, you veer away from the ditch and proceed upwards to the broad summit of Knocknafallia, 668m — a strenuous ascent but you will be rewarded by splendid views from the large cairn which marks the summit. Care and precision are required to find this cairn in mist as it is off the centre of the plateau.

From here you will be able to see the southern side of the ridge for the first time — the River Blackwater meandering southwards towards Youghal Bay, the large grey buildings of Mount Melleray, a Cistercian monastery on the lower slopes of Knocknafallia, and eastwards the Comeragh Mountains.

From Knocknafallia the route now crosses a col and on to the stone-strewn ridge of Knocknagnauv (*Cnoc na gCnabh*, Hill of the Bones, 655m). Here you pick up the wall again with its small summit cairns. Descend now to the col just under Knockmealdown. An ancient ecclesiastical route (St Declan's Way) from Cashel to Ardmore passed through this col, and traces of it are still discernible.

The biggest ascent of the day now awaits you — with Knockmealdown looming up ahead! It is 300m from here to the top of the highest peak in the range, Knockmealdown itself (*Cnoc maol donn*, Bare Brown Mountain, 794m). Follow the wall, which goes steeply to the top where you will be rewarded by excellent views and the knowledge that your day's work is almost done.

The rest of the walk over the Sugarloaf to the Vee Gap is the same as Walk 18.

Distance: 14.5km/9miles. Ascent: 1,000m/3,300ft. Walking time: 6 hours.

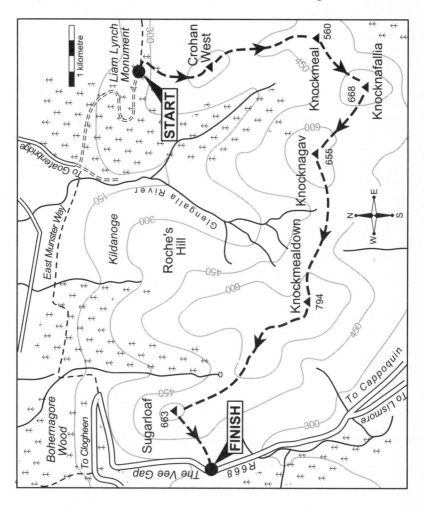

Reference OS Map: Sheet 74 (1:50,000).

20. TEMPLE HILL–MONABRACK HORSESHOE

Driving east from Kilbeheny on the N8 take the second road on the left. After about 2km/1.2miles you will pass a pump-house and just beyond this the road forks and you should take the right option. There is some parking at the end of the tarred section of the road, near the corner of the wood (868 197).

Here you are at an elevation of over 300m and a clear day will enable you to enjoy the splendid views in all directions — particularly scenic and including my favourite section of the Galtees with long, deep valleys from which rise the grassy-sloped peaks. The lower slopes are densely forested.

After you have lingered awhile admiring the peaks you should walk northeastwards in the direction of Monabrack — the 629m peak which is unnamed on the OS map — for 400m along a dirt track. Take the first gateway on the left and follow a contouring track to the ruins of a farmhouse. From here, it is advisable to take a sharp left turn in order to avoid a deep ravine and other obstructions and go straight down (southwest) through three small fields. This brings you to a cart track on the banks of the Behanagh River.

Proceed north along this track, cross a bridge, go through double gates and take the left-hand valley in a westerly direction. The going is easier if you keep the stream on your left. Soon, the valley swings north past the curious outcrop of Pigeon Rock on the slopes of Knocknascrow.

This is a delightful little place with its interlocking spurs, totally cutting off all views except the enclosing mountains — a perfect spot to rest and listen to the sounds of the birds and sheep who inhabit this wilderness paradise by the rushing waters of the Pigeon Rock River.

Just beyond Pigeon Rock the slope eases and you can now begin to ascend along a minor stream bed in a northwest direction. Now, views of Knockaterriff and beyond, the summit cone of Galtymore, unfold. The top of the ridge is soon reached, giving extensive valley views in all directions.

Proceeding along the ridge in a direction west of north, the great summit cairn of Temple Hill is soon reached, 785m. Descending eastwards from Temple Hill, swing slightly south to avoid the gullies running into the Glen of Aherlow. After reaching the Temple Hill–Knockaterriff col, proceed in a northeast direction to the col south of Lyracappul.

From here a short climb up a grassy slope brings you to the summit rocks of Lyracappul (Confluence of the Horse, 825m). Now follow the wall for about 1km and take a sharp turn in the direction just east of south towards Monabrack, 629m.

Time to pause again and view the evidence of turf cutting in the past, much of it for burning in the local creameries. To the northwest, there are further cuttings at 670m between Lyracappul and Knockaterriff, and a path to the area can still be discerned. Horse sleighs used to bring out the turf over the grassy terrain can still be found in local barns.

A short rise will take you to the broad summit plateau of Monabrack. Descending from here and heading south you will soon cross a fence from where you should be able to pick out your vehicle ahead of you.

Make for the right-hand side of the small clump of trees, and from here a cart track leads you directly back to your starting point.

Distance: 14.5km/9miles. Ascent: 730m/2,400ft. Walking time: 5½ hours.

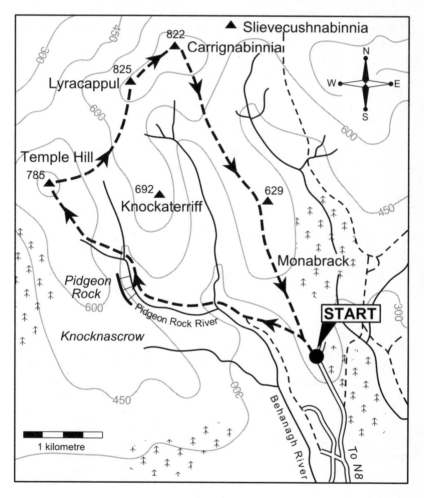

Reference OS Map: Sheet 74 (1:50,000).

21. GALTYMORE, GALTYBEG, O'LOUGHNAN'S CASTLE FROM MOUNTAIN LODGE YOUTH HOSTEL

This route is very popular among hill-walkers using Mountain Lodge Youth Hostel as a base. The hostel is situated deep in Glengara Wood 3.2km/2miles off the N8, 12.9km/8miles west of Cahir on the southern slopes of the Galtees. Occasionally in summer the Wood gate maybe locked, in which case you will have more opportunities to enjoy the grandeur of this wood by walking from its edge. Glengara means Rough Glen and walkers not familiar with the wood are advised to keep to the path!

Starting from the main bridge near the youth hostel (922 209), follow the forest road uphill on the east bank of the stream. This forest road after about 2km leads to the northwest corner of Glengara Wood. Leave the road at an extremely acute right-hand bend where open ground is less than 50m away.

Cross the first stream where the bank is low, at least 100m from the corner of the wood. Continue in a westerly direction and cross another stream. Bearing northwest you should soon pick up traces of an old track going your way, eventually joining the Black Road at the col north of Knockeenatoung.

Follow the Black Road the short distance north to its end; then bear northwest, rising very slightly, and you will pick up a slightly worn path leading to the col between Galtybeg and Galtymore. A few hundred metres below the col on the northern side is Lake Diheen (Tub) said to be inhabited by a snake banished there by St Patrick for eternity.

From the col your route rises sharply westwards to Galtymore, 919m, frequented by Spenser who called it 'Old Father Mole'.

After a short rest, retrace your steps towards Galtybeg and if you are thirsty keep an eagle eye open for the spring on the east slope of Galtymore. Having reached the col once again prepare for the short ascent of Galtybeg, 799m. Here the ridge is at its narrowest and you can at once enjoy views on both north and south sides.

Continue eastwards to the next col and ascend the gradual slopes towards O'Loughnan's Castle, a rocky outcrop at the east end of a broad plateau. This particular spot offers excellent shelter and is a favourite place to rest and restore lost energy. A short stroll over to the edge of the cliffs will be rewarded by an excellent view of Lake Muskry. The outcrop itself is a clearly visible landmark from many of the roads to the north and southwest.

Bearing southwest will bring you to the northern edge of Glengara Wood where you should re-enter the wood at your point of exit.

Distance: 14.5km/9miles. Ascent: 880m/2,900ft. Walking time: 5½ hours.

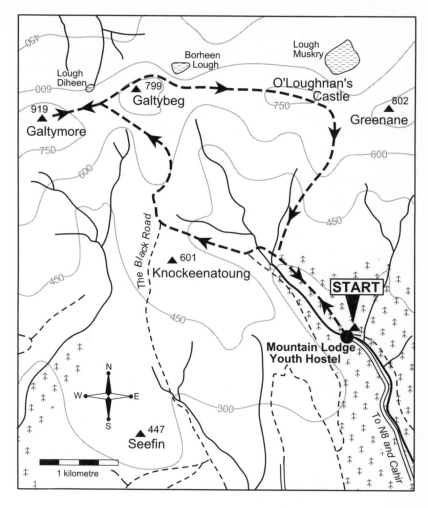

Reference OS Map: Sheet 74 (1:50,000).

22. CIRCUIT OF LAKE MUSKRY

Lake Muskry is the largest of the Galty lakes and was formerly known as Lough Bel Sead (Lake with the Jewel Mouth, the name being taken from a story in the Speckled Book of the MacEgans*). This told of the lake being the dwelling place of lovely maidens who were transformed into birds, every second year, one in particular becoming the most beautiful in the world. In keeping with her position she was allowed to wear a gold necklace which had a large jewel sparkling in it — and the name of the lake derives from this.*

Leave the N24 (Cahir–Tipperary road) at Bansha and take the road running southwest into the scenic Glen of Aherlow to the village of Rossadrehid (927 292).

Take the road running south from the village and as you enter the wood turn right along a contouring forest track. Drive about 500m/0.3mile as far as a triangular section of woodland. Turn left through the barrier and go to a small, grey, brick building on the right. Park here.

Follow the main forest in a direction at first east of south and then south along the west bank of the large stream. As you leave the woods, a rising rough track gives excellent views of the Lake Muskry Cliffs topped by O'Loughnan's Castle — a rocky outcrop of glacial origin. The track levels out after a while and shortly leads you directly to Lake Muskry.

There are a number of possibilities now. If time and energy are limited, you can walk around the lake and return by the route you came.

Alternatively, climb to the top of the ridge by the steep grassy slope to the right of the cliffs, after which a short walk to the southeast will take you to O'Loughnan's Castle, the curious outcrop perched in the middle of peat hags that resembles an old building.

From here, rising gently, make your way eastwards towards Greenane (*An Grianan*, The Summer Bower, 802m), a flat summit with a triangulation pillar.

Continue in a northeast direction for 1.5km across a broad plateau until you reach what is possibly a ruined booley — Farbreaga. Booleying (farmers living in small stone shelters and grazing their cattle on the hillsides during the summer) took place here until the middle of the last century.

From here, head northwest and re-enter the woods at your exit point.

a) To Lake Muskry and back
Distance: 9.6km/6miles. Ascent: 400m/1,300ft. Walking time: 3½ hours.

b) Circuit of the Corrie
Distance: 13km/8miles. Ascent: 760m/2,500ft. Walking time: 5 hours.

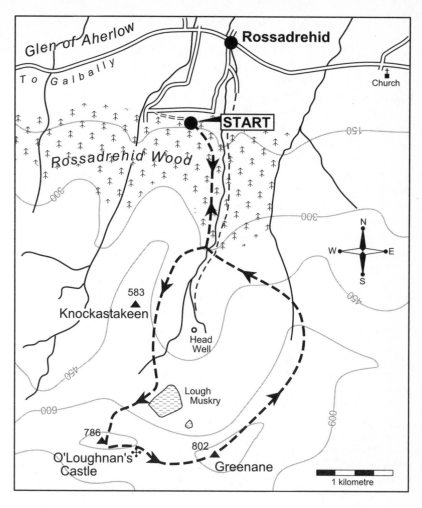

Reference OS Map: Sheet 74 (1:50,000).

23. GOUGANE BARRA–BUNANE

This walk would be suited to someone journeying between the youth hostels at Ballingeary and Bunane. The walk was devised originally by members of the Cork Mountaineering Club who proposed three days' walking over Easter weekends, connecting the Glanmore and Allihies Hostels. This first leg is a long walk requiring some fitness but it is a very good introduction to the area, both West Cork and Kerry, the mountain ridge being the county boundary.

The start is, conveniently, that of the path called *Sli Sleibhe* (Mountain Path), one of the six Walks in the National Park, beginning from the most westerly picnic area. To reach the start, you must enter the Park, paying the standard entry charge — although you could avoid this by reversing the walk! Leave the picnic area by crossing a footbridge over one of the streams which merge in the Park to form the River Lee. Once on *Sli Sleibhe*, you cross the same (descending) stream three times and follow to the upper edge of the forest to emerge onto open mountain. Ascend northwest and as you reach the top of the ridge, *Muing Mor* (Wide Long-grassed Expanse) valley opens to the west ahead of you with Knockantoreen (*Cnoc an Tuairin*, Hill of Sheep Grazing) standing to the right. The rusty red of a shed roof is clearly visible at the end. Aiming left of this, take the ridge which leads to the V of the Borlin Valley road.

From here, ascend between the coum of Lough Nambrackderg (*Loch na mBreac Dearg*, Lake of the Red Trout — a name regularly met in mountain areas) and Caoinkeen. At first, a wire fence can be followed but you should depart from it as it swings left towards the coum and follow the rising ground along the cliff edge until you can sit, swollen perhaps with satisfaction, at the 695m top, with Lough Akinkeen 425m below. Now turn south down to a boggy saddle and up to Knockboy (707m). As you ascend, a vast panorama opens both on the left and the right while behind you the MacGillycuddy's Reeks dominate the skyline to the northwest. From the peak, the whole of Bantry Bay appears to be beneath you with, on the right, Glengarriff Harbour.

Descend southwest to the Priest's Leap (579m). A number of legends exist to explain the name. The most commonly accepted one relates how a Father James Archer SJ, in search of volunteers for the defence of the O'Sullivan Beara castle at Dunboy in 1602, was chased across the mountains by enemy soldiers. From the rock here, he is said to have jumped his horse onto a rock a mile from Bantry town. As you reach the road below, you meet an iron cross erected to commemorate the feat.

Ascend now over point 519m and along the ridge with a rise of 80m to point 456m. From here, Barraboy is clearly visible and it may seem at first glance that the course is to go right to join the shoulder up to the top. Trust the map — it is correct. Keep south of west and descend to the two lakes nestling among the rocks in the saddle below. Influenced perhaps by tales of mountain chases, one easily imagines this secluded spot to be the home of a bold rapparee. From the lakes, the line up Barraboy is obvious and from there, one can with care follow a fairly steep grassy slope down to the road and across the Bunane Bridge. At time of writing there is an independent hostel, which I believe provides evening meals if booked in advance. Check with a Tourist Information Office for telephone number and current grading.

Distance: 21km/13miles. Ascent: 1,020m/3,350ft. Walking time: 8 hours.

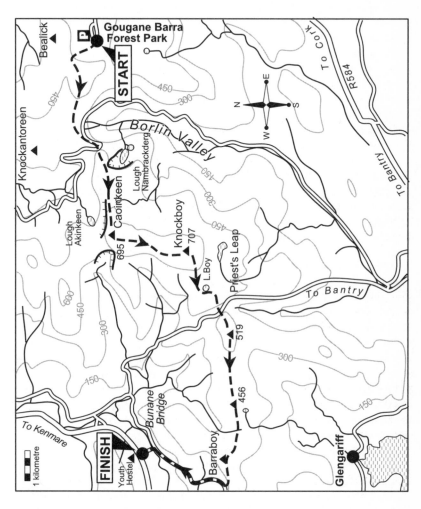

Reference OS Map: Sheet 85 (1:50,000).

24. HUNGRY HILL

The sheer bulk of Hungry Hill (686m) dominates its surroundings and, being the highest peak in the Beara Peninsula, acts as a magnet for hill-walkers. There are a number of routes offering a climb to suit everyone's taste. I give three routes for those new to the area while those more experienced will be able to plot their own variations.

(a) From Rossmacowen

About 7km/4.5miles west of Adrigole on the R572, I would disregard the first fingerpost for Hungry Hill at the Rossmacowen River bridge and continue past the former Rossmacowen School (now bearing a Youth Organisation sign) and church. Turn north on the road commencing at the gable end of the shop premises which stand beside the church, continue north at the T-junction on surfaced road through a farmyard and (seeking permission) leave your car between the house and the sheep-wire gate where it will not cause an obstruction.

From here (740 484), a green road which provides very easy walking winds almost 3km uphill. I assume this to be a road made to give access to the bogs for turf-cutting during World War II when fuel was scarce. The ascent is so gentle that there is plenty of opportunity for admiring the views all around you — Knocknagree and Maulin ahead, Hungry Hill on your right and the expanse of Bantry Bay behind. The Rossmacowen River valley is below you on the right and in the early stages of the road ascent, in the inner end of the valley, you can see a house apparently perched on an isolated rock shelf — somebody's idea of getting away from it all.

The road takes one quickly to the 400m level, very close to the Glas Loughs (*glas*, green), a generic name for small lakes high in the hills. Even if you decide not to proceed further, the walk so far will have been worthwhile. You now have views north into the Glanmore Valley and over Kenmare River onto the Iveragh Peninsula. Bear Island (a base for the British Fleet until 1921) still shows signs of military use — with a pair of binoculars you will be able to see the flag pole in the army camp. The name reminds us of the epic mid-winter march of O'Sullivan Beara who, after the fall of Dunboy Castle, left Glengarriff on 31 December 1602 with a band of 1,000 soldiers, men, women and children, and arrived in Leitrim with only thirty-five followers fifteen days later. The majority of the others had died, victims of the weather, the terrain and enemies, along the 500km route.

If that thought is not too wearying, you can continue your much shorter journey by taking the obvious ridge east, leading up to the north summit of Hungry Hill (656m). The route is roughly that of the Cork–Kerry border — shown by the dotted line on the map: do not expect to find a path! You meet here the greatest expression of the Beara phenomenon — benches or rock shelves which unfortunately cross your course and seem to add to the

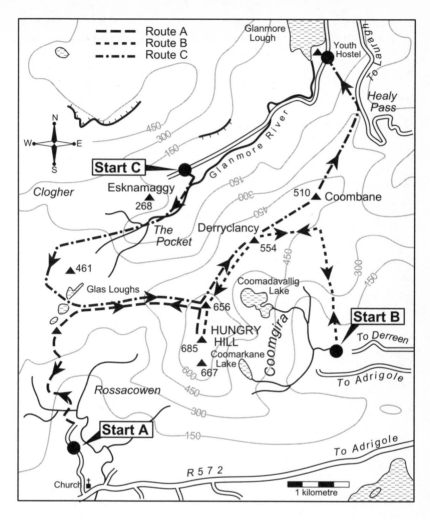

Reference OS Map: Sheet 84 (1:50,000).

length of the walk. However, the green road has so eased the early part of the walk and the views at this stage are so attractive that the ascent is still enjoyable. From the north summit, there is only a short rise south to the main summit (685m) which has an Ordnance Survey trigonometrical station. The view from here, particularly over the West Cork coast with its many islands and inlets, is limited only by the visibility. The finest summer days are understandably hazy but you may have been lucky enough to travel on a day when the air is clear.

The descent on this occasion is by the way you came. It will have been obvious from the views on the ascent that you should not try to go directly from the south summit to the ridge but must return to the north summit first.

Distance: 12km/7.5miles. Ascent: 610m/2,000ft. Walking time: 4½ hours.

(b) Coomgira/Hungry Hill Waterfall

While the first route is the easiest one onto Hungry Hill, many walkers dislike retracing their steps. For that reason, a walk termed Coomgira Horseshoe featured in past printings of this book. The line is shown still on the map for illustration purposes only.

Each side of Reen Bridge to the south of Adrigole village are byroads leading east. It is now pointless to drive in the southern one as the landowner has withdrawn permission to go through his land. Whatever may be your feeling, I ask that you do not press through, a course that may impact on fellow-walkers. We can keep an eye on the situation and perhaps it may some day be possible to resume a circuit beginning at the earlier point (784 493). Before deciding on an alternative approach onto Hungry Hill from the Adrigole side, read below.

Signposts for Hungry Hill Waterfall direct you along the (very narrow) northern byroad. There is a parking spot just before the end and you should use it. Going any further may mean an awkward reversing operation! Walk west to the gate at the end of the road (784 496) and from there follow the markers over 1km to the base of the waterfall itself. Nestled under flanks of the hill, the cascade is a magnificent sight and it may be that a stop here for refreshment, physical or spiritual, may be enough for the day. A *fulacht fia* (ancient cooking place) is shown on the OS map and trying to find and identify it will add interest.

Continuing onto Hungry Hill, in my view, depends on experience. It is worth reflecting that local folklore is that the correct name of the summit is Angry Hill, presumably a title derived from its appearance in bad weather. The alternative theory is that seven of Beara's hills have been named after the seven deadly sins and that Hungry derives its name from one of these. The Irish form is *Cnoc Daod*, Hill of Envy. Anyone with confidence, a proven head for heights, already-honed skills and sufficient time (to avoid taking risks) could find a line (or lines) through the cliffs to circuit Coomadavallig Lake (known locally as North Lake) and onto the summit. The more prudent course would be to go east initially onto the spur and from there over Derryclancy (556m). I will not be any more specific, nor give distances, etc., as any walk from this direction is for those who can navigate and have prepared a route card.

(c) Northern Horseshoe

For those using the Glanmore Youth Hostel, an approach from that side would obviously be more convenient.

You can walk or drive southwest almost 4km to the final T-junction (758 524) in the Glanmore Valley (*Gleann Mor*, Large Glen) from where you can walk into the pocket south of the spur Esknamaggy (306m). This is The Pocket; the name has been incorrectly shown on some maps at Cummeengeera, in the Drimminboy River valley, to the northwest. The walk into The Pocket is beside the Upper Glanmore River and I recommend leaving the road to follow the river bank and admire the many patterns eroded on the rocks. Then, ascend west beside the series of waterfalls behind the house to the flat plain of Clogher with its many meandering rivers. This is an area ideally suited to those seeking solitude — indeed, we have found the traces of what looked like a hippy encampment. Then swing south to the saddle between Knocknagree (586m) and point 461m, southeast to Glas Loughs and east up the ridge already described in Walk 24(a) to the twin summits of Hungry Hill.

Using extreme care, a descent is just possible into The Pocket from the saddle before Derryclancy. However, I recommend going over Derryclancy (see advice in Walk 24(b) and don't be drawn into the cliffs right) and Coombane (510m) and across *Eisc na gCorp* to the top of the Healy Pass. Incidentally, somewhere on the ridge between Hungry Hill and the Healy Pass is a lake, possibly seasonal and not shown on some maps. I have met it while travelling in thick fog (a course not recommended if unused to map and compass), am uncertain now where it is and have been told by others that they could not find it in summer. I mention it in case you get alarmed on finding it and might doubt that you were on the correct course.

Distance (hostel to hostel): 14.5km/9miles. Ascent: 730m/2,400ft.
Walking time: 5½ hours.

25. GLANINCHIQUIN

The lake-filled glens carved into the mountains are a feature of the northwest-facing side of the Beara Peninsula. Obviously, ice lasted longer and was more effective in scouring out coums on northern slopes protected from the sun. A glen that might claim to be the most attractive is that containing Cloonee Loughs and Lough Inchiquin and our next walk gives plenty of scope for enjoying it.

Turn off the R571 (Tuosist–Kenmare) road at the signpost for Inchiquin Lakes. The drive of approximately 7km/4.5miles on the north shore of the lakes (right at the Y-junction of the surfaced roads), and ending in front of the waterfall (locally called the Cascade), sets the scene. Use the car park provided (856 622), offering to pay for the facilities and promising yourself that you will return to the teashop at the end of the walk. From there you can follow the 'tourist road' west for a short distance. Your walk is a longer circuit, at a higher level. Leave the road to walk northwest towards the spine leading up to point 483m known locally as Eskana (and shown on OS maps as Cummeenanimma). There is a clear line to the left of the spine. Underfoot, it is rocky and fern-covered with the result that the going is rough. However, the gain in height in a short time is spectacular. To the right of the spine as you travel upwards is the Robber's Den. Local tradition is that a robber was chased from this den and shot on the Bunane side of the hills. In the chase, he is said to have dropped a golden boot in the river pool beside your starting point.

By the time you reach the top of Eskana, there are views all around but you may decide to cross the turf banks to the cairn (or is it a small fallen sheep shelter?) at the top of Coomnadiha (644m) before taking a break for lunch. Glantrasna and Lauragh are below to the southwest. Beyond the Kenmare River, Scariff Island lies in the Atlantic beyond Lamb's Head. The Baurearagh Valley stretches to the northeast. But it is the view north and northwest that is most spectacular. In fact, this would be a perfect site for a lesson on the effects of the Ice Age. While Templenoe, centre of the ice cap which shaped much of the area, is not in view (it is east of the inlet of Sneem, clearly seen), the signs of the movement from there are obvious. You are looking north through the dramatic gash of the Gap of Dunloe carved out by the ice floe, while to the northwest is the Gap of Ballaghbeama, through which the ice moved to Caragh Lake and, beyond, Dingle Bay.

Immediately north of you is Cummeenadillure. Local tradition is that it was formerly *Coimin an Fhiolair* (Small Coum of the Eagle). The eagle's nest was high above the lake which is 490m below you. There is a mini-coum above the main one and **this steep area must at all costs be avoided**. Taking a last look at Bantry Bay, set a course more or less directly east — the descent here is still a little steep but quite safe — towards the lake on the saddle below. As you descend, you can see clearly a sheep path leading from the lake north across the face of the ridge on your course. In good conditions, this is a good route but if wet, the lichen makes the rock slippery. It adds little to the journey to take the wide grassy slope leading from the lake to the right of the path. Either way, you reach the top of the saddle looking down into the Baurearagh Valley and can see how close the road comes at this point.

While it is possible to descend by the Cascade (to the north of the *Staca*, Stack), I suggest continuing north-northeast over Knocknagorraveela (*Cnoc na gCorra-mhiola*, Hill of Midges — none were in evidence while we were there) to follow the Maulagowna River. On the east bank of the river, you meet an almost complete ring ditch, possibly a cattle enclosure. Nearby are the traces of wide ridges, signs of tillage at a former settlement. A few ruins of stone houses still stand. There were apparently thirteen houses here and these may have been frame ones as there is a tradition that all neighbours gathered together to erect a 'cowluck' (very likely *cabhlach*, house frame) in a day. Look for the signs of the foundations of one house which seemingly never went beyond that stage. The Maulagowna River joins the Glaninchiquin close to where you parked your car.

Distance: 9km/6miles. Ascent: 720m/2,350ft. Walking time: 4 hours.

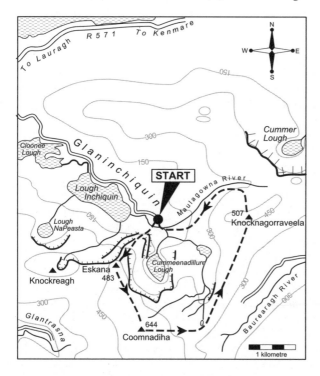

Reference OS Maps: Sheets 84 and 85 (1:50,000).

26. CUMMEENGEERA

My favourite part of Beara is still that around Lauragh. The contrasts of rich wood, wild bog and mountain, lonely glen, lake, river and ever-present sea never fail to please. The distance from a centre of population adds to the attraction. The next walk gives a bird's-eye view of this wonderful land- and sea-scape while the walk in the glen described afterwards is a gentle introduction to the folk history of the area.

(a) Cummeengeera Horseshoe

Travel less than 0.7km/0.45miles west of Lauragh School on the R571 and take the road south, which leads to Glanmore Lake and Shronebirrane, for a distance of 6.5km/0.4miles. (Incidentally, this walk can be shortened — see below.) Watch for two gates side by side on the right of the road on a slight left-hand bend. That on the right leads via a rhododendron avenue to a two-storey house. A path to the left of the house (763 575) leads through a small wood (mainly holly) to open mountain beyond. Cross the wire fence ahead with care, and the ascent of the benches will quickly give views behind of Kilmakilloge Harbour with the renowned gardens of Dereen House at the inner end. To the left is the lower end of Glanmore Lake and across the slope above it, the ribbon of the Healy Pass Road. The views increase as you ascend to the top of Cummeennahillan (356m) where you can sit to study the rock structure exposed on the ridge, which runs from the north to the aptly named Knocknaveacal (*Cnoc na bhFiacal*, Hill of Teeth).

The undergrowth up to now has consisted of long grass, but crossing the saddle from Cummeennahillan, this changes to heather, dense in summer, which can be tiring. On a really hot day, I have succumbed and used the escape route left into the hanging valley from which one can zig-zag carefully to the right of the waterfall into Shronebirrane, the reverse of this being the alternative start suggested above (753 552). However, it is worth pushing on. After the molars of Knocknaveacal (513m), the heather disappears to allow quicker progress across turf and rock. The ridge runs from the 'Hill of Teeth' to Tooth Mountain (590m) but my practice has been to contour (traverse at the same level) on a direct line for Coomacloghane (599m), a rounded summit with many pools of water trapped on its rock shelves.

Now descend south to the saddle from which there is a short ascent to point 584m which again can be avoided by contouring (left). A view of Bantry Bay is now opening on your right while below on the left the Drimminboy River winds out of the valley towards the sea. The 600m peak which you pass over is generally known as Eskatarriff (*Eisc a' Tairbh*, Steep Path of the Bull). This, properly speaking, is the name of one of the gullies leading down to the valley floor. You had passed another earlier called *Eisc na mBo* (Path of the Cows) — it leads down to the ruins of abandoned houses to be seen in the inner end of the valley.

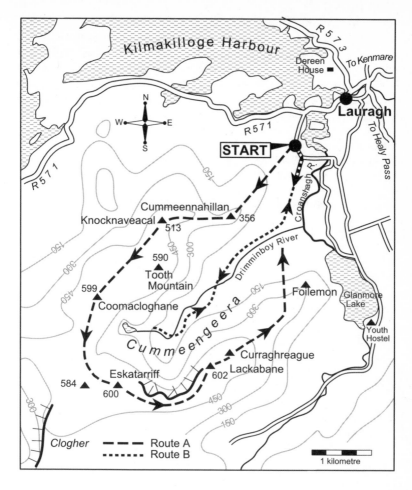

Reference OS Map: Sheet 84 (1:50,000).

Somewhere along the top of the cliffs on which you are now travelling, I recall on a still day producing a triple echo among the cliffs to the north and northwest, the second echo quite clear and the third just heard. Mindful of the friendly rivalry between the two counties and our position right on the border (represented by the dotted line on the OS map), one wit suggested that this was the Kerry method of throwing a Corkman's insult back in his face! On a later journey here, the wind foiled all attempts to produce even one echo.

From the next saddle, there is a stiff ascent to Lackabane (602m), known locally as Bullauns, and its twin peak, Curraghreague, but this is rewarded by fresh views of Kilmakilloge Harbour ahead, the Glanmore Valley on the right, and behind you the inner end of Bantry Bay. Any descent before point 406m, northeast of Curraghreague, should not be attempted. From the shoulder, there is an escape route left — aim for the circular earthen fort from which a path leads to the surfaced road at Shronebirrane.

For those who wish to finish the ridge or to gain the Glanmore road, a route over Foilemon (known locally as Foilcannon) is possible but a course left is still essential. The wooded slope on the eastern side is very steep — it is said that when the trees were being planted, estate workers had to be lowered on to the benches by rope. There is a path east through the wood at the northern end of Glanmore Lake leading to the surfaced road.

Distance: 13.5km/8.5miles. Ascent: 760m/2,500ft. Walking time: 6 hours.

(b) The Rabach's Glen

The walk on the valley floor into the hill-enclosed Cummeengeera (from local pronunciation, probably *Coimin gCaorach*, Sheep Pasture) would be a gentle respite after more serious walking and also suitable for a family group. Shortly after the surfaced road ends, park your car, with consideration, by the last houses in Shronebirrane (753 552) before the stone platform bridge. In a field on the right of the bungalow, you will see a stone circle, a record from prehistory, now a source of mystery to us. The path in the valley is quite clear at first, starting as a green road, crossing a stream and then left of the first rock outcrop which creates a narrow entrance. As the valley opens out, the path is not so distinct but there is an obvious line to the left under the steep slope of Bullauns (Lackabane). The back of the valley is quite green and shows signs of fields and tillage. The Drimminboy River is now easily crossed to reach ruins which, while decayed, are good examples of simple stone dwellings in use in the last century. Surrounded by the towering rock walls of the coum, it is easy to imagine how hard it was to scrape a living here and why the area was eventually abandoned. No road ever reached this spot and the coffin of the last person to die in the valley had to be shouldered up to the road. Life was basic and the story of the Rabach must be viewed in that context.

Cornelius Sullivan *Rabach* (the word in Irish can mean 'violent' or 'vigorous', both of which seem appropriate) lived in one of these ruined dwellings, and locals claim him to be the last man hanged in Munster, in 1831. It seems that a sailor (probably a deserter from the British Navy base on Beara Island, directly south across the hills) arrived at the house, seeking lodgings for the night. Urged on by his father (the Old Rabach), Con murdered the sailor in the belief that he had money. The body was hidden under the hearth stone. A woman neighbour who had risen early to go to the well for fresh water for tea (her husband was a horseman who regularly made the two-day journey to the Cork Butter Exchange, trading his own and neighbour's butter for other provisions) saw the deed through the window but kept silence at the time. During a dispute, she was unfortunate enough to tell the Rabach that she had information that could 'put him away for good'. On her next visit to the hill to tend cows, the Rabach followed her, strangled her with a spancel and left her, head down, in a stream to simulate drowning. This was in 1814. No one else apparently knew of these events until a man, injured in the Allihies mines, confessed on his deathbed in 1830 that he had been on the hill (stealing cows' tails, then a reprehensible crime) and had seen the second murder. The chase was then on, but the Rabach evaded capture by making use of a den in the rocks still known as *Pluais an Rabach*.

The Pluais is above the house to the northwest. The Rabach resorted to the den only in times of danger and he easily outran police sent for him (it is said that an autopsy revealed that he had a double heart). In January 1831, the dead woman's son, who had only been a year old at her death, alerted the police that the Rabach would be at home for the birth of a child and they availed of the opportunity to make their capture.

Despite its history, the glen is today a haven of peace. Having sampled that peace and the atmosphere of the glen, you can return by the route you came.

Distance: 3.5km/2.25miles. Ascent: 110m/350ft. Walking time: 1½ hours.

27. THE PAPS

From wherever they are seen, whether from the N22 (Ballyvourney–Killarney road) or the N72 (Rathmore–Killarney road) or from other summits, it is clear why The Paps (Da Chioch Dhana, Two Breasts of Dana or Anu) received their name. The twin rounded summits surmounted by two cairns provide easy climbing and — due to their relatively isolated position — views over amazingly long distances.

The usual approach has been from the roadway running to the east of the peaks by Lough Glannafreaghaun. However, the erection of *No Trespassing* signs suggests that alternative routes be used. It is possible to approach directly from the south, skirting by a forestry plantation and over Rodger's Rock, or from the north, on a sheep track running from Gortacareen. However, there is a much easier approach, provided you seek permission. If you are new to climbing, you may wish to be modest in your ambitions and this is the drive/walk described.

The N22 crosses the River Flesk at Garries Bridge, 2.5km/1.5miles southeast of Glenflesk (081 836). To the east of the bridge, a byroad enters north. Remain on that surfaced road for 1.1km/0.7miles. Immediately there is a small bridge with, on the far side, a gate and cattle grid. Continue left/straight, i.e. not right. After an S-bend, there is a cottage. There, it would be courtesy to ask the Healy family if it is in order to use their farm road. You should also check if there is a bull loose in the lands beyond. Just beyond the cottage, another cattle grid half crosses the road. Go right through the gate there. This is the first of a series of gates along the farm road which twists uphill for 4km/2.5miles. Each gate should be secured after you pass through.

Some distance on, you meet a new farm building beside stone ruins and there are more ruins later showing that this valley once was home to a number of families. After the second last gate (1994), you ford a stream. Between this and the next gate, the road is grassed over. If wet, it may prove slippery and you may decide to leave your car. If so, park considerately, allowing for farm vehicles which may need access. If there is warning of a bull, you may decide to proceed by car inside the upper gate where only sheep graze. At the end of the road, there is a wide turning point. Again, if using it, park neatly to avoid obstruction.

From this parking spot, it is a very short 'step', with an ascent scarcely more than 150m. A zig-zag course northeast leads to the saddle under the west Pap. The upper ground is a soft carpet, reasonably dry in any weather, of heather, moss and whortleberry shoots. On the summit (690m), the mound and cairn are not as grand as those on the other Pap but the ruined chamber entrance can be seen. The feature of this summit is that to the north, west and south, the views are almost unlimited. Only haze or cloud will prevent you from enjoying a panorama from Kenmare Bay to Dingle Bay and beyond.

The east summit is worth visiting if you wish to pay tribute to our pagan past. This involves a descent to the saddle and an ascent of 110m. A massive mound over 6m high has a cairn of 3m on it. This is believed to be a prehistoric burial chamber. Signs of pagan fertility rites abound in this area. It was claimed that the province of Munster owed its prosperity to the Goddess Anu on whose breast you stand, and, to the north of the peak, in Gortnagan, where a penitential station is shown on the map, is *The City*, a stone fort where rounds (walking in circles while reciting prayers) of a well were made each May Day. The practice is thought to have been associated with one of the sisters of Anu but given a Christian aspect later. Until recent times, sick animals were brought from all over Cork and Kerry to *The City* for the cure available at the well.

Returning to your car, you can contour the east summit to avoid a third climb. Again, don't forget to close all gates as you descend the farm road.

Distance: 5km/3miles. Ascent: 260m/860ft. Walking time: 2½ hours.

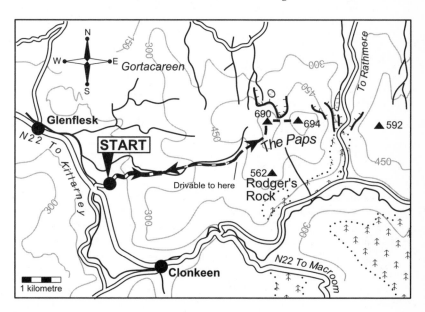

Reference OS Map: Sheet 79 (1:50,000).

28. MANGERTON

Mangerton (839m) offers a fine, fairly short walk amid some magnificent scenery, with a panoramic view of the MacGillycuddy's Reeks to reward you from the summit. For a shorter walk, the Devil's Punchbowl is recommended.

(a) The Tooreencormick Bridle Path

This provides the most gradual ascent. Near Muckross on the N71, take the road left signposted 'Mangerton Viewing Park' and at the upper end of the wood, swing right. Pass the car park and continue to the end of the surfaced road to park by a concrete bridge.

From here (983 848), a path once used as a tourist pony route runs uphill. Initially, it crosses a stream and the Finoulagh River and continues up on the eastern side of the river. On your right is the site of a battle in 1262 in which the McCarthys defeated the Normans. In the battle, Cormac McCarthy fell, thus giving his name to the place. The path shortly swings right to meet an estate boundary fence which runs (left) directly up to the Devil's Punch Bowl. Just before the lake is a small beehive stone shelter, once used by estate gamekeepers.

Go uphill along the north side of the lake to cross the narrow arête between the Punch Bowl and Glenacappul. From there, its is a short journey southwest to the summit cairn. You can descend by the southern edge of the Punch Bowl to rejoin the path at the Bachelor's Well and thus homeward.

Distance: 9.5km/6miles. Ascent: 700m/2,300ft. Walking time: 4 hours.

(b) By Foilacurrane

As an alternative, you can take the much more scenic approach through the shaded slopes of Muckross Forest. The walk is not as gradual as the previous one and at one stage involves some scrambling.

Start from the Torc car park on the N71 Killarney–Kenmare road and follow the attractive tourist footpath up beside the waterfall. At the upper end of the path, swing left on the forest road and continue uphill along the various roads. Getting a copy of the Kerry Orienteers' map of Muckross Forest will aid navigation. At the top end of the upper road, go uphill beside the stream and across the stile on the forest fence to the gorge ahead. This is shown on the map as Barnancurrane (*Bearna an Corrain*, Gap of the Sickle), usually known locally as Foilacurrane (*faill*, cliff). The gorge is a fairly steep scramble, made easier now by the provision of steps. From the top of the gorge, an old fence runs straight ahead (east) — this once separated the tenants' commonage (to the south) from the rest of the demesne, long before it became a National Park. Follow the fence to meet another which you should follow right uphill (now beside the Bridle Path) to reach the Devil's Punch Bowl. Once again, a clockwise circuit of the Bowl is suggested but on this occasion, if you travel directly west from the summit of Mangerton, you will meet the western peak (730m). The cairn marked on the map is in fact a natural rock outcrop.

Here you are looking down on the Owengarriff River which feeds Torc Waterfall. Take the line of your choice down to cross the river (provided it is not in flood, of course) and join the Old Kenmare Road which runs down on the western side of the river and across a bridge (right) to meet the path by which you ascended. On this course, you are almost certain to observe deer, either the native Irish red deer or the imported Japanese sika, which frequent the area — the higher ground in the summer and lower down in winter.

Distance: 11km/7miles: Ascent: 800m/2,650ft. Walking time: 4¾ hours.

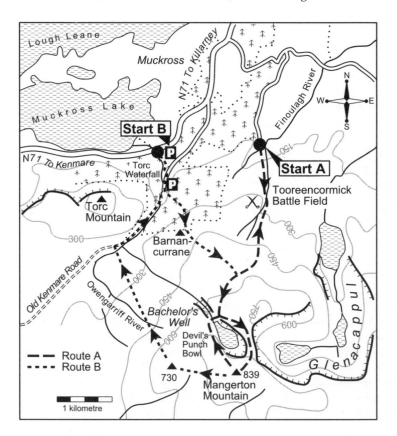

Reference OS Maps: Killarney National Park (1:25,000) or Sheet 78 (1:50,000).

29. TORC MOUNTAIN

For someone seeking a relatively short walk in the Killarney area offering a good viewing point, Torc Mountain (Torc, Wild Boar) provides the answer.

You can walk from Killarney through the grounds of Muckross House following the Kerry Way way-marks or take your car to the car park on the N71 at the bottom of Torc Waterfall (965 847). Ascend by the cascade and follow the yellow Walking Man markers of the Kerry Way along a path with the Owengarriff river below you on the left. Emerging from the woods, continue along the track until you are roughly where the Owengarriff veers away south. Now swing round nearly to north and start climbing. A pit, obviously the source of material for the road, marks the spot. There is a bridle path which can only be discerned in places. However, your line ahead is clear — aim for the shoulder to the left of the peak. In the later stages, short rock-faces cross your path. These force you to zig-zag, the correct thing to do on any ascent.

As you climb, take time to look behind. The area around Cores Hill shows many signs of former habitation — walls, old tillage, etc. In fact, if you had continued further along the Old Kenmare Road, you would have seen a number of ruined houses. These were inhabited until the Clearances — a period when many landlords felt that open land for deer-hunting was more important than the resident tenants, who were simply evicted. It was at that stage that the present Killarney–Kenmare road was built, as the bridges on the Old Road were knocked down to prevent public passage. Behind Cores Hill and between the two branches of the Upper Crinnagh River lies *Inse Baile na mBo* (Inch of the Town of the Cows), presumably the site of a booley village, that is, one inhabited only in the summer when cattle were taken to the higher grazing land.

As you climb, the Upper Killarney Lake comes into view over the shoulder to the left with the sugarloaf of Broaghnabinnia behind it and to the right of that the ridge of the MacGillycuddy's Reeks. The knife-edge of Cummeenapeasta, the centre section of that ridge walk, is clearly seen.

At the top of the Torc (535m), all three Killarney Lakes are in view. To the east is Lough Guitane and to the west Looscaunagh Lough. The sea — the inner end of Dingle Bay — is also to be seen. In fact, a look at the map will show how well situated Torc is as a viewing place — it protrudes out over the lakes from the centre of a crescent created by the peaks of the National Park.

Your descent should be by the course you ascended. However tempting it may seem as a short cut to the bridge, going down by the east side of Torc would be very foolhardy. Keep a keen eye out for deer, usually seen in this area.

Distance: 9.5km/6miles. Ascent: 530m/1,750ft. Walking time: 3¾ hours.

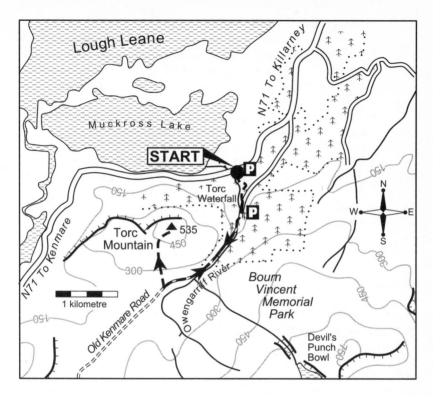

Reference OS Maps: Sheet 78 (1:50,000) or Killarney National Park (1:25,000).

30. PURPLE MOUNTAIN

The Purple Mountain range on the west side of Lough Leane provides very good climbing and viewing points. It can be approached from a number of directions but I am using a south–north attack which would be suitable for anyone leaving the Black Valley Youth Hostel.

From near the turn of the road over the youth hostel (871 833), follow the line of a stream and fence, northeast. A rock wall is on the right and where, after some distance, the stream swings right towards its face, continue with the fence as far as Glas Lough. For some reason, this lake always seems to be nearer the start than expected — a good complaint. It provides a good point to rest for a bite and a view — south over the peaks of Iveragh, southwest into lake-strewn Cummeenduff (the Black Valley) and west down into the ice-carved gorge of the Gap of Dunloe.

At the end of the lake, a heather-clad slope commences and runs up to the right. In fact, the fence conveniently continues on our course for a while. Follow it to the end, from where you bear slightly left to rise to the summit. This slope satisfies one's notions of what a mountain should be like — a fairly steep rock- and scree-covered slope. The sandstone of which the Reeks are made is of various hues and here the rock is definitely purple. Viewed from a distance, in a certain light, this is more distinct. On the ascent, you meet a number of cairns. I judge the fourth heap of stones — really a small circle — to be the peak top (832m). As might be expected, the vistas have expanded.

At the summit, there is a sense of being on the roof of the world. This is the effect of a clear ridge stretching northwest and north over the sheer drops on the right and left. Generally, particularly at the start, there are sheep tracks and one is encouraged to bound along towards Tomies. At the 'complex junction', where the ridge from Shehy Mountain on the east enters, there is a risk of going astray in fog. If this should happen to you, the one thing that must not be done is to go west into the Gap. Almost any other course is safe.

At any rate, there is little point in being here without views. At the junction, you must decide whether to travel east to Shehy Mountain (571m), claimed to be the one vantage point commanding all three Killarney Lakes.

If you are not doing so, continue on to the turf saddle leading to the summit of Tomies (735m). The mounds of stones here are said to mark burial places. Dingle Bay is now seen to the northwest across the plain of mid-Kerry. Across the Gap from you, zig-zagging towards the bare trees on the hill edge, is the track which is the beginning of the Reeks Ridge Walk. Your course ahead is north-northwest (a detour to Tomies Rock is optional) down the heather slope to the L in the river near Kate Kearney's Cottage. Approaching this, I suggest that you continue to the end of the spur, beyond the river, and then swing back on the path leading out beside it to the surfaced road.

Distance: 8km / 5miles. Ascent: 700m / 2,300ft. Walking time: 4 hours. (Please note that this walking time does not include returning through the Gap to the Black Valley which will take another 1½ hours.)

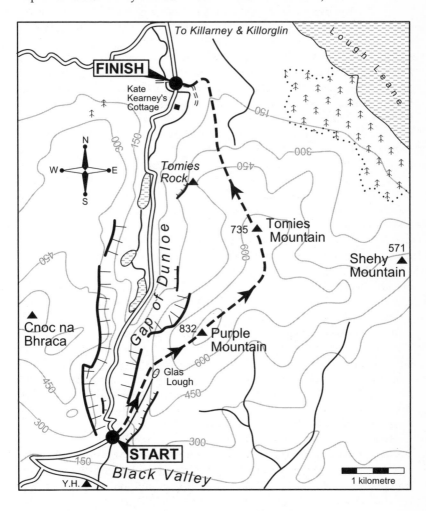

Reference OS Maps: Killarney National Park (1:25,000); MacGillycuddy's Reeks (1:25,000); Sheet 78 (1:50,000).

31. BLACK VALLEY–GLENCAR

This walk takes us through the lonely and rugged glens of mid-Kerry. One mountain pass, on the Lack Road, is at the 365m level and you should be prepared for this. You are following the way-marks of the Kerry Way for the whole of this walk.

The first glen is the Black Valley/Cummeenduff (*Com Ui Dhuibh*, Black Corrie) and as you leave the hostel (865 827) you get your first glimpse of its lake-studded floor. The valley rising northwest towards Lough Googh holds some of the remains of an American Douglas Dakota C47 which hit the ridge in December 1943.

Disregard the unsurfaced road rising uphill to the north, marked unsuitable for traffic — this winds its way through the dramatic ice-carved Gap of Dunloe and could be used as an escape route to Killarney. Continue for some time on the road marked *cul-de-sac* until you reach a Y-junction and go straight on. Near the junction stood a Mass Rock, used for secret worship in Penal times. According to the local legend, the cliffs facing east by the waterfall on your right mark the burial place of the last Viking invader and it is said that a gold hoard lies with him. As the road rises north, swing left at the finger-post, zig-zag at the houses in Cloghernoosh (*Clochar Nuis*, Rock of the New Milk) and follow the markers through a gate. A stony and generally wet path zig-zags by the abandoned houses and continues above stone walls to lead directly to a stile to the left of the gateway into the wood. The path, still stony and wet, winds pleasantly through the wood, which contains enough deciduous trees and holly to mask its commercial intent. As you emerge, enjoy the view southwest, beyond Cummeenduff Lough, of the waterfall on the Upper Cearhameen River. Follow the path (keep right) to the grove of pine trees sheltering the next farmhouse. Please close the gate on the far side when through. A short stretch of surfaced road becomes green road again leading into Curraghmore (*Currach Mor*, Big Marsh).

Pass the last houses in the valley on the marked line. Follow the path (above stone-walled fields and below the wire fence) and continue west to cross the river from Curraghmore Lake by the footbridge. Now on the Bridle (Bridia?) Path, Ireland's highest peak Carrauntuohill (*Corran Tuathail*, Inverted Sickle), 1,039m, lies directly north. The dangers of the ground are obvious and no one should venture to higher levels unless experienced and fully equipped. The cardinal sin is to travel on one's own. As you rise up the path marked by stone cairns, watch for the first of a line of Way marker posts leading right on the approach to the crest of the saddle. The standing stone on the summit is one of an alignment but while it might seem to be a marker for travellers, it would deceitfully lead you through rough grounds and into the fields of the Bridia Valley ahead. The name (*Na Braighde*, the

Prisons) probably arises from the enclosing rock faces. One of the rocks on the saddle has an obvious cluster of St Patrick's Cabbage, *Saxifraga spathularis*, another of the rare Lusitanian flora. Its spatula leaves and pink flower point to its relationship with the domesticated London pride. Do please resist the temptation to pick.

Keeping right with the marked path, the descent through rock benches lends relative justification to the name of the townland on which the next house sits — Cappeenthlarig (*Ceapaigh an Chlaraigh*, Plot of Level Ground). Passing through the farmyard should remind you that you are passing, by

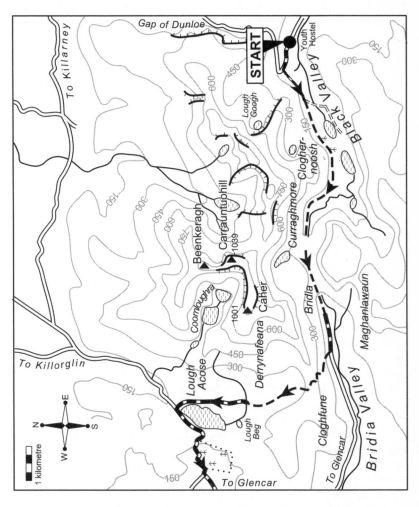

Reference Maps: OS MacGillycuddy's Reeks (1:25,000); Kerry Way Map Guide (1:50,000); OS Sheet 78 (1:50,000).

courtesy of farmers, through their work- and living-place. Please respect all crops, close gates carefully, avoid provocation of working dogs and in case somebody is resting, be as quiet as you can. 2.5km from the house leave the surfaced road at Maghanlawaun (*Macha an Leamhain*, Milking Place of the Elms), the entrance right to the Lack Road being beside a water spout. Despite its name, the trees most seen are the orange-berried rowan/ mountain ash and the birch as well as large bushes of fuchsia with its red bells. I spent some of my school holidays here. One memory is of being able 'to see the weather approach'. The orientation of the valley is such that rain clouds borne by the prevailing south-westerlies could be seen at its far end long before reaching here and if one was engaged in haymaking, by hand of course, there was time to take action.

The surfaced road here is an escape route to Glencar or to accommodation, particularly if mist keeps you off the pass ahead. The Lack Road (*Leac*, Flagstone) was used within living memory for droving cattle to the fairs in Killorglin to the north, a journey starting at midnight to ensure arrival at the fair at 7.30 a.m. Before that, the road was used to transport firkins of butter to market by pack-horse. While it is much clearer later on, the road has been absorbed into fields initially and you must follow the markers and stiles to gain open hillside where the Lack Road intelligently switchbacks to save energy. As you ascend, you have a view southwest of coum-enclosed Cloon Lake. An island on the lake is reputed to be the burial place of William Francis Butler who tells in his book *Red Cloud* of his childhood in Glencar and his later life in America where he joined a Native American tribe. Cloon also has an Early Christian site.

At the stile at the summit of the pass, the view northeast is of the 1,001m Caher (*Cathair*, Stone Fort — perhaps of the Fianna). Beneath you to the north is the amphitheatre of Derrynafeana (*Doire na Feinne*, Oakwood of the Fianna) and Lough Acoose (*Loch an Chuais*, Lake of the Recess). With a view further north to Killorglin and Dingle Bay, the vista lends credence to tales of day-long deer hunts by the Fianna, Ireland's legendary army aided by giant wolfhounds. Keeping left to avoid steeper ground on the right, descend the zig-zag road to join a path which starts where the Cummeenacappul Stream (*Coimin na gCapall*, Small Coum of the Horses), flowing from the slopes of Caher, joins the Gearhanagour Stream (*Gaortha na nGabhar*, Woodland of the Goats).

The path leads to farmhouses, and gradually becomes a road that crosses the Gearhanagour stream and heads for the east shore of Lough Acoose. Incidentally, a pre-bog system (walls, huts, enclosure and a bog trackway) has been located between Lough Beg and Lough Acoose. The road continues along the lake shore and joins the Killorglin–Glencar road. Turn left along this road from which you can enjoy the view east into the magnificent corrie of Coomloughra shaped by the ridge connecting Ireland's highest peaks, Beenkeragh, Carrauntuohill and Caher.

The road left descends beside the Gortmaloon Wood (*Gort Ma Luan*, Field of the Plain of Lambs), through which tumbles the Caraghbeg River. At the Y-junction, bear left to walk 1.6km to the Climbers Inn. The hostelry, which is also the post office, is run by Sean Walsh, an experienced climber. Nearby is Glencar House, formerly Lord Lansdowne's shooting lodge. One of its renowned guests was Father John Sullivan, and it is said that a religious reading overheard at a French window, still preserved, led to his conversion to Roman Catholicism. Assuming that you have pre-booked accommodation, Glencar is an ideal place for an overnight stay.

Note: It is hoped to move the Kerry Way off road by paths to the west of Lough Acoose. If just after passing the second set of buildings on the descent from the Lack Pass you see a Kerry Way marker pointing left (west), you may safely follow it and its successors to Gortmaloon Wood. **In the absence of such a marker please do not attempt to go west of the lake.**

Distance: 20km / 12.5miles. Ascent: 480m / 1,600ft. Walking time: 6¼ hours.

32. COOMLOUGHRA HORSESHOE

Including Ireland's three highest summits, the circuit of Coomloughra must be regarded as the country's finest horseshoe walk. This narrow ridge gives a far greater sense of being 'on top of the world' than other approaches to Carrauntuohill. One word of warning: the route is not for those of a nervous disposition.

Park near the bridge at Breanlee (767 867) on the Killorglin–Glencar road. Go south from the bridge to meet the bohereen leading to a winding path on the western side of the Cottoners River which drains the Coomloughra lakes. Please ensure that you do not encroach on planted fields (or cross fences) and that all gates are closed after you.

The path turns south behind a rock outcrop and then east and very quickly as you climb by the side of the stream, views of the hills on the Dingle Peninsula open behind you; they are most impressive if they have a covering of snow, although this may not be the time of year to undertake the Horseshoe. Cross the stream where it leaves Lough Eighter (*Loch Iochtar*, Lower Lake). At this stage, there is a fine view of the almost sheer walls of the amphitheatre. Carrauntuohill rises over all to the southeast. The hydroelectric scheme here resulted in serious scarring of the hillside during construction. This was not envisaged by the environmentalists or by the planners who welcomed the idea of clean power. One can only hope for rapid revegetation despite the height and short growing season.

Ascend northeast to the sharp summit ahead — this is the shoulder of Skregmore (*Screag Mhor*, Large Rough Hill) and there is a short ridge walk to the peak (848m). From this point, there is a further rise and fall before the ascent to Beenkeragh (*Beann Caorach*, Peak of the Sheep: 1,010m). On the summit, you are already 'above it all' with hills and valleys all around and a view across the plain of mid-Kerry to the north. The ridge to the cairn of Beenkeragh (one upright stone in the centre) has been broad and rocky. Now it becomes almost a knife-edge, a place perhaps to be avoided if rain has made the lichenous rock slippery. It seems best not to travel along the top but to descend slightly to the right to travel on the Coomloughra (west) side at this stage. You should be able to find sheep tracks. Barren as the area seems at first glance, there is flora in abundance. St Patrick's Cabbage is much in evidence. The ridge becomes steeper as you swing north to the peak of Carrauntuohill to take a welcome respite.

From the peak (1,039m), leaving the cairned route to the Devil's Ladder on your left, descend carefully to join the ridge to Caher. You travel west-southwest on sheep tracks to the left of the sheer drop into Coomloughra. There are three summits in Caher, the second (1,001m) being the highest. From the second there is a ridge (left) to Curraghmore, but keep more right to rise up the steep scree slope to the third peak (975m). From there, you can continue northwest to pass over a spur (442m). My preference is to get out of the boulder field as soon as possible by descending carefully before reaching the spur to the eastern end of Lough Eighter and joining the track by which you ascended. The road made beside the pipeline is usable but very steep.

Distance: 12.5km/7.75miles. Ascent: 1,150m/3,750ft.
Walking time: 6–7 hours.

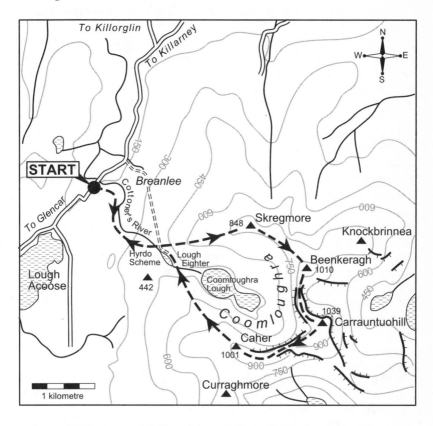

Reference OS Maps: MacGillycuddy's Reeks (1:25,000);
Sheet 78 (1:50,000).

33. MACGILLYCUDDY'S REEKS RIDGE

With no fewer than six peaks over the magical 915m, this is claimed to be the finest ridge walk in the land. An organised walk was, at one time, held each year on the June Bank Holiday, stewarded by the mountaineers of Kerry. However, logistic and environmental considerations led to its abandonment. In any case, it had served its purpose in introducing so many to the Reeks. It is a walk for experienced walkers only and careful calculation must be made of the time required, allowing for the composition of your party.

Park your car opposite Kate Kearney's Cottage (881 887). From there, walk up the road into the Gap of Dunloe for about 0.5km. A green road on the right zig-zags towards the summit of Strickeen Hill (440m). This is a welcome bonus on the first leg of the journey. The road (a turf bog road, in fact) ascends as far as the scarecrow trees on the skyline — you can omit the 440m summit — and then swings south to take you into bogs and in line for the first peak, *Cnoc an Bhraca* (731m). The slope is rich in hurt (whortleberry). This peak is the turning-back stage for some who now realise that they were over-ambitious. If you have cause to return, **do not attempt to descend to the beckoning road below to the east in the Gap of Dunloe** — this course has led to more than one accident.

Having savoured the view south to Kenmare Bay (origin of the Ice-Age flow which shaped the Gap of Dunloe), head west-southwest down to the saddle over lake-dotted Alohart. From there, climbing begins and the steep and sharp scree-covered slope is a good hint of what is to come. On one journey here, a colleague (Father Aengus Fagan of Rochestown College) photographed a circular rainbow broken only at the bottom by his own shadow. This is how a rainbow should appear but those of us who do not fly much and are generally earth-bound do not see rainbows in full. I have a colour slide of Father Aengus photographing the rainbow but why I did not shoot the comparatively rare optical phenomenon itself I could never explain afterwards. The slope ends at the 932m *Cruach Mhor* (Large Stack) which is surmounted by a grotto. An old man living in Ballyledder below is responsible for this — he had to haul everything, even the water, in plastic bags to the top for his act of worship.

The 'interesting' part of the walk now begins. There are two arêtes — knife-edges — lasting for approximately 1.5km. **If your head is not good, do not press on!** The passage can be made easier by dropping down on the first leg to meet a sheep track on the western side, bypassing The Big Gun (939m) in the centre and crossing the ridge top to continue to second leg on its southerly side to arrive at the peak 988m, generally known as Knocknapeasta. This peak is named after the lake-corrie below, Coomeenapeasta (*Coimín na Peiste*, Coum of the Serpent). If the sun catches it, you may see the wing of an American plane which crashed into the lake during World War II. On a course for Cornwall from North Africa, it was flying too far west. Seeing the

35. MULLAGHANATTIN–THE CLOON HORSESHOE

Mullaghanattin (Mullach an Aitinn, Summit of the Gorse) is a 773m peak southwest of the Reeks, high point of the horseshoe walk from Glencar. This offers great variety but you must be prepared to regard it as an all-day walk.

The usual starting point has been from the summit of Ballaghbeama Pass (754 781) from where there is an interesting scramble to the top of Knockavulloge (462m), not named on the OS map, and from there an ascent of over a mile to Mullaghanattin itself. Incidentally, if you have reason to return on this course, instead of heading north to the Pass top at Knockavulloge, a more easterly course is essential to avoid the steeper ground.

A start at Ballaghbeama, while it means that you can complete the entire horseshoe, also means arranging for two cars, one of which can be left at Lettergarriv. If only one car is available to you, I suggest parking it on the main Cloon Valley road near the Owenroe River (725 801), walking up to the houses at Cloghera and seeking permission to walk through the fields (use and close all gates). Mullaghanattin (773m) from this side looks perfectly conical and you walk up the spine between the two gullies, one containing Eskabehy Lough. On my first trip here, I had just been initiated into the joys of plant life. This sharp slope (involving some scrambling, particularly nearing the summit) is rich in some of the rarer plants which I could recognise — sundew, butterwort, St Patrick's Cabbage, to mention a few. I was surprised to see a solitary woodbine apparently growing out of a rock. Given the outline of the mountain from this side, it is surprising on arrival at the summit to find a broad boggy top bare of stone — a few stones have been found to pile on one another as an excuse for a cairn. Views aplenty are given — across the plain north to Caragh Lake and Killorglin, east to Lough Brin (there are stories of a Lough Ness-type monster in that lake) and southeast to the Kenmare River/Bay.

As you descend west-southwest to the next saddle, look south across the pocket. The rocks laid millions of years ago are exposed to view and so crippled that one could imagine them still pliable and moving. Just above this saddle is a tablet commemorating the death here in April 1973 of a Dublinman, Noel Lynch. Noel was an international climber killed in a simple fall while hill-walking.

The next leg of the journey, south over Beoun (752m) and then southwest, is generally a pleasant stroll along a grassy ridge with views south across coum and plain to the sea. If you have tarried earlier and the day is well advanced, do not let smug self-satisfaction overcome you. There is rougher ground ahead. By the time you reach the narrow ridge before Cnnararagh, the nature of the terrain to come is clear. Short rock faces and constant ups and downs seem to add enormously to the journey. Of course, if you are lucky in the day and there is good visibility, there is adequate

Dingle Peninsula, the crew believed that they had overshot their destination and flew south into the Hag's Glen, realising this too late to gain sufficient height to clear the ridge. Further wreckage was found on the Cummeenduff side in an area where rare plants were being catalogued. Continue now west-southwest over points 973m (*Maolan Bui*) and 926m (*Bearna Rua*, Red Gap) to the 958m *Cnoc an Chuilinn* (Hill of the Rolling Incline). From there, the ridge continues west over *Cnoc na Toinne* (846m). There is a wire fence just before this summit and this is a sign that you are well into the second half of the walk. An awkward stile, to the south of the peak itself, leads you on the most 'economical' route across this slope. Note: Most of the names in this paragraph are not on the 1:50,000 map.

From *Cnoc na Toinne*, descend to the boggy saddle over the Devil's Ladder and up the scree slope to Carrauntuohill. Incidentally, there is a well — which unfortunately dries up in the hottest weather — on the cairned line to the summit. From Carrauntuohill, follow the line of the previous walk over Caher down to Breanlee.

Distance: 18km/11miles. Ascent: 1,830m/6,000ft.
Walking time: 7½–9 hours (it has taken 12 hours or longer!)

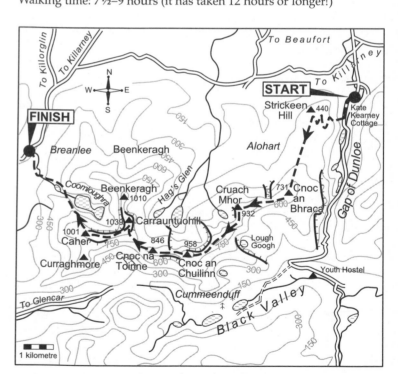

Reference OS Maps: MacGillycuddy's Reeks (1:25,000); Sheet 78 (1:50,000).

34. COOMASAHARN LAKE HORSESHOE

Our next walk is southwest of Glenbeigh village where the Ice Ages have created a dramatic series of six coums in an area of approximately fifteen square kilometres. It needs a fine day because it would be a pity to miss the magnificent views and because coums mean cliffs! I should mention the need to show all courtesies including parking with consideration. As a result of the experience of Coomloughra, the Federation of Mountaineering Clubs of Ireland opposed a hydroelectric scheme planned for this area. Some locals did not agree with the stance taken.

From Glenbeigh, follow the signposts off the N70 to Coomasaharn Lake. Near the lake, the road turns sharply right where a small grove of pine trees surrounds a red-roofed building. Park your car here (635 853).

The name Coomasaharn is puzzling. For years, some thought that the name referred to *Satharn* (Saturday), when people might have gathered at the Mass Rock deep in the coum during the Penal days. It is now accepted that it originated in ancient Irish and the meaning is not certain. Indeed, this area shows signs of the earliest human presence. There is rock art in the field to the right of the surfaced road going right uphill. Your route to the mountain is straight ahead on unsurfaced road to the eastern side of the lake where you will find a gate. This leads to a fairly steep ascent. Zig-zag through rock benches to the 561m top of Knocknaman (*Cnoc na mBan*, Hill of Women). This follows the principle of ascending the steeper ground and descending more gradual ground. Apart from the question of safety, gaining views (for example, that of the main lake and its serrated shore) more quickly is encouraging and on this walk there are two extra bonuses: travelling clockwise gives a better vantage over Dingle Bay later in the day and the prevailing wind will probably be with you at that stage.

From Knocknaman, a gradual rise leads to Meenteog (715m), known locally, simply and aptly, as *Muing* (Flat, Boggy, Long-grassed Place). It is not necessary to go to the summit. You can contour south-southwest (admittedly on a wet, boggy line) until funnelled right on the ridge south of the cliff. If you have kept close to the cliff tops, there is no better place to lunch than over the hanging valley of Coomacullen (*Cum a'Chuilinn*, Coum of the Rolling Incline). This is a haunt for ravens who may entertain as they dive and soar with the air currents. As you sit, there is a spot visible across Coomasaharn Lake with the intriguing name of Tooreentoninairde (literally sheep pasture, backside up). In the inner end of the main coum is a rock where local tradition has it that the last wolf in Ireland was killed (by Mayo bounty hunters who apparently travelled the country for the £5 reward given for each head). Incidentally, if your meal has provoked a lethargy, do not feel tempted to descend here. There is no recommended escape route into Coomacullen.

You are now at the southernmost point. Swing west (or slightly north of west) to follow a very definite feature — a boundary wall of an earlier era consisting in places of a stone wall and in places of a straight cutting (3m wide

or so), presumably where scraws were dug to make an earthen wall, weathered away. Two sheep fences cross your line to the 772m peak, n... on the OS map as Coomacarrea but locally known as Sagart (the Irish w... priest, presumably some connection with the Mass Rock below). Be sure the two gates considerably inserted by the landowner(s) — dipping you in the process to avoid decapitation! Over Coomacarrea, keep to the le... line of upright stones and the wire fences which prevent sheep from war... onto the steep ground and coume to the right. There is a multitude o... here and detailed directions may confuse. The course is northwest ... turfbanks to the rise east of 760m point (Teermoyle Mountain on the OS...

Now, swing north. The spur coming from the right is in view. Th... peak is called Coomreagh on the map but is called Conaire locally ... gained by a short arête (a knife-edge but not too frightening), to reac... you must descend a grassy slope. The corries here come so close ... must see where you are going. If mist has caught you, I can only ... taking a bearing for Gleesk to the northwest. The arête, called *Cein...* gives a magnificent view of the L-shaped amphitheatre with the M... directly across the corrie by the streams.

After the arête, there is a flat, boggy triangle. Head for the left p... views as you travel of the MacGillycuddy's Reeks. Over Conaire ... left on the line of the spur to the outer end of the lake (taking ca... wire fences or, better still, finding the gates) to gain the road.

Distance: 10.5km/6.5miles. Ascent: 730m/2,300ft. Walking time: 5½–...

Reference OS Maps: Sheets 78 and 83 (1:50,000).

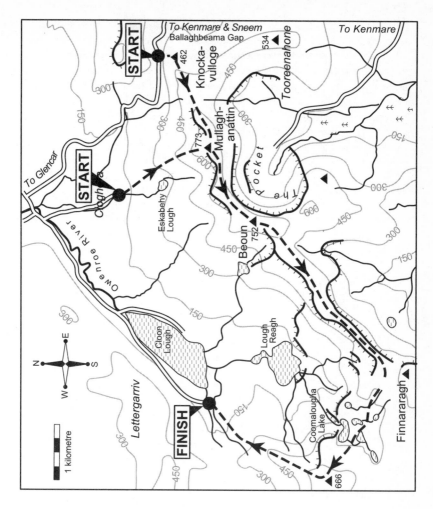

Reference OS Map: Sheet 78 (1:50,000).

compensation. You can bypass Finnararagh and swing northwest on a
bearing to take you to the seven lakes trapped on the rock shelves over the
sheer walls at the back of the coum above Lough Reagh. I repeat sheer walls
— **no attempt should be made to find a descent at this point.** If you are in
need of an escape route, there is a steep gully leading down from the flat
slabs north of Coomalougha Lake. However, on past experience, the
descent is so slow and the route across rough ground west of Lough Reagh
and, worse, the bog between it and Cloon Lough equally slow, that nothing
is gained. It is as well to continue on the horseshoe.

From the lakes, ascend to the unnamed summit of 666m. Before heading north, make sure that you are on the summit — a broad boggy expanse — well above the rock-faces over Lough Reagh. From the top, the line of the shoulder is quite clear and it takes you to the houses at Lettergarriv, some distance from which you will have been forced to park your car. If in the mood for further exploration, you could detour into the bog just south of Cloon Lake to visit an Early Christian site with interesting stone carvings, marked Cillin/burial ground on the map.

There are roads on both sides of Cloon Lake to take you to your parking spot.

Distance: 14.5km/9miles plus road walk. Ascent: 1,040m/3,400ft.
Walking time: 6–7 hours plus time on road.

36. KNOCKNADOBAR

As one travels on the N70 a few miles east of Cahirciveen, the five-mile-long, scree-covered slope of Knocknadobar (Cnoc na dTobar, Hill of Wells) stands invitingly to the north. It presents a number of easy walks, two of which I describe.

(a) The Pilgrims' Route

Off the N70, take the road to Coonanna Harbour and at the col before it, you will see a small grotto at the right-hand side of the road. A sign there reads 'Stations — Next Gate'. Enter the gate (481 828) and the route of the Stations of the Cross is quite clear. The faces of the Stations are painted white as are all through gates. At first, the line is more or less northeast but later it zig-zags (indistinct at times) to ease the ascent and allow time for reflection and prayer.

The fourteen Stations were erected in 1885 by Canon Brosnan, parish priest of Cahirciveen and builder of the O'Connell Memorial Church. Apparently, his second church, sitting under the hill in Foilmore, was de-roofed by severe winds each winter for a number of years. One winter, the roof survived and the Stations were a thanksgiving. Whether there was a tradition of pilgrimage here before then, I do not know. At any rate, there is a Holy Well (at the back of James O'Donoghue's house, the neatly-hedged one before the grotto) dedicated to St Fursey and said to offer a cure for sight complaints. This was the original start of the pilgrimage route but is not used nowadays as it involves crossing fences. The Stations route is generally wet underfoot, a condition which should favour butterwort and sundew. The first is in evidence but, for some reason, not so the second.

If you want to avoid the moisture, you could begin at the Holy Well (ask James O'Donoghue for permission to cross his fences) and ascend by the spine — an interesting scramble over sharp rock, the sharper part of which can be avoided by dropping slightly to the left. On this course you meet only the eleventh and (after a broad barren shoulder) the fourteenth Stations. Either way, following an ascent which gives increasing views with height, you arrive at the High Cross, generally called the Canon's Cross. Here, Mass is said on the pilgrimage revived in recent years.

The Cross is not at the true summit. Continue northwest straight over a turf expanse, eroded to reveal the scree beneath. There is a small cairn on the 690m peak.

If you have not decided to retrace your steps, proceed east to a shoulder and down to an arête over Glendalough Lakes nestling in the coum to the north. Needless to say, care must be taken on this short stretch of narrow ridge which leads down to a fairly broad saddle, known locally as the *Mullach* (Top). Here, the path called *Cnoc na mBo* (Hill of Cows), used for driving cattle from Kells to Cahirciveen Fair, crosses the saddle. Attractive as it may seem, abandon any idea of going north on the path into the coum to follow the route above the sea to Coonanna. This is very rough going and requires a number of detours to avoid deep gullies running down to the sea. Instead, swing right (southwest) to follow the path downhill to meet the line of an old road. This is the *Bothar Ard* (High Road) which ran from Roads (the townland) to Kells Lough to Coonanna. The road is not always fully discernible and in a few places is somewhat overgrown. The line is generally shown by the ruins of stone dwellings. Approaching the Holy Well, the road becomes clearer and even fitted with a stile or two — I imagine it may have been a short cut to the former schoolhouse to the west

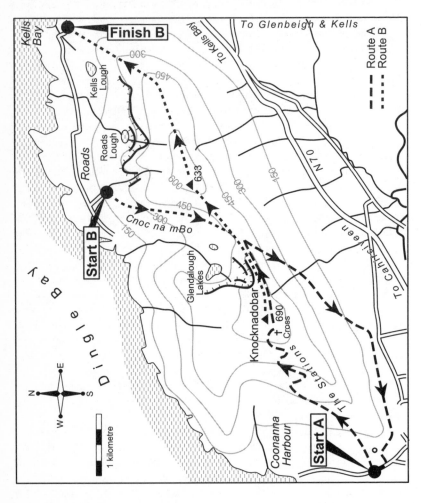

Reference OS Map: Sheet 83 (1:50,000).

Dingle Peninsula, the crew believed that they had overshot their destination and flew south into the Hag's Glen, realising this too late to gain sufficient height to clear the ridge. Further wreckage was found on the Cummeenduff side in an area where rare plants were being catalogued. Continue now west-southwest over points 973m (*Maolan Bui*) and 926m (*Bearna Rua*, Red Gap) to the 958m *Cnoc an Chuilinn* (Hill of the Rolling Incline). From there, the ridge continues west over *Cnoc na Toinne* (846m). There is a wire fence just before this summit and this is a sign that you are well into the second half of the walk. An awkward stile, to the south of the peak itself, leads you on the most 'economical' route across this slope. Note: Most of the names in this paragraph are not on the 1:50,000 map.

From *Cnoc na Toinne*, descend to the boggy saddle over the Devil's Ladder and up the scree slope to Carrauntuohill. Incidentally, there is a well — which unfortunately dries up in the hottest weather — on the cairned line to the summit. From Carrauntuohill, follow the line of the previous walk over Caher down to Breanlee.

Distance: 18km / 11miles. Ascent: 1,830m / 6,000ft.
Walking time: 7½–9 hours (it has taken 12 hours or longer!)

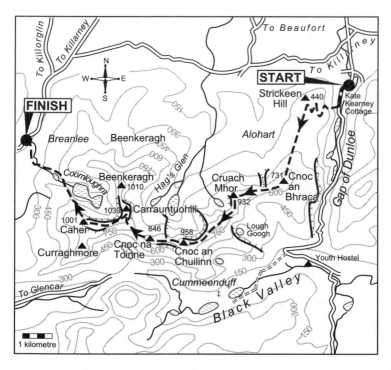

Reference OS Maps: MacGillycuddy's Reeks (1:25,000); Sheet 78 (1:50,000).

34. COOMASAHARN LAKE HORSESHOE

Our next walk is southwest of Glenbeigh village where the Ice Ages have created a dramatic series of six coums in an area of approximately fifteen square kilometres. It needs a fine day because it would be a pity to miss the magnificent views and because coums mean cliffs! I should mention the need to show all courtesies including parking with consideration. As a result of the experience of Coomloughra, the Federation of Mountaineering Clubs of Ireland opposed a hydroelectric scheme planned for this area. Some locals did not agree with the stance taken.

From Glenbeigh, follow the signposts off the N70 to Coomasaharn Lake. Near the lake, the road turns sharply right where a small grove of pine trees surrounds a red-roofed building. Park your car here (635 853).

The name Coomasaharn is puzzling. For years, some thought that the name referred to *Satharn* (Saturday), when people might have gathered at the Mass Rock deep in the coum during the Penal days. It is now accepted that it originated in ancient Irish and the meaning is not certain. Indeed, this area shows signs of the earliest human presence. There is rock art in the field to the right of the surfaced road going right uphill. Your route to the mountain is straight ahead on unsurfaced road to the eastern side of the lake where you will find a gate. This leads to a fairly steep ascent. Zig-zag through rock benches to the 561m top of Knocknaman (*Cnoc na mBan*, Hill of Women). This follows the principle of ascending the steeper ground and descending more gradual ground. Apart from the question of safety, gaining views (for example, that of the main lake and its serrated shore) more quickly is encouraging and on this walk there are two extra bonuses: travelling clockwise gives a better vantage over Dingle Bay later in the day and the prevailing wind will probably be with you at that stage.

From Knocknaman, a gradual rise leads to Meenteog (715m), known locally, simply and aptly, as *Muing* (Flat, Boggy, Long-grassed Place). It is not necessary to go to the summit. You can contour south-southwest (admittedly on a wet, boggy line) until funnelled right on the ridge south of the cliff. If you have kept close to the cliff tops, there is no better place to lunch than over the hanging valley of Coomacullen (*Cum a'Chuilinn*, Coum of the Rolling Incline). This is a haunt for ravens who may entertain as they dive and soar with the air currents. As you sit, there is a spot visible across Coomasaharn Lake with the intriguing name of Tooreentoninairde (literally sheep pasture, backside up). In the inner end of the main coum is a rock where local tradition has it that the last wolf in Ireland was killed (by Mayo bounty hunters who apparently travelled the country for the £5 reward given for each head). Incidentally, if your meal has provoked a lethargy, do not feel tempted to descend here. There is no recommended escape route into Coomacullen.

You are now at the southernmost point. Swing west (or slightly north of west) to follow a very definite feature — a boundary wall of an earlier era consisting in places of a stone wall and in places of a straight cutting (3m wide or so), presumably where scraws were dug to make an earthen wall now weathered away. Two sheep fences cross your line to the 772m peak, marked on the OS map as Coomacarrea but locally known as Sagart (the Irish word for priest, presumably some connection with the Mass Rock below). Be sure to use the two gates considerately inserted by the landowner(s) — dipping your head in the process to avoid decapitation! Over Coomacarrea, keep to the left of the line of upright stones and the wire fences which prevent sheep from wandering onto the steep ground and coume to the right. There is a multitude of fences here and detailed directions may confuse. The course is northwest through turfbanks to the rise east of 760m point (Teermoyle Mountain on the OS map).

Now, swing north. The spur coming from the right is in view. The 513m peak is called Coomreagh on the map but is called Conaire locally. This is gained by a short arête (a knife-edge but not too frightening), to reach which you must descend a grassy slope. The corries here come so close that you must see where you are going. If mist has caught you, I can only suggest taking a bearing for Gleesk to the northwest. The arête, called *Ceimaconaire*, gives a magnificent view of the L-shaped amphitheatre with the Mass Rock directly across the corrie by the streams.

After the arête, there is a flat, boggy triangle. Head for the left peak, with views as you travel of the MacGillycuddy's Reeks. Over Conaire and keep left on the line of the spur to the outer end of the lake (taking care across wire fences or, better still, finding the gates) to gain the road.

Distance: 10.5km / 6.5miles. Ascent: 730m / 2,300ft. Walking time: 5½–6 hours.

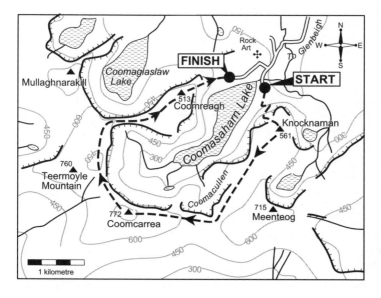

Reference OS Maps: Sheets 78 and 83 (1:50,000).

93

35. MULLAGHANATTIN–THE CLOON HORSESHOE

Mullaghanattin (Mullach an Aitinn, Summit of the Gorse) is a 773m peak southwest of the Reeks, high point of the horseshoe walk from Glencar. This offers great variety but you must be prepared to regard it as an all-day walk.

The usual starting point has been from the summit of Ballaghbeama Pass (754 781) from where there is an interesting scramble to the top of Knockavulloge (462m), not named on the OS map, and from there an ascent of over a mile to Mullaghanattin itself. Incidentally, if you have reason to return on this course, instead of heading north to the Pass top at Knockavulloge, a more easterly course is essential to avoid the steeper ground.

A start at Ballaghbeama, while it means that you can complete the entire horseshoe, also means arranging for two cars, one of which can be left at Lettergarriv. If only one car is available to you, I suggest parking it on the main Cloon Valley road near the Owenroe River (725 801), walking up to the houses at Cloghera and seeking permission to walk through the fields (use and close all gates). Mullaghanattin (773m) from this side looks perfectly conical and you walk up the spine between the two gullies, one containing Eskabehy Lough. On my first trip here, I had just been initiated into the joys of plant life. This sharp slope (involving some scrambling, particularly nearing the summit) is rich in some of the rarer plants which I could recognise — sundew, butterwort, St Patrick's Cabbage, to mention a few. I was surprised to see a solitary woodbine apparently growing out of a rock. Given the outline of the mountain from this side, it is surprising on arrival at the summit to find a broad boggy top bare of stone — a few stones have been found to pile on one another as an excuse for a cairn. Views aplenty are given — across the plain north to Caragh Lake and Killorglin, east to Lough Brin (there are stories of a Lough Ness-type monster in that lake) and southeast to the Kenmare River/Bay.

As you descend west-southwest to the next saddle, look south across the Pocket. The rocks laid millions of years ago are exposed to view and so rippled that one could imagine them still pliable and moving. Just above this saddle is a tablet commemorating the death here in April 1973 of Dublinman, Noel Lynch. Noel was an international climber killed in a simple fall while hill-walking.

The next leg of the journey, south over Beoun (752m) and then southwest, is generally a pleasant stroll along a grassy ridge with views south across coum and plain to the sea. If you have tarried earlier and the day is well advanced, do not let smug self-satisfaction overcome you. There is rougher ground ahead. By the time you reach the narrow ridge before Finnararagh, the nature of the terrain to come is clear. Short rock faces and constant ups and downs seem to add enormously to the journey. Of course, if you are lucky in the day and there is good visibility, there is adequate

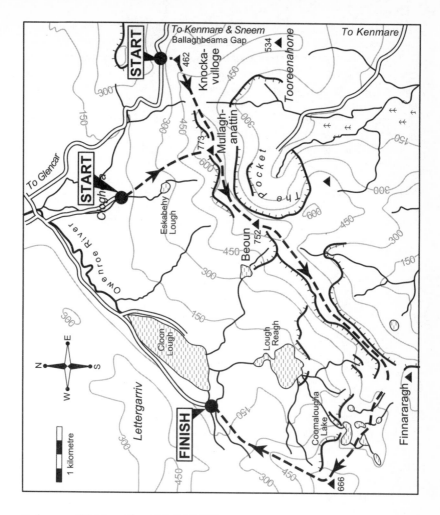

Reference OS Map: Sheet 78 (1:50,000).

compensation. You can bypass Finnararagh and swing northwest on a bearing to take you to the seven lakes trapped on the rock shelves over the sheer walls at the back of the coum above Lough Reagh. I repeat sheer walls — **no attempt should be made to find a descent at this point.** If you are in need of an escape route, there is a steep gully leading down from the flat slabs north of Coomalougha Lake. However, on past experience, the descent is so slow and the route across rough ground west of Lough Reagh and, worse, the bog between it and Cloon Lough equally slow, that nothing is gained. It is as well to continue on the horseshoe.

From the lakes, ascend to the unnamed summit of 666m. Before heading north, make sure that you are on the summit — a broad boggy expanse — well above the rock-faces over Lough Reagh. From the top, the line of the shoulder is quite clear and it takes you to the houses at Lettergarriv, some distance from which you will have been forced to park your car. If in the mood for further exploration, you could detour into the bog just south of Cloon Lake to visit an Early Christian site with interesting stone carvings, marked Cillin/burial ground on the map.

There are roads on both sides of Cloon Lake to take you to your parking spot.

Distance: 14.5km/9miles plus road walk. Ascent: 1,040m/3,400ft.
Walking time: 6–7 hours plus time on road.

36. KNOCKNADOBAR

As one travels on the N70 a few miles east of Cahirciveen, the five-mile-long, scree-covered slope of Knocknadobar (Cnoc na dTobar, Hill of Wells) stands invitingly to the north. It presents a number of easy walks, two of which I describe.

(a) The Pilgrims' Route

Off the N70, take the road to Coonanna Harbour and at the col before it, you will see a small grotto at the right-hand side of the road. A sign there reads 'Stations — Next Gate'. Enter the gate (481 828) and the route of the Stations of the Cross is quite clear. The faces of the Stations are painted white as are all through gates. At first, the line is more or less northeast but later it zig-zags (indistinct at times) to ease the ascent and allow time for reflection and prayer.

The fourteen Stations were erected in 1885 by Canon Brosnan, parish priest of Cahirciveen and builder of the O'Connell Memorial Church. Apparently, his second church, sitting under the hill in Foilmore, was de-roofed by severe winds each winter for a number of years. One winter, the roof survived and the Stations were a thanksgiving. Whether there was a tradition of pilgrimage here before then, I do not know. At any rate, there is a Holy Well (at the back of James O'Donoghue's house, the neatly-hedged one before the grotto) dedicated to St Fursey and said to offer a cure for sight complaints. This was the original start of the pilgrimage route but is not used nowadays as it involves crossing fences. The Stations route is generally wet underfoot, a condition which should favour butterwort and sundew. The first is in evidence but, for some reason, not so the second.

If you want to avoid the moisture, you could begin at the Holy Well (ask James O'Donoghue for permission to cross his fences) and ascend by the spine — an interesting scramble over sharp rock, the sharper part of which can be avoided by dropping slightly to the left. On this course you meet only the eleventh and (after a broad barren shoulder) the fourteenth Stations. Either way, following an ascent which gives increasing views with height, you arrive at the High Cross, generally called the Canon's Cross. Here, Mass is said on the pilgrimage revived in recent years.

The Cross is not at the true summit. Continue northwest straight over a turf expanse, eroded to reveal the scree beneath. There is a small cairn on the 690m peak.

If you have not decided to retrace your steps, proceed east to a shoulder and down to an arête over Glendalough Lakes nestling in the coum to the north. Needless to say, care must be taken on this short stretch of narrow ridge which leads down to a fairly broad saddle, known locally as the *Mullach* (Top). Here, the path called *Cnoc na mBo* (Hill of Cows), used for driving cattle from Kells to Cahirciveen Fair, crosses the saddle. Attractive as it may seem, abandon any idea of going north on the path into the coum to follow the route above the sea to Coonanna. This is very rough going and requires a number of detours to avoid deep gullies running down to the sea. Instead, swing right (southwest) to follow the path downhill to meet the line of an old road. This is the *Bothar Ard* (High Road) which ran from Roads (the townland) to Kells Lough to Coonanna. The road is not always fully discernible and in a few places is somewhat overgrown. The line is generally shown by the ruins of stone dwellings. Approaching the Holy Well, the road becomes clearer and even fitted with a stile or two — I imagine it may have been a short cut to the former schoolhouse to the west

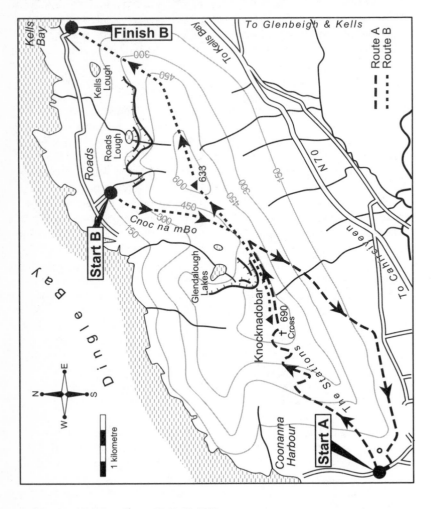

Reference OS Map: Sheet 83 (1:50,000).

(more recently a residence of ex-President O Dalaigh). If you lose the path, you have only to go south through fields to the surfaced road which will lead you back to your car.

Distance: 10km/6.25miles. Ascent: 680m/2,250ft. Walking time: 4½ hours.

(b) From Roads
The second walk would be an ideal one for somebody holidaying in Kells. Roads is the townland to the west of the bay with an intriguing name, *Na Roda*, thought to mean an anchoring place for boats. From here, follow the left-hand road at the Y-junction to join the path of *Cnoc na mBo* (526 871). Along the path as it travels into the coum is a series of stone walls. These are called *Clochans* and were used to support ricks of turf cut nearby for firing by the forty families who lived in this townland in the early part of the last century. The path gives a very gradual ascent to the saddle from which you make your visit to the Canon's Cross.

Your descent can be over the east peak (636m), from which you should travel east and east-northeast to follow the shoulder and avoid the steep descents near Roads Lough.

Distance: 9.5km/6miles. Ascent: 700m/2,300ft. Walking time: 4 hours.

37. MAUGHERNANE CIRCUIT

The Waterville area has been popular as a holiday centre for generations, particularly for fishermen. It has not always been seen as a walking area, which is a pity. The Inny River valley (between Ballaghisheen and Waterville) has a number of lake-filled coums on its eastern side. These provide ample scope for attractive horseshoe walks and the one I have termed the Maughernane Circuit is a sample of what is on offer.

Leave the Waterville–Ballaghisheen road at Dromod and go east on the road through Oughtiv to its end at Maughernane (601 698, Maghygreenane on the OS map). As you drive in, the view directly into the stony coum whets the appetite. Opposite the black and white painted (holiday?) house, there are two gates which lead onto the shoulder. A wire fence which crosses your route has, conveniently, a wooden gate. The next wire fence travels with you to meet another at right angles and at the meeting point there is a further wooden gate. After that, continue up the heather-clad slope for the rock slabs ahead. On reaching these, you find that the line is conveniently with you, taking you very gently to the ridge, where you can look out at the axis of the two coum lakes.

From this boggy expanse, you get your first glimpse of the Kenmare (River) Bay to the southeast and the views are expanded, on reaching summit 642m, to include Beara Peninsula. (There is some confusion about peak names — so I will not use any.) From this point, you can go west following the faint line of a stone fence. Below on your left is the Glanmore Valley, an area rich in folklore. In earlier time, a poet/fisherman lived there and normally fished Lough Iskanagahiny, known locally as *Loch na gCapall* (Lake of the Horses), which is said to have a monster (*ollpeist*) in it. On one occasion, he decided to fish in the two lakes on your right and carried his skin-covered boat on his shoulders from one valley to another. The boat was deliberately damaged and he wrote an amusing satire in Irish (it can still be quoted) about the culprits.

The faint stone fence meets a wire fence which can be followed uphill, passing a small stone sheep shelter, to where it swings left at the flat summit which is the high point of this walk. The map shows two triangulation points (672m and 675m) but this is virtually one flat summit. From its centre, you can look across Cloonaghlin Lough and Lough Namona to the outer end of Derriana Lough. Below, Lough Iskanamacteery is normally called *Loch na hEisce* (Lake of the Esk) after the coum or gully that runs down to it, *Eisc na Machtire* (Steep Path of the Wolf). Half-way down this, a man once lived and the signs of tillage are still to be seen there. The upper lake in the Glen is correctly shown on the map as Lough Nambrackdarrig (*Loch na mBreach Dearg*, Lake of the Red Trout) and the area around it is called *Cum an Aitinn* (Coum of the Gorse). These old names remind us that

our ancestors were by nature what we have to strive to be —
environmentalists.

Continue west from the flat top along the ridge, enjoying views over
Lough Currane and Ballinskelligs Bay. As the direct route down from 675m
is fairly steep and can be slippery when wet, I suggest that you go to the
low point of the ridge before swinging northeast to gain the surfaced road
again.

Distance: 8km/5miles. Ascent: 610m/2,000ft. Walking time: 3½ hours.

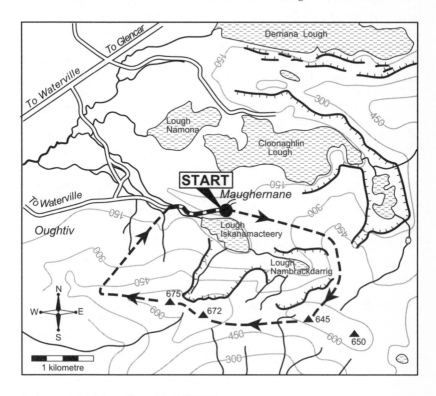

Reference OS Map: Sheet 83 (1:50,000).

38. KNOCKNAGANTEE

For those based in Sneem, there is very pleasant climbing to Eagles Lake with its waterfalls and a scramble if continuing over Knocknagantee.

From the western square of Sneem village (66 69), travel north for almost 6km/3.7miles following the course of the Sneem River. Its twisty course gives the village its name (*snaidhm,* knot). Opposite the football pitch, go left at the Y, left at the T (5km/3.15miles) and over a concrete bridge to park with consideration beyond green farm buildings. This is *Glorach* (Noisy), named for the tumbling streams and the echo by the lake.

To the right of the last house (668 712), a farm road winds uphill. You can go cross-country northeast and north, following the tributary of the Sneem River which drains Eagles Lake or you can follow the farm road north, not forgetting to close the gate. As it swings west, leave the road and go onto the mountain through the sheep-gate, made of two poles held by wire loop. Again don't omit to secure it — sheep may be confined to higher ground for feeding or, if it is lambing time, confined nearer the houses as protection from foxes. Go uphill through long grass and later barer ground with the waterfalls behind the lake coming into view as you ascend. In wetter weather, the separate falls must combine into one solid sheet. Up on the left are the sheer walls under Knocknagantee. Note the fencing along the top of the cliffs. You should heed the inherent warning — farmers do not want their sheep to wander onto this ground and, unlike you, they have four-leg drive. The stream can be easily crossed at the outlet from the lake, at least in summer. The rocks are lichen-covered and you need to be careful if they are wet. In this hidden corrie, you may wish to linger. Wild duck were to be seen on my visit.

From the lake, care must be taken in picking a course. I stayed on the right of the waterfalls, going up the grass slope and then scrambling/rock-climbing under the dark overhanging rocks near the top of the saddle. Here, in wetter ground, were examples of the carnivorous butterwort. Reviewing the course, I feel it would be best to go to the left side of the falls to scramble up the scree slope and boulder field to Lough Coomanassig (*Com an Easaigh,* Corrie of the Waterfall). Keep left above the lake to travel north-northwest avoiding the bull-nose and cliffs west. The stream acts as a handrail to take you onto the wide boggy saddle. Unless you go well east to look down from cliff tops into the Inny Valley, the views here are not great. However, the MacGillycuddy's Reeks show up clearly to the northeast.

From the saddle, swing south to the summit of Knocknagantee, using the fence seen earlier as a second handrail — there's no need to warn you to remain on the right side! Soon the pointed peak (676m) is visible and you can head straight for it. Approaching the cairn, you can see an opening in the wire at the fence corner — open and close it again with care. There is now a

360° panorama — much of Iveragh and Beara Peninsulas. This was one of only three triangulation points on the Iveragh Peninsula for the original Ordnance Survey 1825–33. Dingle Peninsula must also be in sight but I could not judge, owing to the haze on my visit. According to local lore, the name *Cnoc na gCainnte* (Hill of Conversations) arose from the practice of meeting here from various townlands while out checking on sheep. A few generations ago, families were large and 'some had to go out' to make room.

A stile leads west over a fence from the cairn and obviously this is the prudent course — on no account should you aim south. You can either continue west to meet the farm road approaching the saddle or pick a course southwest to join the road at a lower level. Either way, the road eases the way home.

Distance: 8km/5miles. Ascent: 580m/1,900ft. Walking time: 3½ hours.

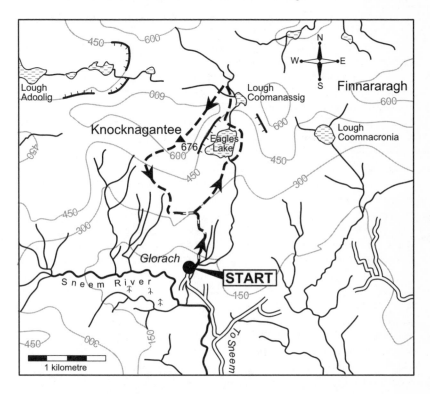

Reference OS Maps: Sheets 78 or 83 (and 84 for approach from village) (1:50,000).

39. DERRYMORE GLEN, BAURTREGAUM AND CAHERCONREE

Our first walk in the Dingle Peninsula is a pleasant gradual one into the coum of Derrymore, suitable for a party of mixed abilities. However, the summits at the head of the glen beckon, and the walk may be extended easily to take in Baurtregaum and even Caherconree. For added enjoyment, the Geological Guide to the Dingle Peninsula *should be taken along.*

Travelling west on the N86 from Tralee, 1.2km/0.8miles beyond Derrymore School is a narrow hump-back bridge. Disregard the unsurfaced road beside this and take the next (surfaced) road left. Pass one house on the left and park near the Y-junction. A neat bungalow is at the end of the surfaced road on the right. Follow a bohereen which starts here (742 108) and shortly swings right to end at a tubular steel gate. Be sure to close it properly. Passing a sheep-dipping tank, follow the fence on the left towards the gorge ahead.

Soon you meet what appears to be a dried-up river bed with an embankment across it. In fact, there are ruins of a mill beside the Derrymore River less than 1km downstream and this was the mill-race which was dammed each night to gather water. As will be seen later, so were the three lakes inside. From the ruin of a stone house above this, look up at the skyline and you will see what is known to locals as *Carraig a' Tae Pot* (Rock of the Tea Pot, what else?). The old mill-race leads to Derrymore River which fed it just below a series of small waterfalls.

Leave the river (the bank is too rough a course) and move right, uphill, to follow a sheep track. There is, in fact, no single defined track but many converging and separating. The ascent through the gorge is gradual. If you are lucky enough to travel on a fine day after rain, the tumbling streams and waterfalls glitter on all sides of this valley, particularly where, after the gorge, the valley opens out to reveal the scree-covered slopes on the right under the cliff columns of Gearhane. Pass a stone wall sheep shelter and continue on a line on the firmer ground at the bottom of the scree, avoiding the wetter ground near the river. Skirting a bowl where the Derrymore River has now diminished to a winding stream, this line leads directly to the first of the three lakes snuggling at the end of the valley. Proceed up the short slope ahead, strewn with massive boulders, to meet the second lake. The southwest corner of this presents an idyllic picture — a small sandy beach under a waterfall with room to pitch a solitary tent. Continue up to the third lake, like the second backed by cliffs.

You might decide to rest on your laurels here but I suggest pressing on. Follow the stream (right) entering the lake from the southwest (sometimes it ripples underground) to enter an amphitheatre where you are in a world of your own. The boulders create many dens. It would be easy to imagine these giving the necessary shelter on a holiday away from it all! Ahead in a clear area below a sheep shelter stands a solitary rock which is, I think, the one known to locals as the King's Table (and presumably also that shown on maps as Finn Mac Cool's Table). The area of course abounds in rocks of all shapes calling for names. What is called the Boat Rock is on the ridge to Gearhane.

Having savoured the isolation, the time has come to return home. The ascent has been so gradual that it may be hard to believe that the inner lake is at the 600m level. This becomes clear when on ascending the rise outside the outer lake, you see — through the gorge by which you entered — the surface of Tralee Bay well below, beckoning you homeward.

For those who want to continue, an easy ascent from the inner end of the walk leads southeast (slightly left) to the saddle (706m) between Baurtregaum *(Barr Tri gCum,* Top of the Three Coums) and Caherconree.

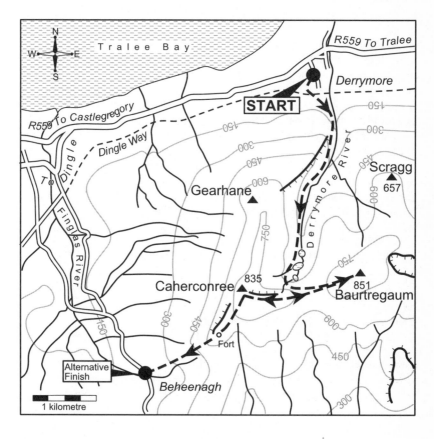

Reference OS Map: Sheet 71 (1:50,000).

From the summit of Baurtregaum, there are the magnificent views of land and sea which are unique to the higher peaks of this peninsula — north across Tralee Bay, northwest to Brandon Bay and south and southwest across Dingle Bay.

Returning to the saddle, the line of the ridge leads westwards towards Caherconree. It should be obvious that there are cliffs to be avoided and, if there is danger of mist, it may be best to reconsider. At any rate, it is necessary to travel west-southwest first, before swinging northwest to the summit (835m), marked by a small cairn. Once again, the views are magnificent.

The main attraction of Caherconree is its legends and it is worth descending southwest to the fort (683m). Promontory forts are common on tongues of sea-cliff and this is one of the few inland ones. Our ancestors made use of the natural cliff outcrop, still below you, and the first feature you meet is the remains of the wall thrown across the 'inland' side of the promontory. If you continue, you will exit through the natural gateway of the fort.

The fort (and the mountain) are called after its supposed builder, Cu Roi Mac Daire, a mythical figure with magical powers. It is said that, each nightfall, he caused the fort walls to spin so that no one could enter the gate. He was killed by a ruse worked by his wife, Blathnaid, who alerted her waiting lover, Cuchulainn, that the way was clear by spilling milk which turned the Finglas River below white. The stories of Cu Roi and the other Red Branch figures abound and it may set the mood if you have read them in advance.

You can either return down the Derrymore Glen or descend south west to Beheenagh on the unclassified road from Camp to Aughils. You could also of course climb Caherconree from Beheenagh and return the same way, but it would be a pity to miss the Derrymore Glen.

Derrymore Glen
Distance: 8km/5miles. Ascent: 640m/2,100ft. Walking time: 3¾ hours.

Baurtregaum
Distance: 11.5km/7miles. Ascent: 790m/2,600ft. Walking time: 5 hours.

Caherconree (with return by Derrymore)
Distance: 15km/9.5miles. Ascent: 920m/3,020ft. Walking time: 6½ hours.

Caherconree (with descent to Beheenagh)
Distance: 10km/6.2miles. Ascent: 920m/3,020ft. Walking time: 5 hours.
(Allow at least 2 hours for return to your vehicle by road and Dingle Way.)

Slea Head on the Dingle Peninsula
(Bord Fáilte — Irish Tourist Board)

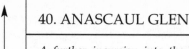

40. ANASCAUL GLEN

A further incursion into the legends which are such a part of this peninsula is provided by the circuit of Anascaul Glen.

Turn off the N86 west of Anascaul village on the road signposted to the lake. Park at the car park (581 051). Ascend northwest (initially southwest to clear Carrigblagher Cliffs) to Knockmulanane (*Cnoc Mhaoilionáin*, 593m). The ascent is a long, even one with views that become ever more extensive.

Eventually, you arrive at a gully down which you can look directly at the green road beside Lough Anascaul. *Loch an Scáil* is named after Scál Ní Mhurnáin, one of the many women in whose affairs the legendary Cuchulainn took an interest. It seems that a giant came to take her away and she sought the hero-warrior's assistance. He stood on Dromavalla Mountain, east across the lake, and the giant stood somewhere on this side, exchanging fire–boulders no less. After a week of fighting, Cuchulainn was hit and gave a loud groan. Scál, thinking him killed, drowned herself in the lake.

From the cliff edge, travel west passing the peak and over fences (no standing on the wire, please) to descend to the saddle. From here a descent can be picked to meet tracks, visible from above, running northeast above the Garrivagh River. At the top of the saddle over Maghanaboe (*Macha na mBó*, Cattle-field), join the green road zig-zagging up from the south.

That road now could be an escape route if you wish to shorten your day. It descends pleasantly by a series of waterfalls, of interest to the photographer. Folklore abounds. Apart from stories of a lake (no longer there) fitted with a sunken round tower and once producing eels 5.5kg in weight — as well as a chalk carcass that might have been a turtle's — locals tell of Sagart Rock, a V-shaped Mass rock near which is a well named *Tobairín na gComaoineach* (Well of the Communicants). They also tell of splits inside *Faill Dubh* (Black Cliff) 6m long and said to be 60m deep. This green road could also be used to reach Beenoskee (826m) and Stradbally (798m) Mountains, the slopes of which rise to the northeast.

However, we are on the trail of Cuchulainn and will continue southeast from the saddle by the tumbling stream to the cliff edge where we get a spectacular view down the wooded Glanteenassig (*Gleannta an Easaig*, Glens of the Waterfall) and across Tralee Bay to Fenit and Banna Strand. On our first visit here, we were puzzled by a cleared belt which ran along the cliff tops at the 530m level. Rejecting the idea of movement of the earth's surface, we decided that it must be a forest fire-break, obviously a good idea to prevent gorse fires being spread into the plantations by the prevailing southwesterlies. This opinion was later confirmed to be correct by the late Tom Hayes of Killorglin who was forester-in-charge when the work was done in the 1950s.

The flat top of Dromavalla Mountain (533m), now within easy reach, shows a line of standing stones. Locals term them sentries guarding Cuchulainn's House, the large mound of stones which proves to be hollow in the centre. I thought it a natural deposit but archaeologists now think that it might be a burial mound, the hollow due to the collapse of the inner chamber. We must leave legend behind and descend the gorse-covered slope southwards. Rather than cross the river in the boggy ground to the south of Lough Anascaul, it is best to follow the track east of the lake and cross the river north of the body of water, gaining the green road that leads you back to the car park.

Distance: 12.5km/7.8miles. Ascent: 890m/2,900ft. Walking time: 5½–6 hours.

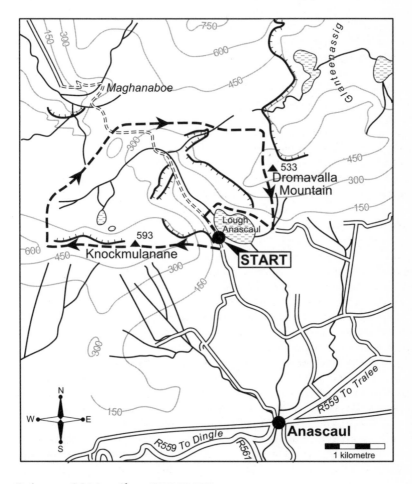

Reference OS Map: Sheet 70 (1:50,000).

41. DINGLE–SLEA HEAD (DINGLE WAY)

While our walks in Kerry so far have introduced us to folklore, archaeology and geology, in my view you are about to sample a more intense experience walking west of Dingle. Apart from the fact that the culture is different, this being a Gaelic-speaking area, the scenery is much more rugged and history seems to invest the very landscape.

From Dingle town (44 01), travel west — either along the seafront or past the hospital — onto the Slea Head road by crossing Milltown Bridge. Your view across the harbour is of Eask Hill with its finger post tower and beneath it the woods of Burnham enclosing the former residence of Lord Ventry, now an Irish-speaking college for girls, *Colaiste Ide*. Travel straight through the crossroads. As you approach the crest of the hill, opposite the graveyard is a standing stone oddly juxtapositioned with a pseudo-Georgian house. This is part of a complex of two standing stones, a pair known locally as *Geatai na Gloire* (Gates of Paradise) — the remains of a megalithic tomb — and a boulder decorated with rock art.

Just over the hill, go off the Slea Head–Ventry road by continuing straight onto a byroad, bordered by fuchsia, honeysuckle and blackberry. Once again, uphill through a crossroads onto a road now bordered in season with the rich orange flower, montbretia. The profusion of flower and hedgerow in West Kerry is encouraged by the temperate climate. There is a second slight ascent on the surfaced road before you go right (beside the house with the red-tile roof after the 'Slow. Children Crossing' sign) onto another surfaced byroad. About 400m on, watch for a green road on the left. As you travel, you will find this genuinely green with fern, rushes, foxglove, thistle and nettle — you may need to cover up if in shorts! Continue northwest up *Bothar a' Chinn* (Road of the Head). The high stone walls, well mossed and covered in plant life, restrict views but as you approach the top before turning west, a lower fence line allows views right of Dingle and, stretching north, the Brandon Ridge. At the crest, Rathinnane Castle comes into view. The line of *Bothar a' Chinn* continues past the castle onto Ballyferriter but your course ahead will be along the coast to the south of Croaghmarhin (behind the castle) and Mount Eagle (to its left). Leaving the saddle, go right across a stone stile by a wire and fishing-net fence and, still on green road, swing left to gain your first glimpse of Ventry Strand.

As you continue, you meet a gate; keep straight on over unsurfaced road. 60m west of the gate, set in the stone wall on the left of the road, is a cross-inscribed slab. In the field to the south is an Early Christian church site, Kilcolman (*Cill na gColman*). If you have not seen ogham writing, search out a large boulder with two inscribed crosses. The writing consists of strokes along a stem line up the left side of the face and across the top, interpreted as (translation) 'My name is Colman, pilgrim' thus giving the site its name.

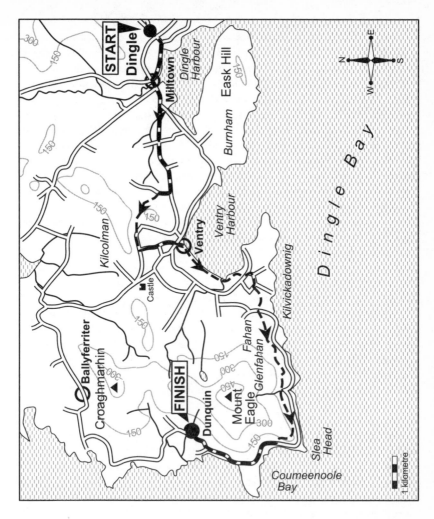

Reference Maps: OS Sheet 70 (1:50,000) or Dingle Way Map Guide (1:50,000).

As you walk west, the full extent of Ventry Harbour comes into view and 0.75km from the gate, just as the descent begins and the ruin of Rathinnane Castle again becomes visible, watch for a green road on the left, with plenty of evidence of daily use by cows, which will take you onto surfaced road and directly to the harbour. (Before entering the green road, you may consider continuing a few metres west to view the neat sheep-gate built into the stone fence on the right.) At the crossroads, the village is on the left and the Dingle Way continues onto the beach straight ahead. I recommend

111

going right, to the Bradan Feasa Café for refreshment. You can also invest in pottery and educate yourself in the myths of Ireland through the murals and, if possible, have a chat with the owner, Maurice Sheehy, who as well as being one of the developers of the Dingle Way is a writer of guide books.

You are at the location of the Battle of Ventry, fought between the Fianna, Ireland's legendary standing army, on one side and the fleets of the King of Spain and the King of the World on the other. It lasted a year and a day with massive losses on both sides. If the tide is high, it may not be possible to travel on the beach. In that event, follow the green arrows directing you past the Bradan Feasa Café along fuchsia-lined roads to meet the Way again before Caheratrant. Otherwise, go west along the beach across two streams and leave it before the loop to the pier for a sandy track leading to surfaced road where you go straight/leftish and then right at a T-junction into a cluster of houses, right again at the next T to end at a farmyard and house with neat fuchsia hedge at Caheratrant. To the right of the house is a green road which travels northwest before swinging to loop west between narrow walls. You can understand how in winter or even on a clear summer night it deserved the name *Bothar Dorcha* (Dark Road). This was the route to the school at Kilvickadownig, clearly seen as you emerge.

Just before the school, you meet the Slea Head road again. The Way goes left and, almost immediately, crosses the road to enter a short stretch of green road beginning between the gables of two bungalows. If this is not marked, Mrs O'Shea at the B & B at the corner will give directions. Go through the gate and at the end of the road, cross a stile, go straight across the field and over a stone fence to regain the green road. The Dingle Way now continues west more or less parallel to, but above, the motor road, giving you even better views than those the coach passengers must pay for. It is said that this area has the greatest concentration of archaeological remains in Ireland and with little detour you will be able to sample two. Descend through fuchsia bushes to Fahan village onto a short stretch of surfaced road which can be used for access to Dunbeg (*Dun Beag*, Small Fort), which is below on the left across the main road. Excavation of the promontory fort suggested habitation from 550 BC to the tenth or eleventh century AD.

Leave the surfaced road after 150m or so to go right onto green road, meeting the first of the specially-designed tubular steel pole stiles. Bearing left to follow the clear path west on the hill side of the stone wall, ascend to the saddle and pause for the views — behind is all of Dingle Bay and the Brandon Ridge; ahead, the Atlantic with one of the Blasket Islands (west) and the Skellig Rocks (southwest). The Way, confirmed by marker posts and stiles, continues on an ascending line outside stone walls until you cross Glenfahan Stream at a minor ford. Shortly afterwards, two abandoned houses below you indicate the line of the former road and, as directed by markers, you descend to that line and resume a westerly course. Shortly, the second Blasket Island comes into view and, as the third appears, you are rounding Slea Head and are in 'the nearest parish to America'. Landowners have had problems on this leg. Firstly, large numbers of walkers have arrived by coach, neglected to use the stiles provided and caused damage to fences. Despite advice to the contrary, individuals have travelled the ground with dogs, causing sheep to scatter. None the less, the Dingle Way Committee and landowners have cooperated to put in place a line over the nose of Mount Eagle/Beenacouma that runs down to Slea Head. Simply follow markers and stiles and do avoid crossing fences.

With the cliffs of Coumeenoole in view, you will exit through a gate onto the surfaced road. You have the choice of going left to make a visit to Slea Head with its Calvary grotto before going right to Dunquin. If you have been lucky enough to reserve accommodation at Dunquin, I recommend an overnight stop here but if you are hostelling, you will have to continue a few more kilometres north.

As marking at this point may be scarce, if you are travelling the Dingle Way in reverse, go through the gate and bear right uphill by the stone wall to meet the first steel pole stile and marker.

Distance: 20km/12.5miles. Ascent: 345m/1,130ft.
Walking time: 6½ hours.

42. MOUNT BRANDON

Outside of the MacGillycuddy's Reeks, Mount Brandon at 952m is the country's highest peak and, in many ways, it is the finest climb. There are rewards for the lover of scenery, for the geologist and for the botanist, and the mountain deserves repeated visits. A ridge walk can be added by those with time and energy.

(a) Direct Routes

There are two direct routes of ascent and one traverse, and I leave it to you to combine them as you like. Given the opportunity, the eastern ascent (from Faha, a townland on the slope above Cloghane village) is without doubt the better and more spectacular. Follow the signposts from Cloghane and park your car above the severe S-bend at the upper end of the surfaced road (496 118) near Miss O'Connor's house. There is a telephone here and it would be wise to leave a note on your windscreen (route and expected time of arrival) in case of an emergency. Here, a further signpost directs you to a grotto from which a line of poles leads along the shoulder. These were erected to guide those taking part in the pilgrimage to the oratory above. As you contour along below the skyline, you are walking under the site of a number of aircraft crashes. These occurred in the early days of flying, and wreckage can still be seen if you care to detour. The wrecks include one of a German fighter plane which belly-landed and exploded in 1940.

During the traverse of the shoulder, a perfectly-shaped peak stands ahead — this is Brandon Peak. The boulder field descending to a wide scree field is known locally as *Gran Ceol* — Grain Music or Ugly Music: the 'music' is created as rocks tumble during a storm.

It is when you reach the turning point at the *Tobar* (a spring well — a welcome amenity if your trip is on a hot day) that the interest really begins. You now sit over Lough Cruttia (*Loch Cruite*, Harp Lake) and Lough Nalacken (*Loch na Lacha*, Duck Lake) and these in their rock setting give a hint of what is to come. The path now continues northwest in the side of the narrow ice-carved glen. Any description of mine would fail to do justice to the geological grandeur created by the scree slopes and the sheer walls, their curved rock layers laid bare for our inspection, towering above the line of paternoster lakes. The *Geological Guide to the Dingle Peninsula* gives all the technical data.

For the botanist, there are equal pleasures. Already, the insectivorous butterwort (plentiful) and sundew (less in evidence) were to be seen along the slope above Faha. Now, St Patrick's Cabbage can be seen among the rocks by the path and the primitive club moss is to be found by the inner lakes. But it is at the end of the valley inside the two last small lakes that the rarest alpine flora (survivors on uncovered peaks during the Ice Age) are to be found — just to the left of the path as it commences to rise up the esk.

Each plant may be found in one or two other areas in these islands but it is only in Brandon that all are to be seen in close proximity.

My first incursion here was in snow and these seemed ideal conditions to appreciate what the Ice Age had created. It also led to another experience — the smell of a fox who had just passed by and had left fresh pad marks on the snow at the bottom of the esk. The smell (like burning rubber is the best description I can give) was still there on our return an hour or so later.

Beyond the lakes, the path swings (right) up the esk/steep gully to take you to the saddle north of the peak. This is a good spot to look back and see how the lakes beside which you travelled have been trapped on rock shelves. Here, the western end of the Dingle Peninsula and the Blasket Islands lie before you and you can look down on the perfect amphitheatre of Maughanveel to the northeast.

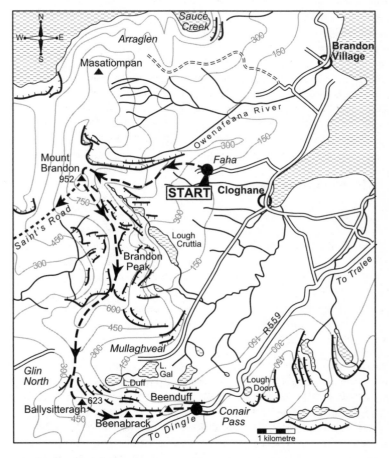

Reference OS Map: Sheet 70 (1:50,000).

115

A short rise of 90m or so (now over an almost sheer drop of 300m — please be careful) takes you to the summit marked by the remains of *Teampaillin Breanainn*/St Brendan's Oratory, another rectangular building and a holy well. No date has been put on the constructions but it is suggested that building continued in phases over 1,400 years. St Brendan (the Navigator) is supposed to have reflected here before setting out with a band of fellow-monks in a frail currach on their journey to Greenland and America. *Sliabh Daidche* was the peak's name in pre-Christian times and it was apparently the site of a Celtic harvest celebration. If there are views (Brandon is termed a wet mountain and generally has a cloud sitting on its summit), these are understandably magnificent — sea, land, rock and lake.

From the peak you may decide to retrace your steps — take care on the esk. Alternatively, you can descend in a south-westerly direction roughly on the line of the Saints Road. Care should be taken leaving the top — the western side is rounded and the lie of the land may pull you into the corries on either side. Keep to the centre of the shoulder. The boggy top changes to a steeper, rockier section before levelling off again to bog, marked with a few standing stones. A path is now somewhat discernible and it runs down to the right of a deep-cut stream (a dried-up stream bed at times) and finally crosses it to meet the stony bohereen which leads to Ballybrack.

While this is a favourite haunt, I must record a few complaints. The markers on the early part of the path are of dubious value, merely encouraging those better-off on low-level routes. The whitewashing brush used to paint the rocks along the pilgrims' route may, I think, have been applied too liberally. On the summit, the tubular steel cross looks obscene — a small stone plaque would be much more appropriate. Lastly, a doubt rather than a complaint: the new plantation to the north of Lough Cruttia may not be an improvement from the visual point of view. One could argue that trees once covered this entire area and there is also the question of employment provided. However, particularly when looking from the Conair Pass road beside the perfect coum of Lough Doon (Pedlar's Lake) where the effects of Ice Age glaciation were first recognised in Ireland, the barrenness emphasises the scouring and carving effects of the ice. But these are small matters — nature has worked on such a grand scale that man's puny efforts have little effect. Mount Brandon still remains one of my favourite climbs.

(b) Ridge Walk

The alternative to the descent by the Saints Road is to go along the great ridge curving round to the Conair Pass, and if you have the time and energy, I strongly recommend it.

Descending from Mount Brandon, the route follows a perfectly visible stone wall which goes southeast and south virtually the whole way to Brandon Peak (840m). Approaching the Peak, left below you is Lough

Cruttia with the boulder field (*Gran Ceol*) running into it. As I write, the first wire sheep fence on the ridge is met just before the Peak. You could contour once again to the west but it would be a pity to miss the opportunity of sitting on the top and admiring the view. On a fine summer day, the blue waters of Brandon Bay with the lush vegetation at Fermoyle sweeping down to an almost white beach take on a Caribbean look. To the southeast are the MacGillycuddy's Reeks and you are looking directly into Coomloughra enclosed by part of the highest ridge walk in Ireland. The Blasket Islands and Skellig Rocks stand in the Atlantic to the west and southwest. It is encouraging also to look behind you at this stage and appreciate how far you have travelled. The summit of the Peak consists of a mini-arête and after it, you meet the second wire fence, considerately provided with a gate. Lough Doon is directly in view across the Conair Pass road. The ridge now swings southwest to descend to a boggy plateau which suffers from wind erosion. The tracks of tractor wheels are visible and if the weather or time dictates, there is a farm road offering an escape route east into Mullaghveal Valley, only about 5km from Cloghane. Approaching the saddle, keep to the right of the wire fence by using (and closing) the gate. An old road, not visible on the saddle but quite clear lower down, connected Mullaghveal and Glin North, well serviced by bog roads to the west. This gives another escape route and, if you had studied your map in advance, you might have decided on having transport here for a pick-up.

We will continue over the summit named Ballysitteragh on the OS map (625m). During the ascent, the lakes in Mullaghveal, five below you and one behind, come gradually into view, the names of two — Lough Gal (*Loch Geal*, Bright Lake) and Lough Duff (*Loch Dubh*, Black Lake) — reflecting the light in this narrow coum. Once over the summit, you will see the mouth of Dingle Harbour. The inner harbour and the town gradually come into view and the panorama of Iveragh Peninsula should spur you east over the soft ground across the few slight rises of Beennabrack (*Beanna Breac*, Speckled Peaks) and Beenduff (*Beann Dubh*, Black Peak). The peaks stand over the walls of Mullaghveal and you might pause for the view down before completing a course almost parallel with the road rising from Dingle to the car park at the top of the Conair Pass (490 055).

Another possibility is to start the traverse at the col between Mount Brandon and Masatiompan, reached by the Dingle Way (Walk 43), and climb the north ridge.

Distance (Faha to Ballybrack): 7.5km / 4.5miles. Ascent: 780m / 2,550ft. Walking time: 4–5 hours.

Distance (Faha to Conair Pass): 14km / 9miles. Ascent: 1,370m / 4,500ft. Walking time: 7–8 hours.

43. FEOHANAGH–CLOGHANE (DINGLE WAY)

This walk takes you high and wild over a 650m pass. Although the Dingle Way markers will help you keep direction, the area is subject to mist and you should be careful that both the weather and you are fit for it. You will be rewarded with splendid views.

Leave Feohanagh (39 09) on a northerly course across the bridge and uphill to a T-junction. Go right to travel east under another World War II watch hut on craggy Ballydavid Head, with the cliffs over Brandon Creek coming into view. Stay right with the surfaced road at the Y, then straight through the crossroads (right is an escape route to Dingle) and left to the end of surfaced road at Tiduff (*Tir Dubh*, Black Country, a placename not marked on OS map). You could bring a car this far and save 6km/4miles. West is Brandon Creek, from where legend says St Brendan set sail in his fragile craft to discover America centuries before Christopher Columbus, a sailing feat repeated by the explorer/writer Tim Severin in recent years. Off the surfaced road, go right through a gate. The green road to the saddle can be seen and to gain it, you should depart (right) from the mountain road inside the gate and remain close to the wire fence. Gradually, the built-up form of the military road will become clearer and as you reach the first saddle, you will be pleasantly surprised to find that you are half-way to the main saddle. Beennaman to your left is described in the *Geological Guide to the Dingle Peninsula*. To the east of it and north of your line of travel is a steep valley running down to the sea known to locals as 'the green fields', otherwise Fohernamanagh (*Fothair na Manach*, Deep Glen of the Monks). St Brendan is said to have established a monastery on this site, chosen no doubt for its isolation. You will see field walls below by carefully picking your steps to the edge, but a descent and return would be outside the range of the average walker. The Archaeological Survey report does not contain details of any finds, stating that the ecclesiastical nature of the settlement is suggested only by the name and folklore.

While the military road is at times less clear (absorbed into the bog) as you ascend further on the Way, you should have no trouble staying on course east until you arrive beside the ogham stone/monument on the saddle below Masatiompan and the ruins of the signal tower to the west. Take a last look west at The Three Sisters and Ballydavid Head before taking in the view east — the sweep of Brandon Bay, the Magharees and Tralee Bay by which you will travel if continuing on the Way. From the saddle follow the markers (there was no track at the time of writing) east downhill, through Arraglen and with sight of the safe haven of Brandon pier encouraging you on, down the bog road to reach the gable end of O'Neill's shop.

(If you are on a return trip from the west and you have the appetite, a circular tour can be achieved by picking steps carefully along the more precipitous route from Arraglen, contouring well above the steep cliffs of Sauce Creek and then south of Bookeen to the car park at Brandon Point. I would not recommend this unless you are sure of your navigation.)

At the shop, go left on the surfaced road and left again, still on surfaced road, to loop clockwise down to meet a T-junction, where you go right for Brandon village. Farran ringfort, now much overgrown, is in a field left of the road approaching the junction. It features in a folktale of the locality

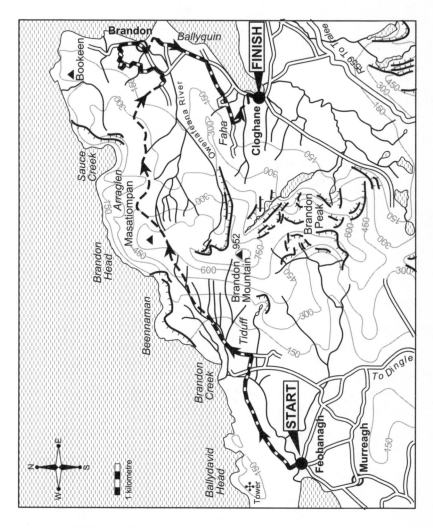

Reference OS Maps: Sheet 70 (1:50,000) or Dingle Way Map Guide (1:50,000).

which tells of crying, heard on the death of an infant, travelling through the townland and dying away only on entering the fort. You may wish to pause for refreshment in the village or detour to the pier to view the fishing boats or buy fish. Continue to the post office and go behind it to the foot-bridge across the Owennafeana River. Go left through the small gate at the end of the footbridge and 20m along the beach to meet tractor-tyre tracks and exit at a gate to surfaced road serving beach-goers. Keep straight/rightish and travel through Ballyquin to rejoin the road from Brandon village to Cloghane. Over the crest of the road with view ahead of the inlet, turn right at the crossroads to follow the signs for *Cnoc Breanainn*/Brandon Mountain. The next leg of the marked route could be very wet in winter and, if your footwear is unsuitable, you have the choice of continuing through the crossroads to Cloghane. Assuming you are remaining on the Way, your journey is 2km uphill on surfaced road, disregarding surfaced roads left and right — although after 0.5km, you could detour right onto a byroad to reach the Cloonsharragh stone alignment, orientated on the rising sun at the summer solstice but claimed by locals to be the headstones of kings. Travelling uphill, the village of Cloghane and church ruin are in view below on the left before you meet the turn-off. Reaching the two-storey house on the right, you hear a stream and can enter left just beyond it — don't be deterred by the overgrown entrance. Go right immediately, through the small gate, and travel downhill with the wire fence on your left until you meet a gap in the fence and stepping-stones leading back over the stream. Follow the muddy path down to the left along by the river, cross at the foot-bridge and, keeping the church tower in view, go through the fields to *Bothar an Teampaill* (Road of the Church). (Incidentally, if you are travelling the Dingle Way in reverse from Cloghane, take the first gate right after the gate left into the churchyard — don't follow the green road, unless of course a change of route has been clearly marked.) The ruins of the thirteenth-century church are worth a visit if only to view the unexpected pagan relic. At eye-level, projecting from the internal southern wall, is the face of the Celtic harvest god, Crom Dubh. (As I write, the stone relic has been removed by vandals and not traced.)

Cloghane is well endowed with hostelries although if you are in need of overnight accommodation, it is best to have booked in advance.

Distance: 28km/17.5miles. Ascent: 790m/2,600ft. Walking time: 9 hours.

44. CAHER VALLEY AND GLENINAGH MOUNTAIN

This is a long but fairly easy walk which is an excellent introduction to the Burren, a limestone karst area whose flora, a unique mixture of arctic and lusitanian species, is internationally famous. Gleninagh Mountain offers fine views west to the Aran Islands and north across Galway Bay to the Connemara mountains.

The Burren Code: It is illegal to remove or pick flowers. Also you should not add to the existing stone cairns or make new ones.

From Ballyvaughan, drive along the R477 and park beside the road about 100m beyond a cottage at 190 100, just west of Gleninagh Castle (*Gleann eidhneach*, Ivied Glen). Walk back towards the cottage for about 80m to a stile on the right-hand side, beside a field gate. Cross the stile to a track (an old mass path to the ruined parish church near Gleninagh Castle) which will take you over the col between Cappanawalla and Gleninagh Mountain. The track is narrow and rough in places but the going is easy and views of Galway Bay, Connemara and north Clare open up as you mount. To the east the extensive sand and mud flats of Ballyvaughan Bay are exposed at low tide and it is here that many migrating birds fuel up in spring and autumn on their way to or from their breeding grounds. It is here, also, that Brent Geese, all the way from Arctic Canada, spend the winter months.

The track winds up the hill to the col, short heather and bracken on each side. As you cross a wall at the top of the col, a broad vista of bare, terraced limestone, cradling extraordinarily lush pastureland and hazel scrub, opens up before you. This rich valley is a surprising and heartening sight in an otherwise barren expanse of rock. Follow the track into the valley, passing the ruins of a ring fort to your right, skirting along the east side of the walled fields until you sight the first cottage, where you join a more substantial track leading to Feenagh.

Take the track to the right up the hill — you are now on the Burren Way. At the high point you will come upon an ancient stone ruin (*Cathair an Aird Rios*) where local lore tells us there used to be a chapel and a shebeen together. It commands a fine view up the Caher Valley to the important caving areas centred on Polnagollum (*Poll na gColm*, Hole of the Doves) and Pollelva (*Poll Eilbhe*, Hole of Elva).

Descend the broad track to the road down beside the Caher River, unique in the Burren in flowing above ground; mostly the streams have cut their way down through the limestone and run underground. Road and river descend through a gorge (locally known as the 'Khyber Pass'), passing on the north side a glacial moraine and large boulders deposited by a glacier to the main road at Fanore Bridge.

Turn right along the road, but leave it for a lane to the right near bungalows. This is actually the old road and you walk it for about 1.2km

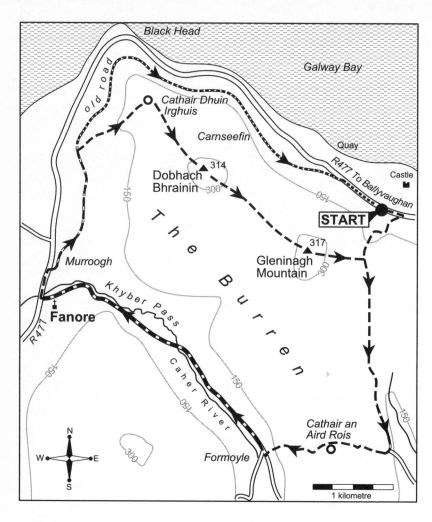

Reference Maps: OS Sheet 51 (1:50,000); The Burren (1:31,680).

before bearing right up a spur that leads to the main ridge at a ring fort *Cathair Dhúin Irghuis*. Turn right and follow the rough, terraced ridge over Pt 314m (*Dobhach Bhrainin*) to the summit of Gleninagh Mountain (317m, *Cnoc Achadh na Glinne*). There are many 'grikes' (crevices) in the limestone pavement — be careful not to put a foot down one! Also, while it is easy to pick your way *up* through gaps in the terracing, it requires some care in finding a descent route. From this ridge are the views north and west I promised you in the introduction, but it is also worthwhile to look south to Slieve Elva, its dark summit of heather on shale rock contrasting with the white limestone below. It is at the junction of the shale and the limestone that the caves begin. From Gleninagh Mountain descend east to the col, passing a 'dolin' — a depression formed by a collapsed cave roof — and return along your outgoing track to the starting point.

Instead of climbing up to the ridge, it is also possible to continue along the old road that contours below the north side of Gleninagh Mountain and joins the main road about a kilometre from the start of the walk — an easier walk but you miss the views. Or for a short walk, reverse this and return over Gleninagh Mountain.

Long walk
Distance: 17km/10.5miles. Ascent: 670m/2,200ft approx.
Walking time: 6–6½ hours.

Short walk
Distance: 10km/6miles. Ascent: 400m/1,300ft approx.
Walking time: 3½–4 hours.

45. ERRISBEG

Errisbeg (Iorrus beag, Small Western Peninsula: 301m) is a low hill to the west of the attractive village of Roundstone. It is sometimes called Roundstone Hill by those under the misapprehension that there is a relationship between the village name and the shape of the hill. In fact the Irish name for the village is Cloch na Ron, *Seal Rock.*

Follow the coast road (R341) from Roundstone westwards for 5km/3miles to a sharp bend in the road (684 397), just before a quarry on the south side of the road. Here there is parking space and access to open ground through a gate.

Take any route past the lake and up to the summit ridge, picking your way carefully through the crags and angular boulders. There are three summits on this very entertaining ridge with its small gorges, crags and sheltered hollows. Return by the same route.

I cannot but agree with many other authors who consider the view from Errisbeg one of the finest in the region — the Bens, Maumturks, the lakes, the coastline, the scatter of offshore rocks and islets, and Clifden with its two prominent spires. To the south is the classic tombolo, composed of the shells of countless microscopic animals, which joins a low granite island to the shore, forming Gorteen Bay (*Goirtin*, Little Garden; also known as *Port na Feadoige*, Plover's Shore) to the east and Dog's Bay to the west.

I would find it hard to recommend a better short hill walk in the whole region.

Distance: 3km/2miles. Ascent: 240m/800ft. Walking time: 1½ hours.

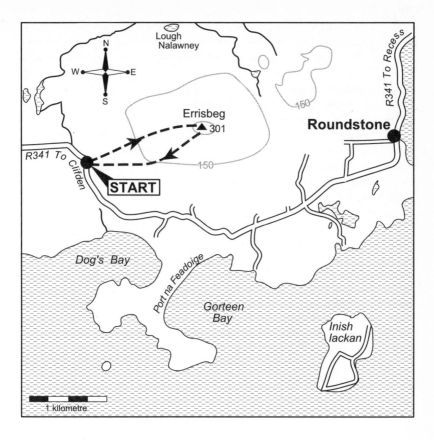

Reference Maps: Connemara (1:63,360) or OS Sheet 44 (1:50,000).

46. MUCKANAGHT AND BENBAUN

This walk will take you to the hub of the Bens. At the northern end of the Recess–Kylemore road (R344), take the westward road below Barnaheskabaunia, cross the new bridge and park near the start of the rough track which runs parallel to the Kylemore River. It leads eventually to one of the most isolated habitations in the area, at Glencorbet.

Take the track to its end point at the farm and continue along the bank of the river where the ground is moderately dry. To your left the bog extends to the foot of the Knockpasheemore–Benbaun ridge but to the right it has been transformed into a sea of green conifers.

Follow the line of the left fork of the stream to the col between Benbrack (*Binn Bhreac*, Speckled Hill) and Muckanaght (*Meacanach*, Place of Lumps and Ridges: 654m). The dryish ground gives way to eroded and very wet peat, but contemplation of the ancient stumps of 'bog deal' revealed by the erosion should take your mind off any brief discomfort. What was this valley like when it was forested? Which animals inhabited the forest? Could 'prehistoric climbers' have penetrated the forests to reach the summits of the Bens? Will future climbers be able to reach the peaks once current planting schemes are complete?

Muckanaght rises to your left, steep, smooth and green in contrast to its grey, craggy neighbours. It is the most inaccessible of the Bens and is probably one of the least visited of the group. From the col the summit is reached by a route starting at an obvious ramp between two small crags. Care should be taken because the ground is steep and the short vegetation is often greasy.

From the summit there is a fine all-round view of Connemara. Looking down on the col from which you ascended you will notice that the northern face is craggy. This, along with other crags, is shown on the *Mountains of Connemara* map, but the OS map (although the contours are superior) shows neither this, nor any of the numerous other crags in the Bens and Maumturks.

Descend to the next col with caution and take the easy ground to the minor summit of Benfree (638m) and then follow the curved ridge to the scree-bound peak of Galway's highest mountain, Benbaun (*Beann Ban*, White Mountain: 729m). It is the hub from which all the main ridges of the Bens radiate and it rightly commands one of the most comprehensive views in the whole region.

Return via the ridge leading to Knockpasheemore (*Binn Charrach*, Rock-encrusted Peak) and descend to Glencorbet by the small stream flowing from the minor col below the knoll of 456m.

Distance: 10.5km/6.5miles. Ascent: 870m/2,850ft.
Walking time: 5–5½ hours.

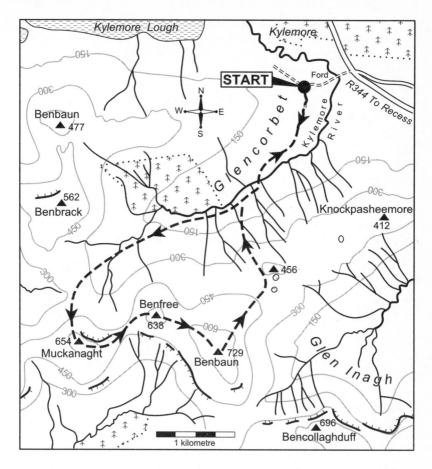

Reference Maps: Mountains of Connemara (1:50,000); OS Sheet 37 (1:50,000); Connemara Superwalker (1:30,000).

47. THE GLENCOAGHAN HORSESHOE

The Glencoaghan Horseshoe takes in the six peaks of Derryclare (677m), Bencorr (711m), Bencollaghduff (698m), Benbreen (691m), Bengower (664m) and Benlettery (577m). It is one of the best known and most popular walks in Connemara, particularly with walkers staying at Benlettery youth hostel. The youth hostel is reached by taking the N59 from Recess towards Clifden. The hostel is obvious as the road runs beside Ballynahinch Lake. Park by the roadside.

It makes little difference whether you do the walk clockwise or anti-clockwise. However, I prefer to start at Derryclare because when I come off the last peak, Benlettery, perhaps tired and aching, shelter, rest and refreshment can be close at hand. When descending from Derryclare you are faced with a long road walk which can be hard on already sore feet, whereas the same road walk at the beginning of the day serves to warm you up for coming exertions.

From the youth hostel go east along the Recess road (N59) for about 1.5km; turn left onto a bohereen, follow it across a bridge and through a farmyard. Leave the road where the slopes of Derryclare loom on your right. The summit can be reached via Lop Rock and the long ridge or, more directly, up one of the steep gullies which rise near the head of the road. From the summit of Bencorr, a steep rocky descent brings you onto Devil's Col which overlooks some of the longest rock climbs in Ireland at the head of Glen Inagh. A broad expanse of smooth bare rock eases you onto the Bencollaghduff ridge which rises to the summit at 698m and then sweeps down to the col below Benbreen.

From the col, take the southerly ridge leading to the first minor summit of Benbreen. The ground is rocky and heathery and steep enough in places to take one's mind off the strain of the upward slog. And the natural route runs close to the edge of impressive cliffs which plunge almost sheer into the Owenglin Valley — so tread warily. The summit ridge is semi-circular, and beyond the summit of Benbreen (*Binn Bhraoin*) it leads into a spur which will take you back to Glencoaghan. Therefore it is advisable, particularly in mist, to determine your route to Bengower (*Binn Ghabhair*, Peak of the Goat) with a compass.

The steep descent from Benbreen can be greatly accelerated by a scree run which lands you slightly to the left of the crest of the col. Bengower is steep and steplike and offers good, but generally avoidable, scrambling. From here the walking is easy and once Benlettery is surmounted the descent to the hostel, although steep and rocky in places, is quickly achieved.

Distance: 16km / 10miles (including road walk). Ascent: 1,500m / 5,000ft approx. Walking time: 7½–9 hours.

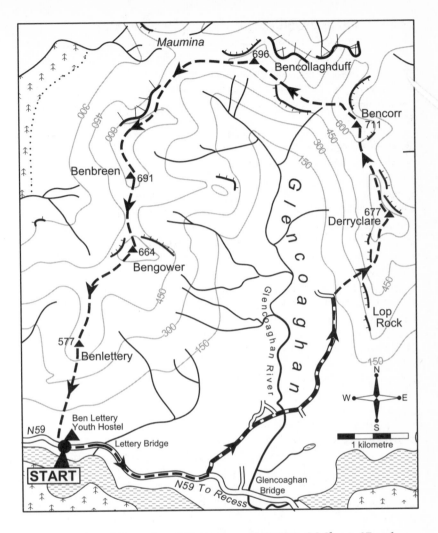

Reference Maps: Mountains of Connemara (1:50,000); OS Sheets 37 and 44 (1:50,000); Connemara Superwalker (1:30,000).

48. BENCHOONA

Benchoona (Binn Chuanna, Peak of the Corner: 581m) is one of the nearest hills to the Rosroe (Gubbadanbo; Gob an Dambha, Point of the Spit) youth hostel. Start at the bend in the Tully Cross–Leenane road where the bridge crosses the stream flowing from Lough Fee to Lough Muck (Loch Muc, Lake of the Pig) (780 621).

Take the direct route up the steep grassy slope facing you or, if this is too slippery for comfort, as it can be in damp conditions, follow an easier line onto the ridge below the north-facing crags.

Taking the first route you will come to a small plateau at about 120m where you can stop and take note of your surroundings, Inishturk to the northwest, the Maumturks to the southeast, ancient potato ridges to the north of Lough Muck and again on the southwest side of Lough Fee. Below you and to the north there is a ring fort atop a mound — a strategic position overlooking the pass linking Killary Harbour's main pier at Rosroe with the hinterland.

As you ascend the ridge, the Inagh Valley, cradled by the Maumturks and the Bens, directs your view across the bogs of Connemara to Galway Bay in the south. And to the north, Mweelrea, Clare Island and the host of rocky islets which break up the Atlantic rollers as they approach the sandy Mayo shore come into view.

To the right of your route the ground steepens into dangerous wet and broken crags which are best left to the agile feral goats which make their living on the high ground.

From the top of the ridge, you will be able to look down on Little Killary Bay, with its fringe of oakwoods in the foreground, the small Protestant church and the remarkable graveyard nearby where once it was customary for mourners to smoke clay pipes after burials and then leave them at the grave. The graveyard is well worth a visit just to enjoy the inscriptions on some of the headstones! At the northeast corner of Little Killary you should be able to discern a pillar of rock standing out from the main cliff. This is known as the Pinnacle and, like the neighbouring cliffs, it offers a number of rock climbs ranging from Very Difficult to Very Severe. If you want to develop your climbing skills or experience any other outdoor pursuits you should visit the Adventure Centre a few kilometres away off the road to Leenane.

From the summit plateau you can continue to Garraun (598m) and return via the obvious ridge to the south shore of Lough Fee, or traverse Benchoona and descend the steep northern slope to stepping stones across the river on the seaward side of Lough Muck.

Distance: 5.5km / 3.5miles (both routes). Ascent: 600m / 2,000ft approx.
Walking time: 3 hours.

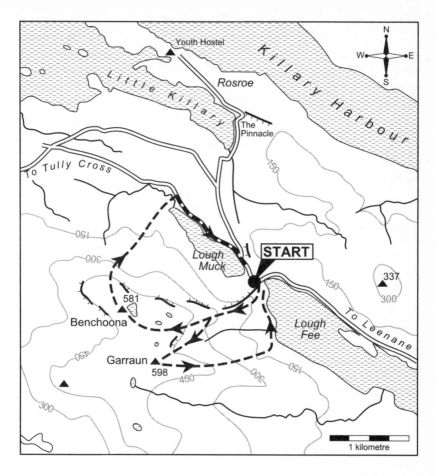

Reference Maps: Mountains of Connemara (1:50,000); OS Sheet 37
(1:50,000); Connemara Superwalker (1:30,000).

49. DOUGHRUAGH

*When I first travelled the road from Letterfrack to Leenane (N59) I was
taken completely by surprise when I came upon the magnificent edifice
of Kylemore Abbey, virtually built into the hillside of Doughruagh, surrounded by
oakwoods and overlooking a most beautiful lake. It was built originally by a wealthy
Liverpool merchant, Mitchell Henry, in the nineteenth century, but today it is a
convent school for girls.*

Start from the car park (there's a charge) of Kylemore Abbey (*Coill Mhor*,
Big Wood). Walk beside the lake in front of the Abbey along a track which
joins the main road at the west end of Kylemore Lough. Follow the road for
about 100m, then slant left up the hillside along a faint path. When you
reach a stream turn left and climb directly to open ground. The mass of
Doughruagh is on your left (west). Head directly for it over mixed boggy
and rocky ground. Your route crosses an old track and climbs steeply to the
summit plateau. This is a wilderness of loughans and rocky knolls, and the
summit (526m) is well to the north side.

From the summit there is a less familiar view of the Bens, in which the
minor peaks of Little Benbaun (Maolan), Binn Bhreac and Diamond figure
prominently, with the main ridges a distant backdrop. Across the bog to the
north the surf-edged rocky islets at the mouth of Killary Harbour are
backed by the grey-blue shapes of Clare Island and Achill.

On the return journey head directly south towards the hidden Abbey. As
you come over the edge of the plateau you will see below you a white statue
of the Sacred Heart. Pause for the view — very different from the summit
view — of the Kylemore valley, before picking your way carefully down the
steep slopes, avoiding the many small crags, to the statue. In 1996 there
were some rock slides on the direct descent and it is no longer
recommended except for very experienced walkers. Instead, retrace your
steps as far as the old track you crossed on the ascent, turn right and follow
the track to the statue. From the statue a path leads back through the
rhododendrons to the Abbey. Do not attempt to descend anywhere else;
you can spend hours forcing your way through the rhododendron bushes!
Back at the car park, remember its prime purpose is for visitors to the
Abbey complex, and treat yourself to a cup of coffee!

Distance: 4.5km/3miles. Ascent: 500m/1,700ft. Walking time: 2½ hours.

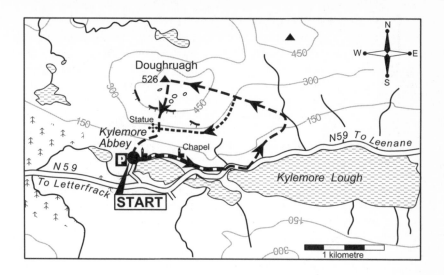

Reference Maps: Mountains of Connemara (1:50,000); OS Sheet 37
(1:50,000); Connemara Superwalker (1:30,000).

50. THE MAUMTURKS WALK

Lloyd Praeger, in his classic book The Way that I Went, *describes the traverse of the Maumturk Mountains from Maam Cross to Leenane as a 'glorious day's walking'. And so it is. But 24km of the roughest terrain in the country with about 2,300m ascent (plus 60m more descent, because the finish is at sea level) is not an expedition to be taken lightly and walkers are advised to be well equipped and competent with a map and compass. The ridge may look fairly straightforward on the map, but in mist even experienced walkers are known to have gone astray. And remember, if you have to abandon the ridge part way, there is still a lot of ground to cover before you reach base.*

Start from a parking place off the R336 on the Maum side of the Maam Cross — Maum col at 969 496 (not from the new parking area overlooking Maumwee Lough). Walk across the bog towards the high, rounded crags. Move left onto a ramp before you reach the crags and head for an old fence which will guide you to the summit (609m) of Leckavrea Mountain or Corcogemore (*Corcog*). The summit offers a comprehensive view of Joyce's country, upper Lough Corrib and south Connemara.

Continue north-westwards down the ridge, bearing west at the appropriate point to reach the col. To your right a steep rocky corrie drops away into the bog-bound Failmore Valley and to your left a longer, narrower valley plunges down to the forested slopes above Lough Shindilla.

The remains of the fence continue to serve as a useful guide up the steep slope to the west summit (*Mullach Glas*: 622m). From here the going is a bit easier but in misty conditions navigation can sometimes be rather tricky. Continue along the ridge to the third major summit (*Binn Mhor*: 661m) which lies on the south side of the plateau, and bear north-westwards again and descend by the steep spur, aiming to the left of the small lake which lies in a hollow below St Patrick's Bed and Holy Well.

From the col take the steep but easy grassy ridge up to *Binn Chaonaigh* (633m). From here the ridge to *Binn Idir an Da Log* (702m) is easy going in good weather and provides a commanding view of the Inagh Valley and the Bens. But be careful if mist comes down because it is easy to descend into the Failmore Valley before you reach *Binn Idir an Da Log*, without realising your mistake until it is too late.

From *Binn Idir an Da Log* descend north-westwards to *Loch Mham Ochoige*. This is an ideal place to camp if you wish to do the walk in two stages. Cross the col and then take the broken slope westwards to Knocknahillion (*Cnoc na hUilleann*, 607m) taking care to avoid the crags to your right. From the summit there is a fine view of the Inagh Valley and the Lehanagh Loughs in the bog below you to the south. Lissoughter (*Lios Uachtair*, Upper Fort), the site of a now derelict Connemara marble quarry, lies further south while to the west Loughs Inagh and Derryclare are set against a background of dark green coniferous trees capped by the grey ridges of Derryclare and Bencorr.

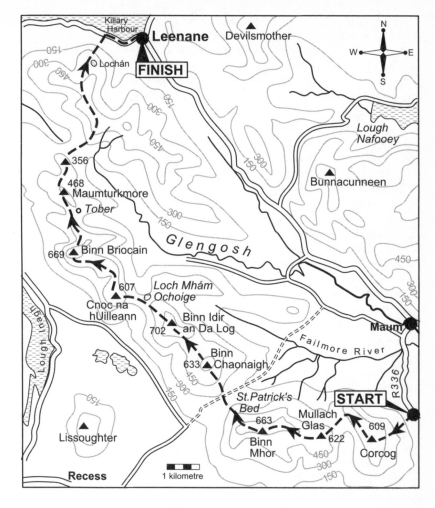

Reference Maps: Mountains of Connemara (1:50,000); OS Sheets 37, 38 and 45 (1:50,000); Connemara Superwalker (1:30,000).

N.B. Only Letterbreckaun and Maumturkmore are named on the OS map. The names in the text are from the *Mountains of Connemara* map.

Turning northwards, descend to the ridge, following its gentle curve westwards past the small lake and then climb to the summit cairn of Letterbreckaun (*Leitir Brecan/Binn Bhriocain*, Brecan's Hillside: 667m) which stands out prominently well to the west of the natural route along the ridge. From this vantage point there is a panoramic view of the hills to the north, and to the west Ben Baun can be seen clearly, standing sentinel at the head of Glen Inagh.

Beyond Letterbreckaun the hills change in character and soften somewhat as the geology changes from quartzite to Silurian sedimentary rocks and, underfoot, bare rock and loose boulders give way to springy turf and wet bog. But you still need your wits about you because the ridge winds backwards and forwards between Letterbreckaun and the col at the head of Glenglosh in a way which may lead you to underestimate the difficulty of this section. For example, to avoid a deep and dispiriting valley between Maumturkmore (*Binn Bhan*: 468m) and the unnamed point 356m you are advised to contour the hills northwards from Tober to the col, rather than cross the two summits.

The steep climb up from the col takes you onto a peat-hagged plateau with a high point at around 578m. Take a direct route across this towards Leenane, passing the lake on your left and taking care not to venture too close to the cliffs on your right. A steep and often slippery slope brings you down to the road by the Leenane Hotel.

Most years, in early May, the University College Galway Mountaineering Club runs a 'Maumturks Walk' for experienced walkers. It is well organised, with many check points along the route, a mountain rescue team on hand and refreshments at the finish. It is done alternately from south to north and north to south, to minimise the environmental effects. Further details can be obtained from the Secretary of the Mountaineering Club, University College, Galway.

Distance: 24km/15miles. Ascent: 2,300m/7,500ft approx.
Walking time: 10–14 hours.

Maumturk Mountains, Connemara, Co. Galway
(Bord Fáilte — Irish Tourist Board)

51. CNOC NA hUILLEANN AND BINN BHRIOCAIN

To sample the wild white quartzite summits of the Maumturks without committing yourself to walking the whole ridge, I can recommend this walk which takes you into the heart of the range and has magnificent views of the Twelve Bens across Glen Inagh, as well as vistas of the Maumturks summits stretching away to north and south.

Cnoc na hUilleann (607m) is approached from Ilion West (*An Uillinn Thiar*) on the minor road linking Tullywee Bridge on the Maam Cross–Recess road (N59) and the Inagh Lodge Hotel. Park at any convenient widening of the road somewhere near 868 524.

Cross the bog and join a stream which flows from the southern flanks of *Cnoc na hUilleann*. Head for the grassy col, passing limestone crags on your left. Amongst these crags are some of the few small potholes in Connemara. To your right bare quartzite cliffs rise sharply, guarding the approach to *Binn Idir an Da Log* (702m), the highest peak in the Maumturks. At the col there is a lake, L. *Mham Ochoige* which marks the crossroads of several routes. It is also an ideal place to camp for anyone taking two days to complete the Maumturks walk. Ascend the broken slope to the summit of *Cnoc na hUilleann* from where you will have a fine view of the Inagh Valley, with Lehanagh Loughs in the bog below you to the south. Lissoughter (*Lios Uachtar*, the Upper Fort), the site of a now derelict Connemara marble quarry, lies further south while to the west Loughs Inagh and Derryclare are set against a background of dark green coniferous trees capped by the grey ridges of *Binn Doire Chlair* and *Binn Chorr*.

Turning northwards, descend to the ridge, following its gentle curve westwards, pass the small lake and then climb to the summit cairn of *Binn Bhriocain* (667m) (Letterbreckaun on the OS map) which stands out prominently well to the west of the natural route along the ridge. From this vantage point there is a panoramic view of the hills to the north and, to the west *Binn Bhan* can be seen clearly, standing sentinel at the head of Glen Inagh.

Return by the same route as far as the first col and descend the steep rocky slope westwards, picking up a stream on your way. This stream will bring you to the Western Way, and after a few minutes walk south along it, to the minor road, and after a further 1.5km to your vehicle.

Distance: 8.5km/5.5miles. Ascent: 730m/2,400ft. Walking time: 4 hours.

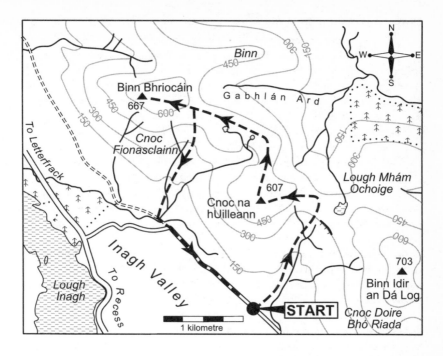

Reference Maps: Mountains of Connemara (1:50,000); OS Sheet 37 (1:50,000); Connemara Superwalker (1:30,000).

N.B. Names are from the *Mountains of Connemara* map.

52. BUCKAUN

Descending from Maumtrasna (the pass between Lough Nafooey and Lough Mask) on the road to Tourmakeady, take the second turning left to Killateeaun. Continue to the shop/petrol pumps, cross the bridge over the Owenbrin River and take the next turning left, signposted 'Factory'. Bear left at the fork, leaving the tarred road, cross the bridge and continue to the end of the track at the turf banks just short of Dirkbeg Lough (Dearc Beag, Small Cave) where the limestone chippings give way to a boulder and sand track.

Had you taken the first turning left along the 'high road' you would have arrived at Lough Nadirkmore, an ideal starting point for a circuit of the southern corrie of Buckaun. However, I prefer to take a more northerly route from the 'low road' (003 657) which offers the possibility of a traverse to Lough Glenawough without too much tramping over bog on the return journey.

Move off southwards across the deep gorge and climb the heathery gully ahead of you to the top of the central spur. The gully is steep in places and can be slippery in wet conditions. From the ridge there is a fine view of lower Lough Mask and its islands. Below you, in the broad valley, the peat-covered moraine is deeply incised by the Owenbrin River and its tributaries. Neat ranks of turf banks are the product of recent human activity which has exposed the many hectares of ancient 'bog deal' stumps, testimony to the valley's wooded past. To the south the two lakes glisten in the early sun, but take on a forbidding air as the sun passes behind the mountains. Together with Dirkbeg Lough these loughs are known as the Dirks and they enjoy a fair measure of popularity with local fishermen.

The ridge is easy going but it narrows and steepens towards the summit and care should be taken in strong winds. To the northwest the familiar face of Croagh Patrick comes into view with the hills of north Mayo in the distance. The single cairn at the top of the ridge is not the summit, but it serves as a useful guide to the exit route down the ridge for those who might find themselves lost in mist on the featureless plateau. The summit is marked by two cairns, a couple of hundred metres to the west.

Follow the rim of the northern corrie northwards across the undulating plateau, over boulder fields and around peat hags, to the precipitous cliffs encircling Glenawough Lough 300m below. The lough is accessible from the northwest but the valley route is always wet and boggy and so the approach from the east is usually more satisfying.

Return either along the northern ridge above the forestry plantation, descending to the valley along one of the firebreaks or take the steep descent into the Owenbrin gorge and then a short walk over the bog to base.

Distance: 7.3km/4.5miles. Ascent: 490m/1,600ft approx.
Walking time: 3 hours.

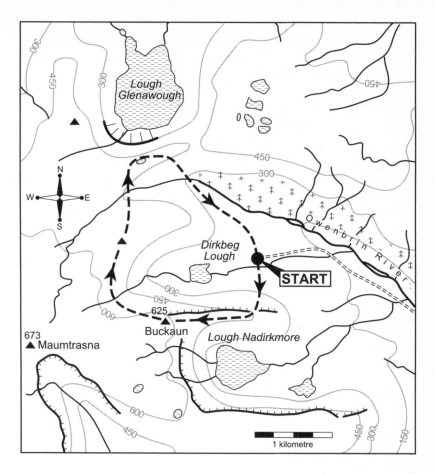

Reference OS Map: Sheet 38 (1:50,000).

53. BEN GORM

Start at the car park on the Aasleagh–Louisburgh road (R335) near the picturesque Aasleagh Falls (893 643) — a place where you might chance to see salmon leaping (Eas Liath, *Grey Waterfall*).

Take the track to the north of the river for a short distance and then cut off up the hill outside the fence past three isolated Scots pine trees.

On reaching the ridge at about 270m you will gain your first clear view of the steep ice-picked corrie wall with its sparkling stream cascading from the summit plateau to the lake below. To the east the buttress of the Devils Mother marks the beginning of the Partry Mountains which stretch north-eastwards, towering over the Erriff Valley and directing your gaze towards the plains of Murrisk. Beneath you, when the tide is low, the flat sandy expanses at the head of Killary Harbour echo with the calls of curlew, redshanks and gulls. And to the south the little village of Leenane rests comfortably between high hills and deep water.

The ridge steepens as you ascend and drops away sharply to your right into a moraine-filled valley. Ahead, the Kylemore Pass permits a view of the western bogs and the sea on a clear day. But the jumble of summits of the Bens, silhouetted against an afternoon sun, surpasses any other view from Ben Gorm (*Beann Gorm*, Blue Peak).

The summit plateau is fairly level but deep peat hags can make navigation difficult in mist and it is easy to take a wrong and possibly dangerous line of descent. The summit cairn is not actually the highest point on the plateau.

From the summit of Ben Gorm there are several routes by which you can return to Aasleagh. The fit and very enthusiastic may continue to Ben Creggan via the grassy col and past the remains of an old shepherd's hut and then descend the ridge overlooking Glenummera (*Gleann Iomaire*, Ridge Glen), returning to base across the lower part of the central spur and nearly two miles of bog — the sort that is none too sympathetic to aching legs. Alternatively, a descent of the steep, narrow central ridge followed by a shorter bog walk can be most rewarding, and certainly less wearing on the temper.

Distance (via Ben Creggan): 10.5km / 6.5miles. Ascent: 800m / 2,600ft. Walking time: 4½ hours.

Distance (short route): 7.3km / 4.5miles. Ascent 700m / 2,300ft. Walking time: 3½ hours.

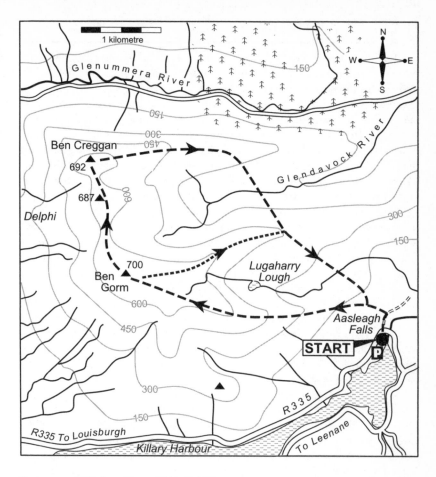

Reference OS Map: Sheet 37 (1:50,000).

54. MWEELREA

Mweelrea (An Maol Riabhach, Grey Bald Mountain: 814m) is the highest mountain in Connaught. It provides a variety of climbing and scenery unsurpassed in the west of Ireland. To describe only one route to the summit would do an injustice to this remote grit and sandstone massif, and in mentioning two I am leaving plenty to the ingenuity of the individual walker.

1. The Horseshoe I prefer to do the complete horseshoe from Delphi on the Aasleagh–Louisburgh road (R335), crossing the Bundorragha River north of Delphi Lodge by a footbridge beside a sluice gate just below the outflow from Doolough. There is a quarry nearby for parking. (There is no access to Mweelrea via Delphi Lodge!) This route leads to steep ground quickly and brings you onto the main ridge early in the climb. In mist be careful not to make the common mistake of taking the spur which runs southeast from Ben Lugmore (803m) (unnamed on the OS map) — it can be a costly mistake on such a long route! The ridge is broad and undulating but to your right the steep cliffs overlooking the Doolough Pass (incidentally, one of the few remaining passes largely unpolluted by electricity wires) may take you by surprise if you are new to the area and relying only on an old map to interpret the scenery. The rest of the walk is simply a matter of following the ridge to the summit of Mweelrea (magnificent panorama of ocean and mountain to west and south) and returning along the undulating southern arm of the horseshoe. Do not be tempted to cut back to your car across the Owennaglogh Valley — it is horribly boggy!

2. By Coum Dubh The most dramatic approach to Mweelrea is via the main corrie (Coum Dubh) on the north side of the mountain. Starting from the north end of Doolough on the R335 to Louisburgh (825 696) cross the stream flowing from Glencullin Lough and then pick up and follow the stream which flows from the valley into the northwest corner of Doolough. At the head of the corrie a broad ramp running up to your right above some featureless vertical cliffs leads you to a relatively easy gully which lands you on the main ridge below Ben Bury (795m), a peak which can be circumvented on the way to the summit.

Returning, you can descend by the steep northern spur which leaves the ridge about 100m east of Ben Bury. The upper sections are steep and require careful navigation and it is advisable to have a rope at hand (for an ascent as well, if you choose to do this route in reverse). Alternatively, the longer, but technically easier, north spur of Ben Lugmore will bring you back safely to base, provided you pick a careful route between the crags which litter this part of the mountain.

Whichever route you select to climb Mweelrea, be well prepared for a long, hard climb. Give yourself plenty of time for a safe descent in daylight — Mweelrea is a most inhospitable mountain in the dark.

The many crags on Mweelrea offer considerable scope for the rock climber and in the winter the gullies on the north face provide some of the few sites for snow climbing in the west of Ireland.

1. Complete horseshoe
Distance: 15.3km/9.5miles. Ascent: 1,200m/4,000ft. Walking time: 7 hours.

2A. Return by the Ben Bury spur
Distance: 10.5km/6.5miles. Ascent: 900m/3,000ft. Walking time: 5 hours.

2B. Return by the Ben Lugmore spur
Distance: 12km/7.5miles. Ascent: 1,000m/3,300ft. Walking time: 5½ hours.

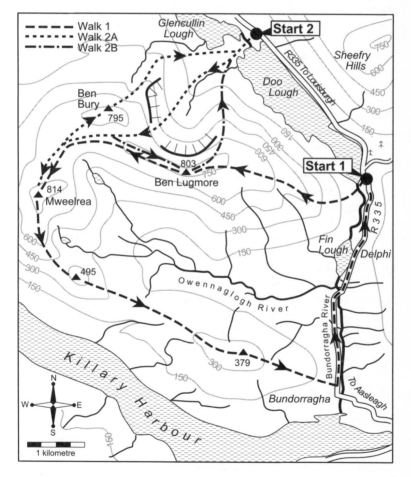

Reference OS Map: Sheet 37 (1:50,000).

55. CROAGH PATRICK

Croagh Patrick, otherwise known as The Reek (764m), is the most climbed mountain in Ireland. Each year on the last Sunday in July thousands of people from all over the country climb the rough pilgrim path to the small chapel at the summit where they pray, hear Mass and receive Communion. In the past most pilgrims made the ascent at night carrying burning torches. But regrettably the Church has stopped this practice, thereby denying us one of the most unusual spectacles to be seen on the western mountains.

(a) **Pilgrim Path** The start of the pilgrim path is signposted at 920 824 beside the car park on the Westport–Louisburgh road (R335). On the opposite side of the road, by the sea, is Murrisk Abbey (*Muirisc*, Marshy Seashore). You will require no direction to reach the summit by this route, but take care on the rough, rocky track — particularly on the final summit approach where it steepens considerably. I always marvel at the variety of bits and pieces of inappropriate footwear which remain on the track after the pilgrimage — even stiletto heels! But I can only admire the pilgrims who climb The Reek barefooted. If the track isn't to your liking, then I suggest that you cut off to the west before reaching the ridge and traverse the heathery hillside to the scree-covered slopes which, with a bit of scrambling, will take you directly to the summit by your own original route.

(b) **Ridge Walk** Alternatively, The Reek can provide an enjoyable ridge walk which will give the walker plenty of time to absorb the magnificent views all around — the bogs and mountains to the south, drumlin-studded Clew Bay and the Mayo mountains to the north, and Clare Island, Inishturk and Achill to the west. Continue along the coast road through Leckanvy and turn left at an unsignposted junction with an attractive slate-roofed cottage on the eastern corner (874 820) and opposite a modern house with a slate roof on the sea side of the road. About 1.1km up the road turn left up a rough tarred road, 'elegantly' lined with telegraph poles, towards a small hamlet at the foot of the hill. Take to the ridge where the road bears right (and where you are joined by the electricity poles!), climb to the first peak, thence onto the ridge which leads to the top of Ben Goram (355m, not marked on the OS map) from where you can follow the main ridge to the summit of Croagh Patrick.

Descend by the track to the road, or, after descending the steep section of the track, continue along the ridge and descend the steep spur to the road east of Murrisk (935 823).

Pilgrim Path
Distance: 3.2km/2miles. Ascent: 750m/2,500ft. Walking time: 3 hours.

Ridge Walk (excluding return along road)
Distance: 8km/5miles. Ascent: 750m/2,500ft. Walking time: 4 hours.

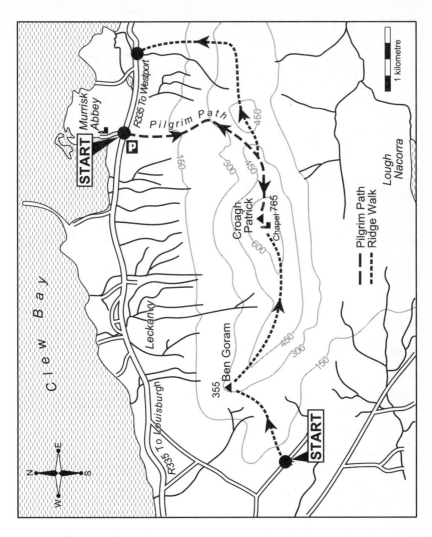

Reference OS Maps: Sheets 30, 31 and 37 (1:50,000).

N.B. You can get by on the Pilgrim Path with Sheet 30 (or no map at all!)

56. CROAGHAUN

Croaghaun (Cruachan, Round Hill: 688m) is the most westerly hill in the region and also the site of some of the most spectacular cliffs in the country, which plunge steeply to the sea almost from the summit cairn. Unfortunately, they can only be viewed properly from the sea or from the knife-edge ridge which forms Achill Head.

The best walk, taking in Croaghaun, starts at the secluded strand at Keem Bay (560 045). Climb up the grassy slope to the south towards the derelict Marconi signal tower atop Moyteoge Head. Follow the ridge westwards, taking in two steep benches and keeping a wary eye on the precipitous gullies which offer unrestricted passage to the sea for those who make a careless move.

From the high point on Benmore descend to the boggy valley which leads you on to the steep, craggy and broken slopes of Croaghaun. A detour via Achill Head should satisfy those with surplus adrenalin. The south summit cairn is soon reached and from it you can see the mountains and islands of Connemara in the south, the cliff tops of the north Mayo coast and all prominent stations in between. Continue along the cliff top over the north summit nearly to Lough Bunnafreeva West, perched right on the edge of the cliff. Then turn southeast to the rim of the large, sharply ribbed corrie which dramatically cradles Lough Acorrymore (*Loch an Corrie Mor*, Lough of the Big Corrie). This now serves as a reservoir and the road serving it takes you easily and quickly back to the coast road and your starting point. Alternatively, you can cut off the corner by crossing the hill and joining the coast road nearer to Keem Strand.

Distance: 11.3km/7miles. Ascent: 750m/2,500ft approx.
Walking time: 5 hours.

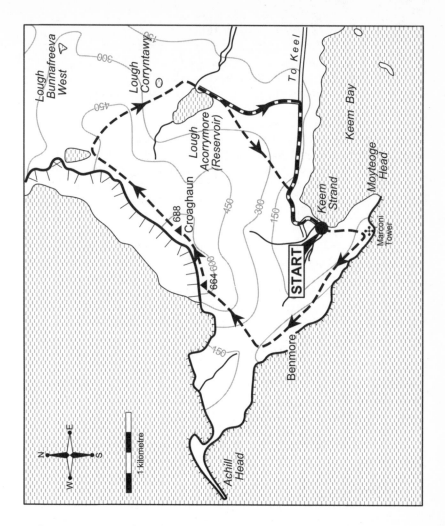

Reference OS Map: Sheet 30 (1:50,000).

57. NORTH MAYO CLIFFS

The walk from the small fishing village of Porturlin to Belderg Harbour offers some of the most spectacular coast walking in the west of Ireland. Contorted Precambrian metamorphic rocks rise steeply from the sea, at some points to a height of about 300m.

To avoid difficulties reaching the cliff from the harbour start from the track to the southeast (890 418) and head directly across the bog to the cliff top. From here you have magnificent, contrasting views which will enchant you throughout the walk. Looking north-eastwards across the open sea you can see Donegal and the great cliffs of Slieve League and to the northwest the almost pyramidal Stags of Broadhaven in their glorious isolation. Inland the vastness of the north Mayo bogs is breathtaking. Only the scattering of cottages and new forestry plantations give scale to this unique landscape.

The walking is reasonably easy but steep in places, a mixture of grass and sedge sward and low heather with some peat hagging on the higher ground.

Seabird life on the cliffs is sparse, fulmars being the main occupants of the cliff ledges in summer. But peregrines also frequent the cliffs — where sea eagles once bred. Diminutive, dowdy and uncommon twites (*Carduelis [Acanthis] flavirostris*) breed on the cliff-top slopes.

Forestry plantations, many of their trees browned by the salt air, are filling up the low ground below Skelp and here they are swallowing up old cottages, surely some of the remotest dwellings even in this sparsely populated area.

Beyond Skelp the cliff turns northwards into a promontory below which you can see the whale-backed island of Illanmaster, a bird sanctuary and the home of many thousands of storm petrels and puffins which nest in burrows on the grassy slopes. Then, after a steep descent you take the broad sweep up to Glinsk, the high point of the walk. The descent takes you to Moista Sound, a spectacular gash in the cliff where a softer igneous dyke has succumbed to the forces of the sea. From here you can follow the long stretch of bog down to Belderg, bypassing Benwee Geevraun Point on the way. Ahead you can see the lowlands of Ballycastle with Doonbristy, a now isolated stack defiantly standing alone at the point of Downpatrick Head.

In Belderg you should visit the excavated remains of Neolithic and Bronze Age farms and, if you have time, the Ceide Fields at Behy, about 6.5km/4miles east on the road to Ballycastle. From the Interpretative Centre on the cliff edge, you overlook 1,000 hectares of prehistoric walled fields overlain by peatbog, which have been either excavated or located by sounding through the peat. It is difficult to imagine that this area was more heavily populated with farming people five thousand years ago than it is today!

Distance (Porturlin–Belderg): 11.3km / 7miles. Ascent: 600m / 2,000ft. Walking time: 4½ hours.

Distance (including return to Porturlin by the track): 22.6km / 14miles. Ascent: 600m / 2,000ft. Walking time: 7 hours.

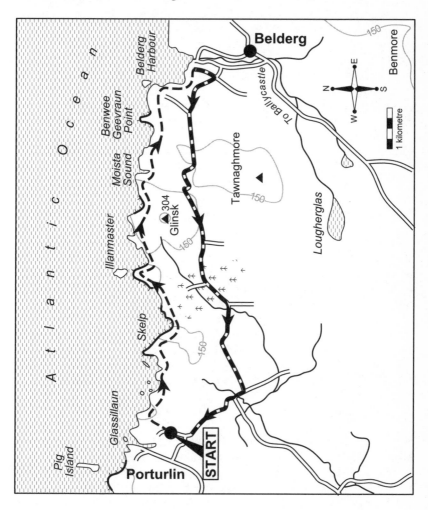

Reference OS Map: Sheet 23 (1:50,000).

58. CUILCAGH MOUNTAIN

Cuilcagh (Cailceach, Chalky: 665m) presides benignly over south Fermanagh, sharing the county boundary with Cavan. The long flat-topped ridge (pronounced Kulk-yach) is easily identifiable on the southern skyline on the approaches to Enniskillen, from where it has an implacable presence, 19km/12miles southwest of the town.

The described route is made either from the Sligo direction on the N16 via Blacklion, or from the north, via Enniskillen. Using the latter route, the starting point off the Marlbank Loop road above Claddagh Glen is by turning right at a crossroads off the Enniskillen–Swanlinbar road (A32). Follow the signs for 'Marble Arch Caves' (8km/5miles) past the Florencecourt Demesne and turn left on to the Marlbank road which rises for 3.2km/2miles, until a sign for Cuilcagh Mountain Park on the left leads to a new car park above the wooded depression of the Monastir Sink. This is one of several depressions caused by collapsed limestone caverns. The drainage system from Cuilcagh's northern slopes of millstone grit displays karstic characteristics, as the two main rivers gradually disappear underground, down the clefts of Pollawaddy and Pollasumera, on reaching the soluble limestone. These rivers reappear after running through 'caverns measureless to man' as the Claddagh River below the Marble Arch cave system and its underground lake. Part of this hidden underworld, opened to the public in 1985, is now a tourist attraction. The entire area was first explored by a Frenchman, E.A. Martel, in 1897, while Gareth Jones has documented the system in *The Caves of Fermanagh and Cavan*.

From the car park cross the stile into Cuilcagh Mountain Park and follow the well-marked track south towards the mountain. (The obvious bite out of the ridge is the Cuilcagh Gap.) This track gives 5km of relatively easy and painless ascent to the summit ridge over what once was very wet and boggy ground. Having gained the ridge, turn southeast to the summit cairn, topped by the OS pillar.

Your panorama on the 'roof' of the Border is expansive, as there is no higher ground between here and the Mourne Mountains. All of the Fermanagh lakeland lies northwards, including Upper Lough Erne and its islands. The conspicuous limestone hills along Cuilcagh's northern foot are known as 'reef-knolls' and are thought to have been formed from shell banks in the seas of the Carboniferous era. Clear weather reveals all the northwest's familiar landmarks, from Slieve League to Muckish, over 100km away. Southwards, the scarped edge diminishes towards the Bellavally Gap, which is backed by the Iron Mountains east of Lough Allen and the central plain.

Leaving the summit, you can choose to walk the 4km along the ridge, taking care to avoid the fissures in the rock above Lough Atona, passing

Cuilcagh Gap, where large blocks of sandstone have fallen away, on to the Tiltinbane cairn at the northwest end of the ridge. The stream rising on the northern slopes of Tiltinbane is the newly discovered source of the River Shannon. The Park authorities prefer walkers to return along the ridge and descend by the way they came up.

Distance: 13km/8miles. Ascent: 480m/1,600ft. Walking time: 4¾ hours.

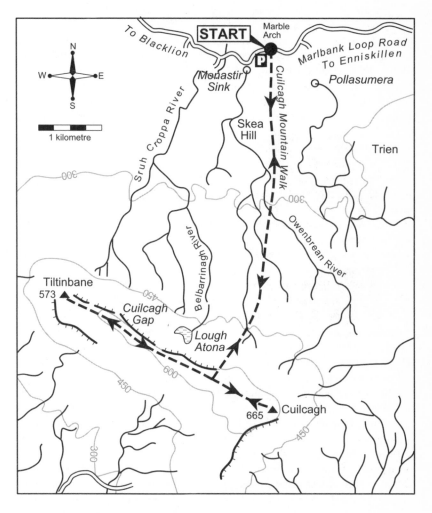

Reference OSNI or OS Map: Sheet 26 (1:50,000). (At time of writing, the OS edition is more up to date.)

59. CASTLEGAL MOUNTAIN

The pale grey carboniferous limestones are the youngest rocks in the northwest. Carved into tablelands and dissected by cliff-walled valleys, they brood dramatically over the coastal lowlands of Co. Sligo, where the intricate play of light and shade on the cliffs and aprons of scree, imparts a unique quality of light to the area.

Castlegal, with its fortress-like cliffs, complements the northern scarped edge of Glencar, perhaps the finest of these valleys. The terrain, which has a quartet of tops, is split equally between Sligo and Leitrim. Castlegal (Caisle Geala, White Castles: 335m) takes its name from the western top. Crockauns (Crocaun, Little Hill: 465m) is the highest point at the east end.

The walk can be done in either direction, with or without return transport. By traversing back along the northern edge in this east-to-west walk, and descending the broad gully opposite the west end of Glencar Lough, you shorten the return road walk.

Starting from the junction of the Glencar and the Sligo–Manorhamilton road (N16) at 780 420 use the gated track a few metres to the left of the N16. It passes a bungalow on the right and continues south through a gate leading to a farm on the left. Ascend through rushy fields towards the lowest point between Crockauns and Hangman's Hill, crossing a small wooded ravine with a ruined house on your right. Climbing up to the left of the forest below the ridge takes you to the upper slopes which are carpeted with primroses in early summer.

The first top gives views eastwards over Hangman's Hill and Keelogyboy. Now follow a ruined wall, going at first downhill and then up along the crest of the cliffs above the forest. Bear left, over green slopes to cross a fence and wall and ascend to the small cairn on Crockauns. Northwards, you look across to the cliffs on the opposite side of Glencar, above which rises Truskmore and the plateau running west to Kings Mountain and Benbulbin Head. Southwards, past the nose of Keelogyboy, lies Lough Gill and the hummocky metamorphic hills culminating in Slieve Daeane.

Your descent to lower heathery ground bypasses a central mound and onwards to the cairnless top of 452m. Further on, the broad gully (mentioned earlier) descends to your right. Continuing west, you pass some limestone knolls to the final grassy summit of Castlegal, where, a little to the west, you have a bird's eye view over the N16.

If return transport is left at this end, it is about half an hour's descent down the left-hand ridge to the road, or by using the track that contours across the face of the hillside. Your return along the northern edge, however, yields the most drama on this walk. A rough path threads through the heather above the vertical cliffs. History relates that a certain Sir Frederick Hamilton from Leitrim came to grief here in 1641 after raiding and burning

Sligo town. Returning home with his men via Castlegal, darkness was falling, and a local shepherd was cajoled to guide the raiders over the mountains. The shepherd cunningly led the horsemen to the cliff edge in darkness, instructing them to gallop over a supposedly narrow ditch ahead. In their haste, Hamilton and his band fell to their deaths, and the place has since been known as Hamilton's Leap.

This promenade, high above the mosaic of fields in lower Glencar is a little exposed in places, so **take care**. Around the first bluff, the limestone knolls overlook the plunging cliffs. Contour the hillside, passing a cluster of detached pinnacles, and cross a gully to the next spur. Continue around the spur to cross another gully via a sheep path. An isolated pinnacle can be seen some way down. Keep ascending to the right, around the next spur, until you reach the edge of the broad green gully, with impressive fans of scree beneath the cliffed face on the opposite side.

You descend steeply at first, following the stream to lower ground, and then over some fields to the main road, a short distance to the west of the county boundary. From here, it is about a 45-minute road walk back to the Glencar road junction.

Distance: 9.6km/6miles. Ascent: 520m/1,700ft. Walking time: 4 hours.

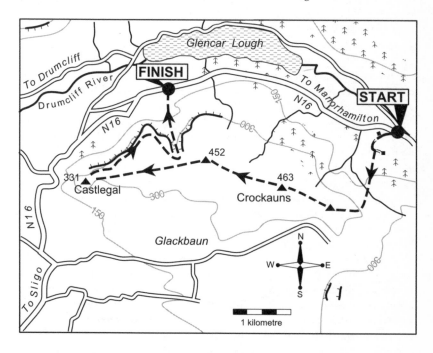

Reference OS Map: Sheet 16 (1:50,000).

60. KINGS MOUNTAIN–BENBULBIN HEAD

Travelling south from Donegal on the N15, the sphinx-like head of Benwhiskin holds your attention beyond Bundoran. Passing Cliffony, the bold scarped edge of Benbulbin (Beann Gulbin, Peak of Gulba) begins to steal the limelight. Further on, in the vicinity of Grange, this famous landmark, immortalised in the poetry of W.B. Yeats, masquerades as a separate mountain, appearing for a few miles to be regally isolated from the main plateau, and making the most of its 526m summit.

This easterly approach from Glendarragh includes Kings Mountain, a high point on the plateau, south of Benbulbin. Turn left (or right if approaching from Sligo) at Mullaghnaneane crossroads (656 473) signposted Ballaghnatrillick, 8.8km/5.5miles. After 2.2km/1.4miles, turn right at a crossroads and proceed for 3.2km/2miles, passing close under the intimidating walls of the north face, whose fluted buttresses are displayed to perfection by the sun's evening rays. The road goes through conifers and over a bridge. It then climbs alongside the river, where you can park beside or across a small bridge above Ardnaglass Upper (at 705 465).

Use the rough track southwards, towards the base of the waterfall descending from the lowest point on the plateau surrounding the spacious embayment between Benwhiskin and Benbulbin. The track peters out, and you bear slightly right, over peat cuttings to ascend either side of the waterfall to gain the plateau. Cross the undulating ground to the top-hatted profile of Kings Mountain (462m), also known as Finn McCool's Table. From the few stones on the summit, you have nice vistas over the scarped southern edge towards Lough Gill and Sligo town, backed by Knocknarea and the distant Ox Mountains.

Now contour the sloping plateau rim to the northwest, around the head of a freshly eroded gully and over a low fence towards the back of Benbulbin Head. Bearing left takes you to the grassy sward on the very edge of the western nose (478m), where the ground plummets dramatically to deciduous and coniferous woodland far below. On a day when a northerly gale battered relentlessly against the cliffs on my right, and huge seas created a white line on the coast, I was able to enjoy a brew-up at this spot in an almost calm vacuum, while absorbing the whole tapestry of the Yeats country beneath my feet.

Keeping as close as possible to the edge of the cliffs and **proceeding with care** will yield sensational views down the most vertical gullies in Ireland. Residual pillars of eroded limestone frame vistas of Benwhiskin's prominent head to the northeast. In early summer you can look for the wide variety of Alpine plants that flourish in the mineral-rich soil. This limestone plateau is the only station in the British Isles of the fringed sandwort (*Arenaria ciliata*) and the only Irish station of the alpine saxifrage (*Saxifraga* *nivalis*). An OS pillar marks Benbulbin's actual summit, south of the eastern nose.

At the end of the north cliffs, turn southeast and continue for a short distance to clear the cliffed edge. You can make an angled descent to Glendarragh and your starting point, via the steep slope with patches of limey shale. Cross the peat cuttings, where a stretch of tarred road leads to the bridge.

Distance: 8.8km/5.5miles. Ascent: 350m/1,150ft. Walking time: 3¼ hours.

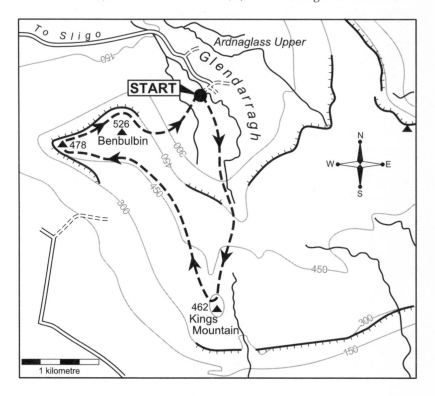

Reference OS Map: Sheet 16 (1:50,000).

157

61. THE CROAGHGORM OR BLUE STACK MOUNTAINS

This is a wild and rugged area of granite uplands north of Lough Eske (Loch Eisc, *Lake of Fish*). *Forming the largest knot of high ground in Donegal, there are few traces of man on these hills — no fences, walls or walkers' paths. Seven summits exceed 600m, only three of which are named on the OS map. In the vicinity of Lough Eske along the main road to Donegal Town, their subdued summits are difficult to distinguish. What they lack in stature and individuality however, is made up for in the display of interesting glacially eroded landforms. Wherever approached, the Blue Stacks will subject the walker to rough, tough and sometimes very boggy conditions.*

The described walk explored the area around Lough Belshade (*Loch Beal Sead*, River Mouth with the Jewels). It commences at the end of a single track road, north of Edergole Bridge. The approach road leaves the N15 southwest of Barnesmore Gap and continues to the head of Lough Eske via its eastern side. Turn right at the top of the hairpin bend and park after 1km/0.6miles beside a barn (970 871) with a walkers' indicator post nearby.

The rough track passes a plantation, falls to cross a stream and continues uphill. Since 1989, the former rather marshy track has been improved and extended up to the river behind the Eas Doonan waterfall, during the construction phase of a small private hydro scheme. This diverts water from the Corabber River (but not enough to dry up the waterfall, even after prolonged dry spells) via a buried pipeline to a power house concealed in the plantation at the head of Lough Eske. From the sluice gate at the top of the track it is worth diverting to the right to view the cascade, which plunges into a black pool at the end of a small gorge containing rare ferns.

Above the falls, follow the left bank of the Corabber, meandering in its grassy valley, passing a few marker posts. You then ascend a rough path up the left bank of a stream draining Lough Belshade. The new small stone weir across the outlet of the lough has raised the surface a little. The buttresses of granite rising above the north shore were once the nesting sites of some of Ireland's last golden eagles. Legend has it that a black cat guards a crock of gold within the boundaries of this tarn.

Your route along the south shore passes a heather-clad island to the base of a stream descending from the ridge to the left of the buttresses. Follow it up into the wild ice-scratched basin, which displays an impressive area of grooved rock and provides a welcome diversion for the scrambler. Bearing slightly right, above the buttresses, this superbly rocky ascent leads to the cairn on Ardnageer (*Ard na Geer*, Height of the Berries: 642m, not named on the OS map). After admiring the panorama over the neighbouring summits, a descent to the east takes you over an expanse of bare granite littered with rocks, and past a large precariously perched boulder overlooking a rock tarn. Beyond this, the ground drops into a trench and then ascends the rock-strewn hillside to the summit of Croaghbann (*Cruach Beann*, Rounded Hill: 641m).

The descent to the south is over a mixture of rocks and heather, passing the head of the Owendoo Valley which is flanked by the Croaghbarnes ridge. With Loughinisland and Lough Fad on the left, continue the descent to the southeast corner of Lough Belshade and retrace your steps down the outlet stream to the Corabber Valley and hence back to Edergole.

Distance: 12km/7.5miles. Ascent: 640m/2,100ft. Walking time: 4½ hours.

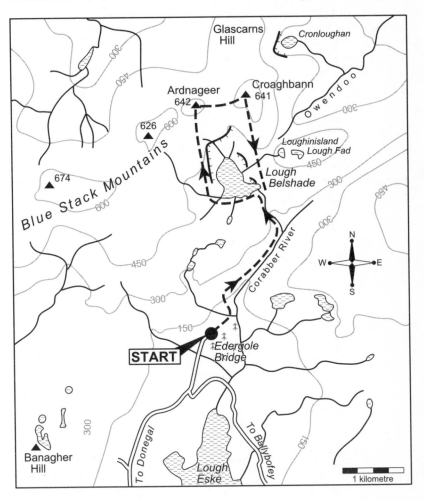

Reference OS Map: Sheet 11 (1:50,000).

62. SLIEVE LEAGUE

Slieve League (Sliabh Liag, Mountain of the Flagstones: 595m) broods over the south Donegal coast. On your approach road (R263) west of Killybegs, it appears as a relatively unassuming lump, giving no indication of its dramatic ocean frontage. There are a number of approaches to the summit, including that via Lough Agh on the northern side, or by the Pilgrim Track past Croleavy Lough to the Holy Well below the east summit, which is signposted (Sliabh Liag) off the Teelin road.

The classic and most popular route which traverses the whole exhilarating crest of the mountain, and the one which draws most walkers time and time again, begins from a car park (575 756) on an adventurous road from Teelin (3km/2miles south of Carrick) to Bunglass (*Bunglas*, End of the Green). As a result of the recent Sustainable Upland Tourism Project carried out in the area, walkers are being asked to park their cars in this new car park and continue the rest of the way to Bunglass on foot. Information boards are also encouraging walkers to return via the Pilgrims' Path, establishing a one-way traffic system which it is hoped will relieve pressure on the badly eroded sections of the cliff-top path. So, continuing on foot, follow the road towards the jagged skyline, giving a foretaste of what lies ahead. In its final stages you traverse the steep hillside high above the sea, with the old signal tower on Carrigan Head on the left. Over the last rise, the road terminates beyond Lough O'Mulligan.

A few steps around the corner at a spot known as *Amharc Mor* (Great View) reveal Slieve League's gigantic facade. Its huge face, extending for some 3km, has been fashioned by the remorseless Atlantic, whittling away at the base of the cliffs over aeons of time. The multi-coloured hues of the schists, slates, quartzites and conglomerates, combined with various mineral ores and the natural vegetation, produce a kaleidoscope of colours. Slieve League is the *pièce de résistance* of the Irish coast. Its only possible rival is the slightly higher Croaghaun cliffs on Achill Island. But they lack the variety of form, and are nowhere displayed to perfection, having no natural balcony like Bunglass.

The actual summit lies west of the dipped arête, which some maps refer to as the One Man's Pass. The rather colourful description in an early guidebook of 'a narrow footway high in the air, with awful abysses yawning on either side' will not daunt today's seasoned walker. A short rib of rock (as illustrated in volume 2 of *Climbing in the British Isles* by H.C. Hart) north of Crockrawer can claim to be the truer 'One Man's Pass'.

Leaving Bunglass, ascend the path, meandering up through crags and heather to Scregeighter (*Screagioctar*, Lower Rocky Ground: 305m). It then follows the elbow of the cliffs over the vertical section of the Eagle's Nest (450m), which **requires caution** in high winds. Far below, white horses

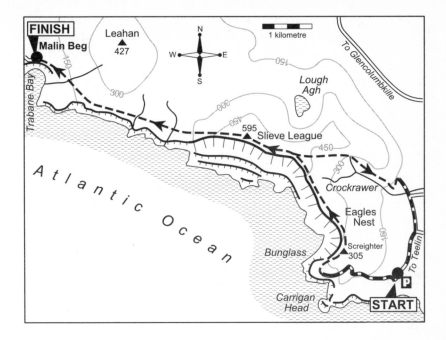

Reference OS Map: Sheet 10 (1:50,000).

surge and suck at the foot of the Giant's Desk and Chair — a pair of sea stacks. The path then drops a little, before rising to contour the slopes of Crockrawer (*Cnoc Reamhar*, Fat Hill).

Continuing up the cliffed edge, the rib of the 'One Man's Pass' is seen above some projections. Angling up for around 10m with a precipitous drop on the seaward side, it will not perturb anyone used to heights, and it can be bypassed on the landward side. Further up, along the crest, past a vertical bluff, grand views extend eastwards over Teelin Harbour to St John's Point. Diverging a little to the north from here takes you to the site of the oratory and wells associated with Saint Assicus, who was a goldsmith to Saint Patrick. This lofty place of worship had its last special pilgrimage in 1909.

Regaining height again, walk over the boulder field, passing the cairn on the east summit. Beyond this, the ground falls slightly to cross the arête above the corrie containing Lough Agh. The gullies above the lough are reputed to support a colony of alpine plants. The level walk across this One Man's Pass presents few difficulties, after which a short rise leads to the OS pillar, which is an unsurpassed belvedere in clear weather.

Your view is high over Donegal Bay, which is backed by the limestone uplands in Fermanagh and Sligo, and right along to Benwee Head and the

Stags of Broadhaven in outermost Mayo. Inland lies the hump of Nephin, and exceptional visibility will reveal conical Croagh Patrick, 120km away. Northwards, over the back of the Slievetooey and Glengesh heights, the unmistakable screes of Errigal and the dome of Slieve Snaght top the northern horizon. Westwards, Rathlin O'Birne Island forms a cornerstone to this delectable coast. A short distance from the summit, where the ridge drops to the west, a series of residual sandstone pinnacles known as the Chimneys invite exploration. They are about 60m below, on the very steep seaward side. Monuments to a vast denudation, they make statuesque foregrounds for the adventurous photographer.

The natural extension to this walk (if not returning to Bunglass) is to descend the west side, following the coast for about 5km to Trabane Bay (*Traig Ban*, White Strand), known as the Silver Strand. You can also make a detour to take in Leahan (427m). Return transport would have to be previously left at the car park (497 800) at the top of the long flight of steps that leads up from the beach.

To return to the car park, retrace your steps over the east summit and bear northeast to pick up the Pilgrim Path near the Holy Well. The path will lead you down towards Teelin, becoming a rough road where the ground flattens out. Take the first turn right which brings you to the Teelin-Bunglass road. Turn right again towards Bunglass on this road and you will soon be back at the car park.

Traverse to Trabane Bay
Distance: 12km/7.5miles. Ascent: 560m/1,710ft. Walking time: 5½ hours.

Return to Car Park
Distance: 12.5km/7.8miles. Ascent: 520m/1,580ft. Walking time: 5½ hours.

Slieve League, Co. Donegal
(Bord Fáilte — Irish Tourist Board)

63. GLENCOLUMBKILLE TO MAGHERA

Between Glencolumbkille (Gleann Cholm Cille, *St Columba's Valley*) *and Maghera* (Machaire, *A Plain*) *some 24km of the iron-bound coast thrusting into the Atlantic was considered by the late Joey Glover of the North West Mountaineering Club to be 'a gourmet's route and a lengthy day, taking in some of Donegal's magnificent cliff scenery'. This particular route along a heritage quality coastline, offers a superb combination of jagged rocks, stacks, cliffs, bays and promontories.* Murray's 1912 Guide to Ireland *stated that all this coast between Teelin and Maghera could 'hardly be excelled by any locality in the British Isles'. Thankfully it still remains remote, inviolate and challenging today.*

Glencolumbkille has long associations with the Saint, and is situated at the seaward end of the most westerly valley in Donegal. The area possesses a wealth of historical antiquities and one of the few fertile strips on this inhospitable coast. With the village as a base, the locality is something of a Mecca for the aspiring archaeologist and the explorer of superb cliff scenery. Inexpensive accommodation is available at Dooey hostel and the Malinmore Adventure Centre.

The view of Glen Head, the bold headland terminating the north side of the valley, is foreshortened on the approach road from Killybegs and Carrick (R263). Further along the road towards Malinmore however, its 222m ochre-coloured face towers over Glen Bay, backed by the residual wedge of the Sturrall (*Sturric*, Pinnacle).

Turn left at the T-junction at the north end of the village and proceed for 2.5km/1.6miles, passing the Church of Ireland and its ancient cross-pillar (one of fifteen stations associated with Columba). Keeping straight on at the next junction, the road crosses the Garveross River (*Garbhros*, Rough Point [of land]), and continues around the valley. Park near a cottage under the craggy slopes of Beefan and Garveross Mountain (279m). Sir Arnold Bax, the composer, during thirty years' association with Glencolumbkille, where many of his works were written, described Beefan as 'a glittering many-coloured surface of rock, bracken and heather'.

A rough track winds up Glen Head gaining height rapidly above the contorted cliffs around Skelpoonagh Bay. There are views over the valley to the thatched roofs of the Folk Village, which are reminiscent of how all the cottages would have once looked. Leaving the track which continues north, bear left and walk across the heathery ground to the old signal tower. This is one of the better preserved of a chain of twelve, built in great haste in the early 1800s to guard the coast against a supposed invasion by Napoleon.

You have an oceanic outlook high over Glen Bay to Rossan Point, backed by Rathlin O'Birne Island. Northwards, beyond the deserted harbour at Port, the view is restricted by the bulk of Slievetooey and Croaghballaghdown. Now follow the sheer cliff high above the inaccessible cove of Camas Binne

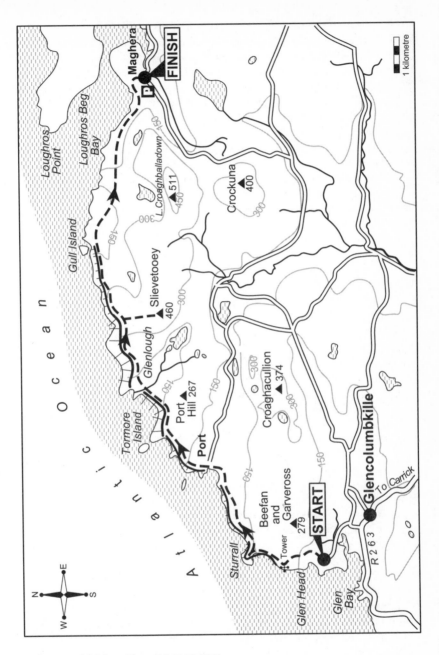

Reference OS Map: Sheet 10 (1:50,000).

(bent cliff). In October, 1870, the cargo ship *Sydney* foundered here with a load of timber en route from Quebec to Greenock. Twenty-seven of the crew perished with only a few managing to struggle up these cliffs to safety. Descending to the right into a small valley, walk over short turf to regain the cliff edge, until you reach the narrow neck connecting the Sturrall with the mainland. Its stupendous face looks impossibly steep, even for grazing sheep. As there is no apparent way across the exposed and shattered crest, the 'back door' to the main top (a blunt pinnacle) is by an adrenaline-producing traverse along the less awesome north side. I would hesitate in recommending it to anyone without a good head for heights.

Keeping the same level as the neck, **exercise care on this section**. The ground is not unduly difficult as you pass below the quartzite wall on your left, after which you angle up to climb over a stone sheep barrier. A scramble up to the left takes you to a small hollow with some fallen blocks. Turning the corner to the right, there is a slight descent, followed by a heather slope on the left, leading to the highest point.

Your dizzy perch has no peer on this coast. With an abysmal drop of 180m on the south side, the majestic Glen Head and the distant Slieve League hold the scene across Camas Binne. On an elemental day the waves exploding relentlessly at the base of the cliffs echo the words of the poet Shelley:

> Around
> Whose caverned base the whirlpools and the waves
> Bursting and eddying irresistibly
> Rage and resound for ever.

It is not possible to proceed along the knife-edge without a rope, so return carefully by the outward route. From here, follow along cliffs of decreasing height leading towards the remote inlet of Port. Further on, a faint bohereen descends to a stone footbridge behind a storm beach with its small concrete jetty, backed by a rock obelisk.

Walk over rising ground behind a number of ruined cottages (one of which has been restored as a holiday home), and angle up the hillside over short turf, above the jetty, to gain the rim of the cliffs overlooking Toralaydon Island. Continuing upwards along a fence brings one to the edge of Port Hill (267m), the outlook from which is impressive.

At the base of these precipitous cliffs, the great rock of Tormore rises like a bastion — the undisputed domain of the sea birds and the rock climber, though there is no record of anyone having scaled its near-vertical walls, to reach the green sloping roof. On the long stony beach to the east, the grey Atlantic seal may occasionally be seen reposing, as on the few other remote beaches along this iron-bound coast.

Leaving Port Hill, follow the cliff edge down a gradual descent of 200m towards the Glenlough River, which drains Lough Anaffrin. This lonely lough used to be the scene where Mass was recited in Penal times. The cluster of sea stacks offshore makes a dramatic foreground for photographing the mighty Tormore from a new angle. It is difficult to reach the beach without a rope. Anywhere here makes a pleasant halt for a snack.

With energy renewed, ascend the steep hillside to the northeast to regain the cliff edge, and continue up to the 300m contour. A short ascent to the south as a diversion to the coastal route takes you to the flat summit of Slievetooey (460m). On returning to the coast, **exercise care** as you move eastwards along the rim. On a stormy day this is Atlantic Ireland at its wildest. The stupendous cliffs excel Slieve League for verticality and in places the crumbling edge testifies to the ongoing erosion, where vast slabs of quartzite have peeled away. The shingle beaches far below are used as hauling out refuges for seals.

Offshore stacks and skerries accompany you as far as the broad green Gull Island. Despite its name, there is a general paucity of sea birds frequenting this coast. Now drop to cross a little ravine cut by the stream issuing from Lough Adoocho, after which there is the option of keeping strictly to the lesser cliffs, or taking the more direct line across the open slopes. The latter route crosses the stream draining Lough Croaghballagh-down. Further on, a narrow sheep path threads through some hillocks to a col, where Maghera beach comes into view. Descend and contour to the hillside towards the beach. Interesting plants such as goldenrod, roseroot and purple saxifrage flourish in this area.

Look carefully for the tenuous sheep path traversing the hillside beyond a bracken-filled hollow. It is a little exposed in places and requires caution. Immediately past a small stream in a mossy crevice, the path angles up to the right, over a rock band, to take a higher route. The base of the cliffed hillside under you is perforated by half-a-dozen caves, accessible at low spring tide. The most interesting and reputedly the longest is *Cuach a' Dorchadais*, or Dark Cave. Continue along the path to a fence at the cliff edge above the beach. Here you descend to the sand dunes, bearing right for Maghera at the end of a rewarding day.

Note: Increased parking of cars by walkers at Maghera has obviously caused some inconvenience to local residents, in that they have now designated a parking area, for which there is a small fee.

Distance: 24km/15miles. Ascent: 770m/2,500ft. Walking time: 7½–8 hours.

64. SLIEVE SNAGHT (DERRYVEAGH)

On the approach road (R251) below Errigal, the granite dome of Slieve Snaght (Sliabh Sneachta, Mountain of the Snows: 678m) broods over the moorland south of Dunlewy and its luxuriant woods. It is flanked to its left by the sombre amphitheatre of the Poisoned Glen, whose glacially smoothed buttresses seamed with gullies invite exploration. There are a number of routes to the summit. The shorter ones, all commencing in the vicinity of Lough Barra on the south side, are more suitable for winter days.

The more classic approach described, and the more convenient for visitors staying at Dunlewy, takes the walker via the grand introduction of the Poisoned Glen. It then progresses into the hub of the Derryveaghs (*Doire Bheathach*, Birch Wood) to savour an optimum combination of wild scenery, rushing rivers, crags and corrie lakes.

Commencing from the road bend (930 189) below the roofless Dunlewy Church, use the short length of track which peters out beyond the old bridge over the Owenwee Burn. Continue up the glen between the enclosing hills, keeping to the left bank of the Cronaniv Burn. The glen may have derived its name from the poisonous Irish spurge (genus *Euphorbia*) reputed to have grown along the banks of the burn. Passing a solitary holly tree, keep the river on your right and cross it where it turns sharp left. Now ascend to the obvious low notch or 'window' on the granite crest, following up through heather and rock beside a small stream to enter a shallow gully. The fortress-like walls to either side were once the haunt of the eagle, but alas they have not been graced by the 'king of the birds' since the turn of the nineteenth century. Emerging on to the ridge, bear right and ascend over rock and heather to pass Lough Maumbeg, a small tarn nestling in a rocky trench. Further up there is an unnamed cairned summit, beyond which lies a larger tarn similar to Maumbeg. A further ascent leads to the summit known as Rocky Cap (not named on the OS map), with a steep gully to the north and an adjacent tarn.

The descent to the west down a rocky slope emerges on to the boulder-strewn platform north of Lough Slievesnaght followed by the final 180m ascent to the cairn on Slieve Snaght's broad summit. As the highest point in the main part of Glenveagh National Park (a separate portion includes part of Errigal) it is a superlative viewpoint. While the stately line of peaks from Errigal to Muckish will hold your gaze to the north, all the coastal features and islands from the Bloody Foreland to Tormore rock at the end of Slievetooey in the far southwest can be picked out.

Descend the steep northwest side, with its smooth slabs, to join the Devlin River at a point below the cascade on its exit from Lough Aganniv. Red deer (*Cervus elephas*) can be seen in this area. The ground levels out and by following the river closely on its right bank the worst of the peat hags can be avoided. The river divides around some islands about a mile further down before entering a shallow gorge which deepens as it descends towards Dunlewy. Rocky bluffs will prevent you keeping to the water's edge all the way through. The gorge in its sequestered highland setting is attractively fringed with oak and some rhododendron, and its refreshing pools will come as a welcome relief after a warm summer descent.

Further down, the river bears left to enter the Dunlewy woods, but you can keep straight on to cross the Cronaniv Burn. If this is in flood, it may be a case of boots off or else using the bridge a little downstream, leading to Dunlewy House.

Distance: 12.8km/8miles. Ascent: 730m/2,400ft. Walking time: 5 hours.

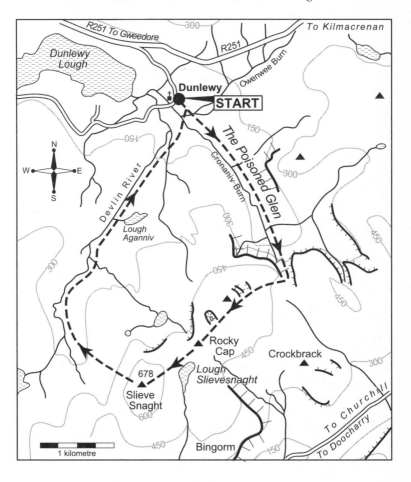

Reference OS Map: Sheet 1 (1:50,000).

65. ERRIGAL

The startling peak of Errigal (Aireagal, Oratory: 751m) dominates the Rosses country. The aspiring hill-walker travelling from the south will have seen glimpses of its upper half, topping the intervening hills. In the vicinity of Gweedore, its pyramidal form, bedecked with frost-shattered scree, is always impressive. These dove-grey quartzite screes often give the illusion of snow, due to refracted light in bright sunshine. Part of the mountain's south side has been incorporated into the Glenveagh National Park.

There are two contrasting ascents to the twin summits. The easier route uses the southeast ridge and starts from the R251 at the new car park, built as part of a road-widening scheme. An information board indicates an 'environmentally preferred' route from the car park, avoiding the boggy moorland that has latterly become very eroded due to popular use. A series of stone cairns now leads the walker slightly to the east of the old 'tourist route', along the firmer, right-hand bank of a burn descending from the western end of Mackoght col. The other more adventurous ascent (not described) is by the airy northwest ridge starting near a small farm (910 211) the access road to which turns right (uphill) at McGeady's pub near Errigal youth hostel and continues for 2km/1.5miles. A winter's day on this ridge can be a real challenge as the world shrinks beneath you and the wind roars and buffets around the crags and you add another day to your experience.

To give a slightly longer day, the route described includes the northeastern satellite of Mackoght (555m) as an appetiser. Some travel writers have erroneously referred to it as 'Little Errigal'. Park at the ruined gateway on the R251 at Carlaghmohane Bridge (952 205) where a faint track leads to the derelict Altan Farm.

Walk up the track, leaving it where it swings right, and then ascend Mackoght's lower slopes. Steep ground continues above a line of old fencing posts and then over quartzite outcrops to the summit cairn perched above the precipitous west face. You have a magnificent prospect of Errigal, which eclipses all its neighbours for dramatic sharpness of form. The entire northeast face, smothered in a chaos of loose scree, displays erosional disintegration on the grand scale. The 'tourist route' can be traced up the skyline ridge.

Leaving the summit, descend through rocks and heather to the broad col between Mackoght and Errigal. A series of moraines below the north side look as fresh as when the last ice sheets melted. The uncompromising climb leads unerringly up the well-scratched track, unfolding a widening panorama. The scalloped face of Aghla Mor or Little Errigal, rising from Altan Lough, heads an entourage of peaks northwards to Muckish. Higher up, past a jutting rock fang, the track turns around the end of the summit ridge to emerge at a circular enclosure to the left of the Glover memorial cairn (erected 1978).

The ridge now dwindles to a narrow crest, providing a degree of exposure, especially under snow. It terminates at the eastern and higher of the twin summits, which is arguably the smallest in Ireland. A short 'one man's path' connects it with the western twin. The highest point in the northwest has a great feeling of aloofness, and on a good day is a breathtaking vantage point. The all-embracing view covers Donegal, its fretted coast and islands, and more than half of Ulster. At one's feet lie the shimmering loughs of Dunlewy and Nacung, divided by a causeway. The stern granite surrounding the plummeting gullies of the Poisoned Glen together with the dome of Slieve Snaght resemble 'the wrinkled hide of a petrified elephant' and form a savage backdrop to the whole Dunlewy scene.

It is best to return by the new 'tourist route', as described earlier, walking west a short distance along the R251 to gain cars parked at the ruined gateway.

Distance: 7.2km/4.5miles. Ascent: 650m/2,131ft. Walking time: 3½ hours.

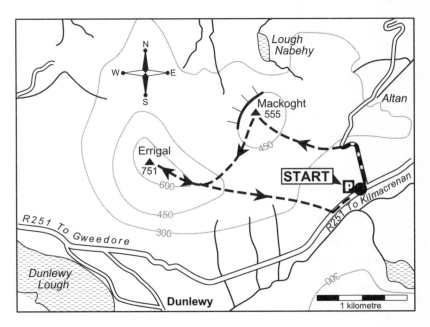

Reference OS Map: Sheet 1 (1:50,000).

66. HORN HEAD COASTAL WALK

The lofty promontory of Horn Head (Corran Binne, *Hook Peak*)
*possesses the highest cliffs on the north Irish coast, and is only rivalled
in grandeur by Slievetooey and Slieve League. The neck of sand dunes stretching
from Tramore Strand to Horn Head Bridge is quite recent; the promontory was an
island in the eighteenth century. Over-cutting of the marram grass in the years
1910–20, combined with storms, led to drifting sands from Tramore virtually
sealing off the tidal waters. The former Rinclevan Strand has been transformed into
the freshwater New Lake, which is now a wild fowl sanctuary.*

The circular scenic road around the headland misses a great deal of the
coastal drama, and short of circumnavigating the cliffs by boat, the hidden
extras can only be discovered on foot. The complete round is a long one, but
it can be shortened in a variety of ways. Here I describe the western half,
starting at Horn Head Bridge, which is reached by bearing right off the N56
in Dunfanaghy. There is space for parking off the road beyond Horn Head
House entrance gates (at 010 376). Return transport can be left, at
Coastguard Hill lay-by, thus saving the 6km road walk back to the bridge.
The walk begins by crossing the extensive sand dunes between the New
Lake and Anloge Hill. Pass through the stone stile and gate at the north end
of the bridge, and walk west to cross a wooden stile at the end of the Horn
Head House plantations. The path turns north for a short distance to cross a
ditch. From here on, a distinct track leads over the dunes, which are
carpeted with wild flowers in early summer. After about 20 minutes you
descend to the north end of the pristine Tramore beach, where the whole
scene is backed by Muckish and its neighbours a few miles inland.

Continue north on a sheep track over short grass. You cross a pair of
small blow holes known as the Two Pistols with a triangular-shaped
entrance cave. Further north, hidden on the surface of the fretted rocks, lies
the better known blow hole of McSwyne's Gun. It is about 200m north of
the small plaque erected in memory of a tragic drowning at the Gun's
entrance in 1982. Old guide books claimed that the noise of compressed air
forced out of the cavern could be heard up to 30km away. Now erosion has
widened the aperture and the Gun has lost some of its boom. This walk is at
its most stimulating when a strong westerly drives the Atlantic combers
with frightening force against this intractable coast, flinging columns of
spray into the air. Then the very ground trembles under the rampaging
waves, expelling their energy with a clap of thunder.

The route now leads to Pollaguill Bay following the coast beside a wall
over which you descend to the beach — an ideal spot for lunch and a
possible bathe, but take heed of the 'Danger — Currents' notice. Continuing
out to the cairn on Pollaguill Point, easy ground leads past Croaghadara
Hill with Harvey's Rocks offshore until you arrive at a grandstand view of
the superb Marble Arch. The sea has carved this 20m high arch through the

base of Templebreaga Head (*Teampaill na Breaga,* Church of Treachery: 126m — not named on the OS map). Cross the wall on the right and either ascend over the Head to view the twin tops of Horn Head to the north, or follow the wall which bypasses the summit. Further on, above a deep chasm, **caution is required** where the cliffs rise again at Crockaclogher before dropping over some rock ledges. Lower ground continues over a fence, from where heather slopes lead out to the horns which are split by a gully. The higher western one plunges in a 200m wall of quartzite to the Atlantic, its numerous ledges providing nesting sites for a variety of sea birds. As an oceanic belvedere it boasts magnificent views along the north coast from Malin Head to the Bloody Foreland.

The closing stages of the walk take you along the crest of the high cliffs to Traghlisk Point, passing the stump of an old signal tower. From the Point walk south and ascend Coastguard Hill. From the derelict look-out post, use the rough path down to the layby at the end of the scenic road.

Distance: 9.6km/6miles. Ascent: 240m/800ft. Walking time: 3½ hours.

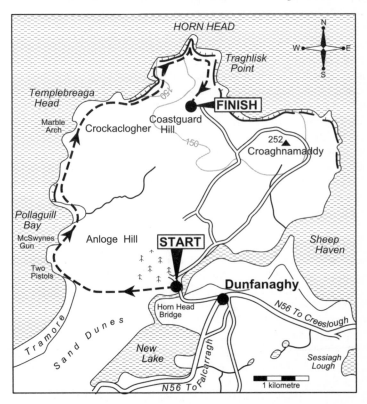

Reference OS Map: Sheet 2 (1:50,000).

173

67. MUCKISH MOUNTAIN

From most parts of the northwest, Muckish (Muc-ais, Pig's Back: 666m) is one of Donegal's landmarks. Rising from the coastal foothills around Sheep Haven, it is visible from the N56 northwards out of Letterkenny. From then on, its distinctive block form dominates the coast as far as the Bloody Foreland, where its finest elevation shows to advantage near Falcarragh. There are two popular routes offering contrasting terrain to the virtually level summit plateau.

(a) Muckish Gap

The first and easier commences from Muckish Gap (240m) on the south side, where an unclassified road from Calabber Bridge on R251 crosses the hills to Falcarragh. Starting from the roadside shrine (998 268), an ascent of around 300m up the grassy southeast ridge opens up impressive views through the glacial breach of the Gap. When you reach the plateau rim, walk over the stony wasteland to the large central cairn, almost as high as the official summit. This is at the northern end, across the boulder field and beyond the OS pillar. It is indicated by a new cross, consecrated in September 2000. It is to be hoped that the lavish use of red paint to mark the Miners Track for those attending will fade in time.

The outlook from this northern sentinel is a panoramic feast as it embraces all the intricacies of the coast from Malin Head to the Bloody Foreland, with Tory Island offshore. Diamond-hard visibility will include the top half of Ben More on Mull over 160km to the north. Southwards, the eye leads over the stark wastes of the plateau to the spine of peaks terminated by Errigal.

The return to Muckish Gap can be made by following the plateau edge westwards where it overlooks the old sand workings, and then by walking south to where the screes fall steeply to the Gap. Retrace your steps down the southeast ridge to the shrine, which is concealed by a knoll as you look from the southern edge.

(b) The 'Miners Track'

This connoisseur's route at the north end has a much more formidable aspect, giving a challenging and pulse-quickening climb, with the added ingredient of a gully descent. It commences at the former sand workings, where fine quality quartzite sand (99% pure silica) used in the manufacture of high quality optical glass was extracted and shipped from nearby Ards pier, until it was officially closed in 1955.

An adequate road leads from the N56, 2km/1.5miles northwest of Creeslough. Turn left (uphill) at a small derelict shop (050 328) and drive for 6km/3.5miles. The route of the Letterkenny and Burtonport railway can be traced on your left. The hard surface ends to the east of Lough Agher.

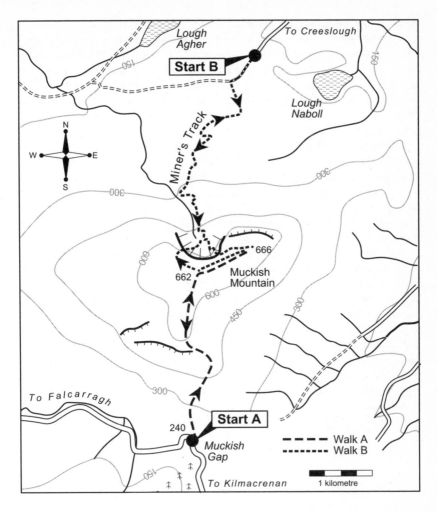

Reference OS Map: Sheet 2 (1:50,000).

Walk up the rough track which zig-zags for 2km to the old loading bays below the conspicuous run of white sand. A rock-fall from the stone-filled gully on the left has engulfed the final section of the track. Cross the stream to the right of the higher loading bay and follow up the broad spur. The climb is a combination of eroded peat and roughly hewn steps. Further up, drop into the left-hand gully and ascend another spur which leads to the base of the rock face. Looking to the right (west) you can see the descent route — a steep but not dangerous gully to the left of the large cave-like opening in the cliff. Continuing upwards, a scant line of posts indicates the path. **This section requires caution.** Above you, vertiginous pinnacles and beetling crags lie below the upper quarry. Further up, the stepped path crosses a small sand-filled gully. The flat floor of the quarry is disfigured with rusting debris. Nowadays, only the plaintive croak of the raven breaks the eerie silence. The inner recesses under the soft friable layers of sandstone provide shelter for a snack.

Leaving the quarry to the left, walk along what was once a stretch of railway and ascend the rough path to the plateau. It is then a level walk over boulders to the OS pillar and the summit plinth. After admiring the view, your return leads northwest above the quarry, where you should descend as far as an outcrop, capped with a flat rock, on the right. It makes a good foreground subject for a 'Miners Track' photo. Two gullies descend from here; the left-hand one ends at the back of the cave (mentioned earlier) and has no through route. Descend the right-hand one and **exercise care with the footwork**. It broadens out into a scree fan, from where you contour across to the stream on the right of the ascent spur. Continue to the top of the white sand run, where a quick scree run finishes at the uppermost loading bay, and hence to the track leading back to the start.

Distance (Muckish Gap): 5.6km/3.5miles. Ascent: 420m/1,400ft.
Walking time: 2½ hours.

Distance ('Miners Track'): 7.2km/4.5miles. Ascent: 450m/1,500ft.
Walking time: 3 hours.

Muckish Mountain, Co. Donegal
(Bord Fáilte — Irish Tourist Board)

68. SLIEVE SNAGHT (INISHOWEN)

Inishowen's reigning summit, Slieve Snaght (Sliabh Sneachta, Mountain of the Snows: 615m) rises as a blunt quartzite dome from spacious moorlands in the heartland of the peninsula, 9km northeast of Buncrana. From the south, the substantial neighbouring hills of Slieve Main (Sliabh Meadon, Middle Mountain: 514m) and Crocknamaddy (Cnoc Maide, Hill of the Strong Stick: 367m) mask its true elevation. This is only seen to advantage in the north in the vicinity of Carndonagh.

This walk includes the outlier of Damph (*Damh,* [like an] Ox: 422m) as well as Slieve Main. Drive north from Buncrana on the main Carndonagh road (R238) and take a right turn for Glentogher. Bear left on to the unclassified road southeast of Damph, passing the scattered houses of Turk. Park about 190m past the last building on the left (a slate-roofed barn) just before the road drops a little (443 369).

An easy gradient takes you to Damph's broad cairnless summit, with extensive vistas over the conifer plantations towards conical Grinlieve beyond Glentogher. Slieve Main and the bulk of Slieve Snaght are in the opposite direction and frame Raghtin More further northwest.

Now follow a fence downhill into a basin between the hills until it turns right. Cross the fence and stream and ascend to the left towards Slieve Main. After topping a subsidiary shoulder, undulating terrain leads over several bumps where it is difficult to ascertain the highest. Southwards, one looks over the ribbed northern slopes of Crocknamaddy towards Buncrana and Lough Swilly. Northwards, Slieve Snaght's smooth flanks dappled with scree loom close at hand, with Slieve Snaght Beg on the left.

Descending to the col where there are a few peat hags, a climb of 200m takes you to the stony summit littered with numerous small cairns. Further on, a dry-stone shelter wall surrounds the OS pillar. A fine day permits a panoramic view over all Inishowen and Lough Foyle, with Lough Swilly backed by the main Donegal Highlands. Far over Inishowen Head, the Hebridean islands of Islay and Jura with its twin Paps can be picked out in exceptional visibility. Looking northwest over the metadolerite outcrops of the King and Queen of the Mintiaghs, the rugged skyline of Urris will hold your gaze.

Slieve Snaght used to be the venue for an annual gathering which took place at the summit spring-well (*Suil-a'-Tobair*). Young people would climb up here, ostensibly to gather heather-berries on the Sunday before 'Gooseberry' fair in Buncrana on 26 July. More often it was a social occasion, with many future weddings resulting. This custom appears to have died out in the early years of the century.

Leaving the cairn, the descent to the east takes you to broken ground, but as there is relatively little bare peat, the going is not arduous. Take a line leading towards the northern end of Damph. Keep the conspicuous rock outcrop on its northwest side to your right. The ground rises for a little and then drops to join the outward route above the road.

Distance: 9.6km/6miles. Ascent: 600m/2,000ft. Walking time: 4 hours.

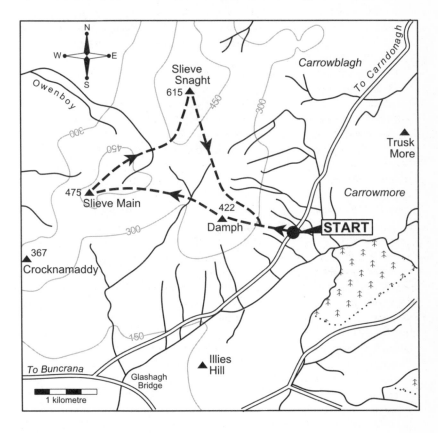

Reference OS Map: Sheet 3 (1:50,000).

69. WHITE PARK BAY TO GIANT'S CAUSEWAY

The Giant's Causeway attracted so many visitors in the eighteenth and nineteenth centuries that, like the Lakes of Killarney, it built up a small industry. *There was an old woman looking after the wishing-well, and there were jarveys and boatmen, and huts and stalls for souvenirs. There were also gates and an entrance charge was made. In 1962 the National Trust, with a grant from the Northern Ireland government, acquired the land, removed the gates and huts, and admitted the public free of charge.*

The Trust then started to obtain access from the farmers along the cliffs. The Ulster farmer loves his land and farms the headlands right to the cliff edge, either with sheep or cattle or in barley. Where the farmer would not sell the strip of coast or cliff, the Trust negotiated an agreement with him and provided fencing and stiles. In this way the Trust has completed a path from Carrick-a-raide to Portballintrae, a distance of about 22.5km, of which this walk takes the middle section.

From the hostel go down to the shore and walk along to Portbraddan, a very pleasant fishing village. There is a tiny, privately built church on the left, which you may see if you seek permission. It is called St Gobhan's after the patron saint of builders. Three hundred yards to the west are the ruins of Templastragh (*Teampul Lasrach*, the Church of the Flame), chiefly of interest for the ancient incised cross-slab built into the remains of the west gable for preservation. These remains are probably of early sixteenth-century date, but there was a seventh-century church on the site.

Continue round the coast past stacks and tiny inlets: Portacallan, Portachornan, Portnabrock (the badger's port), Portninish, the March Foot, the Sandy Ope to Portnaweelan, the port of Dunseverick village. 'Port' means a landing place; curraghs and other small craft may have been able to land in these perilous places. The OSNI map, incidentally, marks Portnabrock near Benbane Head.

Continue for half a mile to Dunseverick Castle, a ruin held by the National Trust. The pear-shaped rock on which the ruin — probably a sixteenth-century gatehouse — stands was fortified from earliest times. Its name, *Dun Sobhairce*, is said in the *Annals of the Four Masters* to be derived from the chieftain who first fortified it. One of the five great roads that radiated from Tara terminated here and the name occurs in many of the ancient Irish tales. St Patrick is said in various accounts to have visited it and blessed it. It was stormed by the Danes in 870 and 924. The site was in the possession of the O'Cahan family in the sixteenth century (perhaps earlier).

You will then come to Portnahastul, Portnahooagh (Port of the Cave), Benadanir (the Dane's Peak), with its fine hexagonal columns, Stac-na-cuil-dubh and Port Moon. Port Moon and Port Fad, a little further on, are still actively used for salmon fishing. The net used is known as a 'bag' net, a Scottish invention introduced to North Antrim in the 1830s.

The remainder of the walk is entirely delightful and in one sense does not need a guide book. But a study of the place names will help. The older name of the Giant's Causeway was *Clachanafomhaire*, the stepping stones of the Fomorians, the small dark men who inhabited Ireland before the Gaelic-

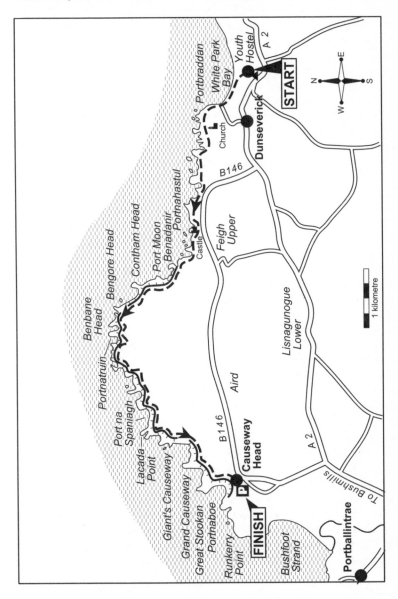

Reference OSNI Map: Sheet 5 (1:50,000).

speaking peoples arrived. The Stookins are rock-like stacks of corn or flax, the same Gaelic word being used. Portnacalliagh is the port of the old woman, while Portnatrachen is the port of lamentation — from the moaning sound made by the wind through a fissure in the rock. Bengore is the peak of the goats, and Portmadagh Ruadh is the port of the red dog, that is, the fox.

You will hear the 'pruck' of the raven. You will see the kestrel and sparrow-hawk and you may see high overhead the peregrine falcon. At nesting times you will see razorbills and guillemots on the cliff ledges. There are puffins in burrows and black guillemots tumbling in the sea below, and the ever-present fulmar petrel gliding on the thermal currents.

You will see fine hexagonal basalt columns at Port Fad and Bengore and again when you round Benbane. Here you begin to see the magnificent series of bays and amphitheatres and stacks that make up the Causeway. You are on the top of the Middle Basalt which is the layer that contains the typical hexagonal columns. The Lower Basalts have no columns; the two series, Lower and Middle, are separated by the very distinctive reddish interbasaltic bed. It is the result of the weathering of the top flow of the Lower Basalts, which took place during a period of quiescence in volcanic activity and which lasted perhaps a million years before the first flow of the Middle layers took place. The bed is 9m to 12m thick and contains fossil plants.

From the top, after you round Benbane, you will see many dykes. Their dark dolerite rock is very hard and resistant. One can be seen cutting through the basalt above Port na Tober (the Port of the Well) and others are on the foreshore at Port na Spaniagh, Port Reostan, Port Noffer (the Giant's Port) and Portnaboe (the Cow's Port).

In September 1588, the *Gerona*, one of the four great galleasses in the Spanish Armada, laden with men and treasure, sank off the Causeway and 264 bodies were washed up in Port na Spaniagh. In 1968 the *Gerona* story was pieced together by the Belgian underwater explorer Robert Stenuit. On an OS map he found 'Spanish Rock', 'Spaniard Cave' and 'Port na Spaniagh'. Since these names had been handed down by generations of fishermen, he searched the seabed below. He eventually found the wreck at Lacada Point (the point of the long flagstone) which you can see lying between Spaniard Cave and Port na Spaniagh. The *Gerona* treasure can now be seen in the Ulster Museum, Belfast.

Continue round Aird Snout and Weir's Snout to Causeway Head. Here there is a National Trust cafe and information centre, where you can obtain an excellent illustrated guide to the Causeway. The Trust operates a minibus service for those wishing to travel by road between Causeway Head and Dunseverick Castle. There is hotel and farmhouse accommodation.

Distance: 12km/7.5miles. Ascent: 120m/400ft. Walking time: 3–4 hours.

70. FAIR HEAD FROM BALLYCASTLE

Fair Head is one of the great headlands of Ireland. It is magnificent when seen from Ballycastle or from any of the headlands on the north coast. The massive basaltic cliff falls sheer for nearly 180m. Its base and face are so inaccessible that a pair of golden eagles was able to nest here and rear two young in 1953. After that their nesting was intermittent and ceased in 1960.

From the harbour walk along the shore of the bay to the east end of the strand and the North Star Dyke and join the little road that runs above the rocks towards Fair Head. Pass the Corrymeela Community Centre, the old coal mine workings, Colliery Bay and Carrickmore, and continue as far as the track will bring you. You now face a very formidable scramble over fallen boulders with overgrown crevices. There is the danger of a sprained ankle, so don't go alone. If any member of the party is not fit for tough scrambling it would be better to climb at once to the moors.

Benmore (the great headland) on Fair Head looks across to Rathlin and to Kintyre. Lower carboniferous sandstones, lying in horizontal beds, were invaded by a mass of molten lava, which squeezed its way in between the layers, forming a solid bed of basalt (dolerite) about 1m thick. Having solidified slowly between two cold surfaces, it has assumed a columnar structure, at right angles to the planes of cooling, as at the Giant's Causeway, but here the columns are some 15m in width and hundreds of feet high. The sandstones which originally formed the cover of the sill have been removed by denudation; only traces of them remain and the wide heathy area on the top of the head is the upper surface of the volcanic intrusion.

Continue round the Head until you see a gap in the cliff, the Grey Man's Path. It is important to find this, as it is the only way of climbing the Head once you have started scrambling round it, unless you go on to Murlough Bay.

Climb up the Grey Man's Path; this is stiff enough, but easier than going down. From the top go down gradually south to Lough na Cranagh and see the crannog, an artificial island or lake-dwelling. It is oval in shape, approximately 36m by 27m and is faced with a dry-built revetment 2m above the water level.

Continue past the lake and climb to Lough Doo. About 300m southwest of this dark lough and 45m from the sea cliff there is a 'sepulchral mound' as it was called on the old OS maps; it is now called a 'cairn'. It is covered with grass and heather, but the cairn stones are visible in places. It appears to be a round passage-grave cairn, 15m in diameter, occupying the sloping top of a 'roche moutonnée' on the glaciated plateau which terminates in Fair Head. The term 'roche moutonnée' was given in 1796 by de Saussure to a glaciated rock outcrop resembling the fleecy, ruffled, curled wig which

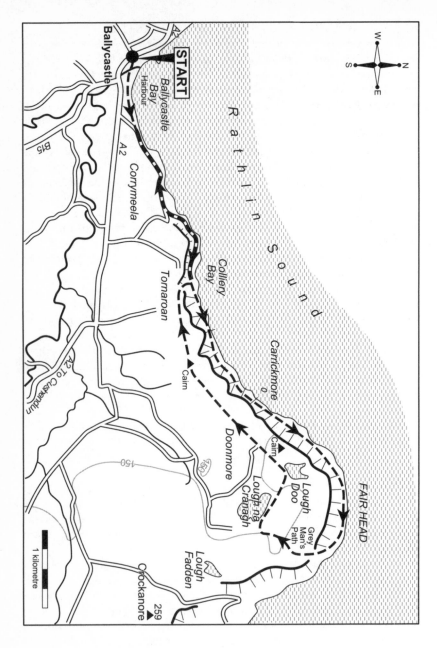

Reference OSNI Map: Sheet 5 (1:50,000).

184

was fashionable during the late eighteenth century. Such rocks have rounded surfaces sloping gently in the direction of the ice movement, with the steeper slopes on the lee side, due to the plucking action of the ice.

Continue south to Doonmore. This is a typical motte and bailey fort carved out of a natural outcrop of basalt probably about 1180 by an early Anglo-Norman settler. It is oval in plan and was originally surrounded by stone walls (1 to 1.2m thick) of which little more than the foundations now remain.

Continue southwest across the moors and parallel to the sea for 1.5km and you will come to a cairn circle, marked on the OSNI map, 300m from the sea. It is 16m in diameter and a number of stones of the peristalith survive, set on edge. There are traces of a megalithic chamber, perhaps a passage grave.

At Tornaroan you can drop down to the coastal path and return by the shore to Ballycastle.

There is an independent hostel in Ballycastle and a number of houses with bed and breakfast accommodation.

Distance: 18km/11miles. Ascent: 250m/800ft. Walking time: 5 hours.

71. GLENAAN AND GLENDUN FROM CUSHENDALL

The Glens of Antrim, which cut deep into the high escarpment that fronts the North Channel, are all beautiful. Traditionally they are counted as nine, but it is possible to distinguish thirteen. Two of these, Glenaan and Glendun, make a very pleasant walk on quiet roads with gradual ascent and descent finishing at the charming village of Cushendun. Here there are many interesting houses around the bay: the Georgian Rockport, *home of the poet, Moira O'Neill; the Italianate* Glenmona *built by Lord Cushendun, Ronald MacNeill, to the design of Clough Williams-Ellis; and the* Maud Cottages, *designed by the same architect in a Cornish style to commemorate Lord Cushendun's wife, Maud, who was born in Penzance.*

From the Cushendall youth hostel go round the north side of Glenville and get to the Glenaan road (221 289) by any of the ways which can be seen on the 1:50,000 OSNI map. A little over half a mile along this road there is a lane on the left leading to Ossian's Grave. This megalithic tomb stands in a field at 135m. It is a segmented gallery grave or 'horned cairn'. The burial gallery, divided into two chambers, opens on to a semi-circular forecourt bounded by two 'horns' of upright stones. It is of Neolithic date (2500 to 2000 B.C.) and is therefore older than Ossian, a warrior and poet of early Christian times.

Continue up Glenaan, following the road which rises to 289m before dropping to the Glendun River. Take the road to the right down Glendun, with Beaghs Forest on your left. In 1963 there was a landslide on the north side of the river and road which did great damage by unleashing a flood down the river. There are four fords by which the two or three farmers who remain on the right bank can get vehicles and animals across, and there are three footbridges. You may use any of the footbridges to explore the right bank, but there is no continuous path on that side. Subject to permission from the farmer, however, you may, by crossing the third foot-bridge (203 318), continue your walk above the right bank right down to Clady Bridge. Take care to close all gates. Do not go down to the viaduct which carries the main Cushendall–Ballycastle road; keep above this road and you will cross it at 222 320. Keep on down to Clady Bridge. Don't cross this, but take a path near it down to the right bank of the river. This path will take you along the meandering river and will bring you over it by a footbridge and out on to the road just below the Roman Catholic church. And so on down to Cushendun. Return to Moneyvart via Knocknacarry and the Layde coast road.

Distance: 26km / 16.25miles. Ascent: 380m / 1,250ft. Walking time: 7¼ hours.

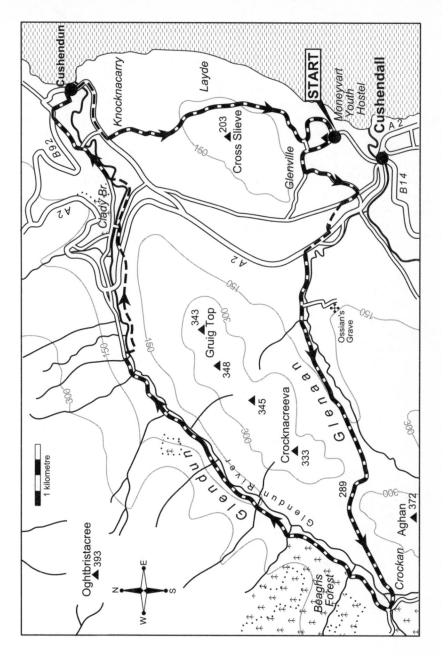

Reference OSNI Map: Sheet 5 (1:50,000).

72. SLIEVE DONARD FROM BLOODY BRIDGE

Slieve Donard (850m) is the highest mountain in the nine counties of Ulster. It is not as attractive as the toothed Bearnagh or the castellated Binnian, but its profile dominates the skyline for most visitors to Co. Down.

Through Down and Armagh the Mournes appear in the landscape in an ever-changing pattern that depends on the traveller's position and the atmosphere and light. They are by any standards a most attractive group of mountains. They are compact; within an elliptical area of about 22km by 11km there are 35 summits over 450m. They roll down to the sea at two places — Newcastle and Rostrevor — and they contain in their valleys and foothills a lively and energetic people still actively engaged in farming.

Opposite the Bloody Bridge car park (389 270) take the National Trust path that leads past a sheep pen over springy ground between granite boulders along the north side of the Bloody Bridge River. On the left is the old bridge, the scene of a massacre in 1641, from which the bridge and river take their name. Here a number of Protestants of Newry with their minister were killed in the troubled year 1641 at the instigation of Sir Conn Magennis. The whin (gorse) growing in the thin soil is brilliant and the sheep nibble its young flowers. Bog myrtle and heather add their scent to that of the whin and the river tumbles downwards in a series of cascades and deep green pools. As W.R. Rodgers wrote:

> . . . There was Bloody River
> Where the granite prickles bristled and blazed, and
> Ebullient water bellied over
> Boulders with the sweep of a bell's shoulders,
> And pancaked out in pools.

The ruined Bloody Bridge youth hostel on the left at 150m was entirely built by the early members of the Youth Hostel Association of Northern Ireland in 1933/34.

Climb past the granite quarry. This granite is very much part of Ulster. Belfast's streets were paved with granite square-sets and Stormont's Parliament Buildings are based on a foundation of Mourne granite. The path here is worn by the boots of quarrymen and of hikers.

Climb to the col between Donard and Chimney Rock. Here you will meet the massive wall of granite built in the days before and after the First World War by the Belfast Water Commissioners to define their catchment area. The wall runs over the tops of 15 mountains and encloses about 3,600ha. The work was started in 1910 and completed in 1922. The Mourne workmen walked to work every day and as the wall progressed their walks were longer. The stones were all quarried on the mountains. The wall is on

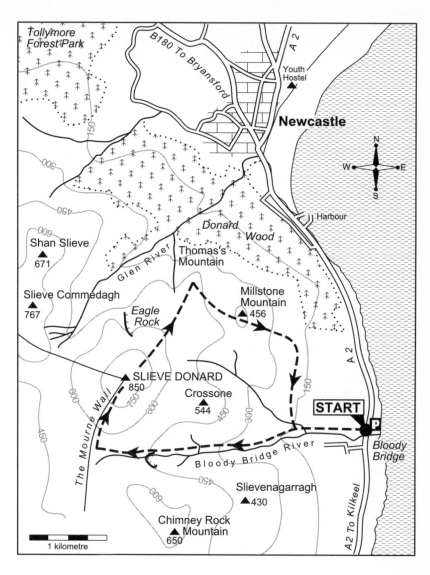

Reference OSNI Maps: Mourne Country (1:25,000) or Sheet 29 (1:50,000).

average 1.5m high and nearly 1m at the base, tapering slightly towards the top; cement was not used except at a few difficult places.

Follow the wall to the top of Donard. This mountain of St Domangard is a massive lump and lacks crags except on its northern side where it overlooks the Glen River on the 450m contour. Of two ruined cairns 250m apart, the one on the summit cannot be distinguished. The other at 830m to the northeast, though mutilated, survives.

The *Annals of the Four Masters*, under Anno Mundi 2,533, has an entry: 'Slainge, son of Partholan, died in this year, and was interred in the carn of Slibh Slanga.' The mountain was for many centuries called by this name. The mountain and the cairn were associated with St Domangard (Donard), a fifth-century follower of Patrick who built a monastery at Maghera, four miles to the north. The cairn was a place of pilgrimage in Colgan's time (1645).

The view from the top is very fine and includes the hills of the Isle of Man, the mountains of Cumberland and southwest Scotland, and the Hill of Howth.

From Donard drop down northeast along the gradual descent in the direction of Newcastle to Thomas's Mountain, a lumpy foothill of Donard, with a cap of baked slate-rocks lying on the granite. From Thomas's mountain turn southeast for Millstone (456m). Then drop to the pipeline (which brings the Mourne water to Belfast). The pipeline is distinguished, about the 210m contour, by small, usually black, gates in the occasional stone walls which mark off the mountain pastures. Continue due south, at the line of the pipeline, until you meet the Bloody Bridge River; then drop down to the car park.

Distance: 11km/7miles. Ascent: 850m/2,800ft. Walking time: 5 hours.

73. SLIEVE BEARNAGH

Bearnagh with its gigantic granite tors is one of the most exciting peaks in the Mournes.

Start from the Cecil Newman car park (or Trassey car park) at 307 308. Follow the track by the Trassey Burn. The ascent is fairly steep till you reach the Spellack (*Speilic*, Splintery Rock), a spur of Slieve Meelmore which overhangs the valley in a towering precipice. The Hare's Gap is straight in front, with a low cliff overhanging it on either side. The stream flows through long pools where tiny trout may be seen darting over the white granite sand. A glen with precipitous sides between Bearnagh and Meelmore now opens to the right; the slope of Meelmore is particularly steep on the right flank of the glen. Climb to the Hare's Gap (400m). This is a notable gap, for it is a kind of grand entrance to the Mournes. As you reach it and cross the wall, you have before you the head of the Kilkeel River — a wilderness of brown bog with the green dome of Donard towering on the left above the lower mountains: Commedagh, Slieve Beg, Cove, Lamagan and Binnian. It is a gateway to the wilderness. Spellack hangs over the valley up which you have come and the placid checkered fields of Down lie spread, with Lough Island Reavey reflecting the sky.

Facing to the right keep round a precipitous escarpment with a flat top and bushes of dwarf juniper. There is now a comparatively smooth but steep slope to the top of Bearnagh (*Sliabh Bearnach*, Gapped Mountain: 739m). Alpine club-moss and dwarf willow grow among the scant turf. The summit is crowned with gigantic granite rocks and from the topmost pinnacle there are spectacular views on every side. This is a fine place for lunch as it is usually possible to get out of the wind on one side or other of a pinnacle.

In her book, *The Mountains of Ireland*, Dr Pochin Mould gives a vivid account of how she saw the Spectre of the Brocken from the top of Bearnagh. She had climbed the mountain from the Hare's Gap and, with the sun behind her, looked across the glen below the ridge of Bearnagh to the opposite slope of Meelmore which was still veiled in cloud.

This phenomenon is the enormously magnified shadow of the observer cast upon a bank of cloud in high mountain regions when the sun is low. The shadow, often accompanied by coloured bands, reproduces every motion of the observer in the form of a gigantic but misty image of himself. It is so named from having been observed in 1780 on the Brocken, the highest point of the Harz Mountains in Saxony.

Strange things have been seen in the mists of Irish mountains. In *Cronicum Scotorum* we read of horse-riders on a mountain in Eireann passing on the clouds in January, 851 A.D. William Leyburn, in his book *The Whole Art of Optics*, published in 1724, speaks of 'the ghosts of Brocken', but

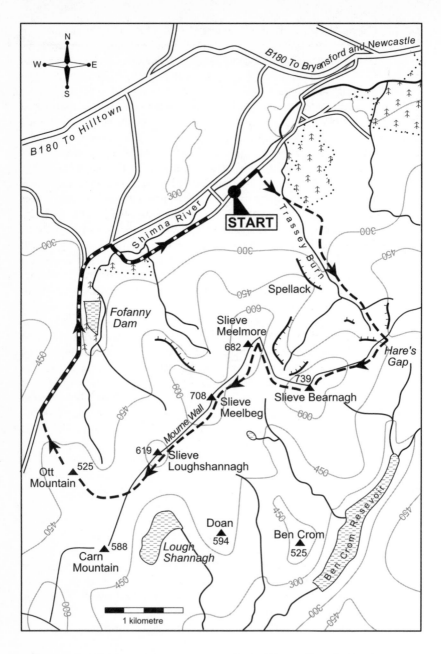

Reference OSNI Maps: Mourne Country (1:25,000) or Sheet 29 (1:50,000).

no doubt the 1780 observation was more exact. Dr Edgar, in the *Irish Mirror* of 1805, tells of something like the Brocken Spectre having been seen on Slieve Donard in 1795. Lieut Murphy, R.E., of the Ordnance Survey, writing to Drummond in 1825, relates that he and his company, passing up Slieve Snaght, in Co. Donegal, were 'shadowed in the clouds'.

From Bearnagh walk down west to the col (520m) between that mountain and Meelmore. At the col turn a little to the right up the slope of Meelmore (*Slieve Maelmor*, Big Bare Mountain). Near the summit there is a vein of amethyst sparkling purple in the granite. The mountain is 680m and thus lower than Meelbeg (*Sliabh Maelbeg*, Little Bare Mountain: 708m). This seems strange, but is probably accounted for by the bigger, stouter appearance of Meelmore when seen from the valleys below; bigness is not merely height. From Meelmore climb down into the hollow and up Meelbeg. You may be tempted to cut short the walk by returning north down Meelmore or Meelbeg, but the way down both these routes is long and arduous and Meelbeg to the northwest is very precipitous. Instead go down southwest towards Slieve Loughshannagh; climb this mountain (called after the long lake on its south side, the lake of the foxes) and here again there is a new and rewarding view.

From here it is an easy climb to Ott (525m). Go down by the track on its northwest flank to the road that runs north out of the Deer's Meadow. And so back to the car park, past the reservoir and the coniferous woods.

Distance: 14.5km/9miles. Ascent: 930m/3,050ft. Walking time: 6 hours.

74. SHANLIEVE, EAGLE MOUNTAIN, SLIEVEMOUGHANMORE, PIGEON ROCK, COCK AND HEN

These six mountains are in the country which is sometimes referred to as the 'Back of the Mournes', the inland part of the mountains away from the more popular north and east. Eagle with its cliffs and rich flora is a rewarding climb.

You should park at the Leitrim Lodge car park (at 224 257) among the Scots pine. Note the very old bridge (probably eighteenth century) made of granite slabs over Shanky's River. Take the track up to Pierce's Castle. This is a great boss of granite and it was here that David McFarland, a Belfast scout leader, sighted the Brocken Spectre on 27 December 1991 (see also Slieve Bearnagh, Walk 73). Walk south-southeast across the Castle Bog past the tiny Shan Lough to Shanlieve (Old Mountain: 626m) and on to Eagle Mountain (638m).

Eagle Mountain has a commanding view of the valley of the White Water, with its patchwork of fields and white houses, down to Kilkeel and the coast. It has a towering precipice which has attracted the peregrine falcon from time to time. The cliff is covered with flowers and grasses, and ferns flourish in the shady nooks. The tiny filmy fern clothes the rocks with dense mats of wiry rhizomes and dark green fronds. On the ledges and at the base of the cliffs the great woodrush grows luxuriantly.

Walk down north to Windy Gap and up to Slievemoughanmore (559m) and then southeast over the broad expanse of Pigeon Rock (533m), so-called after the rock-pigeons which favour it.

Pigeon Rock overlooks the Deer's Meadow. Just as the Happy Valley had to become the Silent Valley Reservoir when it was completed in 1932, so the Deer's Meadow had to become substantially occupied by the Spelga Dam in 1957. The Deer's Meadow is a peneplain of bog-bound land, about five square kilometres in extent, surrounded by green hills. It gets its name from the red deer which formerly grazed here. To these pastures, in the eighteenth century, and probably also in the nineteenth, herds of cattle were driven in the summer from the northern lowlands. This practice was called booleying and traces of booley huts have been found. In *The Antient and Present State of the County of Down* (1744) Harris wrote that the Mourne Mountains 'give pasture to a great number of cattle in the summer, being commons to the adjacent parts of the county. In the bosom of the Mourne Mountains there is a place called the Deer's Meadow, and by some, the King's Meadow (because people have their grazing in it free), extending some miles in length and breadth, to which great numbers of poor people resort in the summer months to graze their cattle. They bring with them their wives, children and little wretched furniture, erect huts, and there live for two months, and sometimes more, and often cut their turf to serve for the next returning season; which done, they return with their cattle to their former habitations'.

From Pigeon Rock walk north-northwest over heathery bog for over a mile to Cock (505m). Drop down northwest and up to Hen (354m), an interesting craggy hill with some good pitches on which to practise rock-climbing. Go down due west to a lane which leads to the Leitrim road at a point near the Rocky River Bridge. Turn left and follow the road for 2.5km to the Leitrim Lodge car park.

Distance: 13.5km/8.5miles. Ascent: 1,100m/3,600ft.
Walking time: 6 hours.

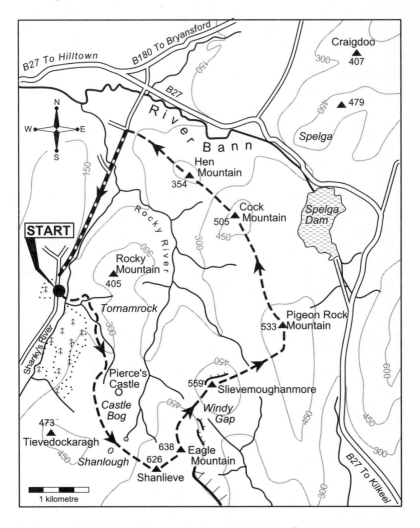

Reference OSNI Maps: Mourne Country (1:25,000); Sheet 29 (1:50,000).

75. THE MOURNE INNER HORSESHOE

This walk covers six peaks in the heart of the Mournes, including Slieve Binnian with its granite tors. From Binnian there are fine views of the sea, the Carlingford Mountains and the chequered landscape towards Kilkeel.

Park your car at Dunnywater Bridge over the Annalong River (354 223). Walk east and take the second track on your left; this will lead you north towards Rocky Mountain, and a minor track will take you almost to the top (525m). Go north in the direction of Donard, but after half a mile turn east and climb Chimney Rock (656m), scrambling over the granite tors which crown it. Go down northwest to the col and along the Brandy Pad towards the Castles of Commedagh. On your left is the Annalong Valley (to be avoided because of its difficult terrain — huge granite boulders, bog and hidden holes). Opposite you is the steep face of Slieve Beg, split from top to bottom by the chasm called the Devil's Coach-road. Looking down the Annalong Valley you now have the crags of Beg, Cove, Lamagan and Binnian on your right. At the southern end of a cliff of Cove there is a long cave which opens through a spur of rock to the mountainside behind, but the passage is almost closed by large fallen granite blocks. Both the lough and the mountain are named from the cave. You will climb Beg, Cove and Lamagan without descending below 500m.

The calm, round tarn, Blue Lough, is below you at 340m and the descent to it is steep and rocky. From Blue Lough climb southwest up the north end of Binnian, whence you will look down on Binnian Lough. It is a mile of springy walking along the top of Binnian with tors and crags and ever-changing views, finally coming to the peak (747m) and its dramatic view of the fields and white houses of the Kingdom of Mourne, spread out between their stone walls towards the sea at Annalong and Kilkeel.

From Binnian and from the map you will see a number of ways of returning to Dunnywater Bridge. Which one you take will depend on how much road walking you want at the end of a strenuous walk. If you want to stay on the mountain, follow the wall and come down by the Annalong River.

Distance: 21km/13miles. Ascent: 1,330m/4,250ft. Walking time: 8½ hours.

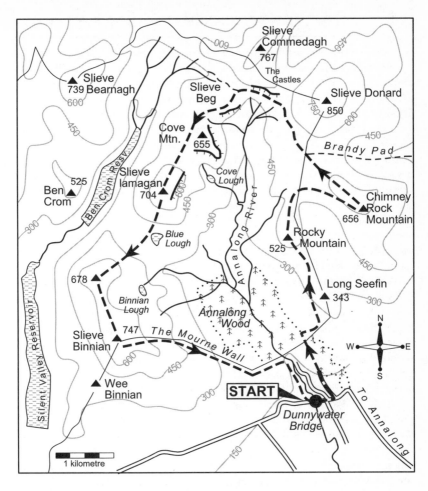

Reference OSNI Maps: Mourne Country (1:25,000); Sheet 29 (1:50,000).

76. SLIEVE FOYE (CARLINGFORD MOUNTAIN)

Start your walk in Carlingford, one of the most interesting small Irish towns, a Danish foundation. It contains King John's Castle (thirteenth century); the Tholsel or Corporation House, originally one of the town gates; the Mint (fifteenth century) with pre-Norman Celtic motifs on the mullioned windows; Taaffe's Castle (sixteenth century); and a fourteenth-century Dominican Friary.

Slieve Foye lies like a giant sleeping above the fiord, the serrated top stretching for a mile and a quarter, from the head (589m) to the toe (520m).

Start the walk at the Information Office and follow the waymarks of the Tain Way through the town towards Dundalk, past the church and up a lane on to the open hillside. Keep walking the Way until you reach the crest of the ridge (the Golyin Pass) where you turn right and follow the ridge, a steady, pleasant climb to the top where the view is most rewarding: the Mournes; the fjord with Greenore Point reaching out for Greencastle on the northern side; all the Cuchulain country, the Cooley Peninsula and Slieve Gullion; and the Hill of Howth far away to the south.

Walk along the ridge to the toe and then go west to the Split Rock and the Ravens Rock. Continue over a small hill (384m) and drop down to the Windy Gap and the site of the Long Woman's Grave. The grave was a megalithic chamber, but was destroyed by the road makers when they drove this road through the Gap. One Lorcan O'Hanlon, who came from this hollow in the hills, is said to have sought the hand of a very tall and beautiful Spanish lady called Cathleen. He told her that back in Ireland he could stand on a mountain from which everything he could see was his own. She consented to marry him and when he brought her to Ireland he took her here and showed her the rocks all around. She dropped dead on the spot and he buried her here, the place ever since being known as the Long Woman's Grave. Take the right-hand fork for Omeath, at the next junction fork right, rejoining the Tain Way, and continue down to the coast road (R173). For the rest of your route back to Carlingford, follow the waymarks, first along the road for 1.5km, and then along forest tracks until you come out above Carlingford, with fine views of the old town, which you rejoin by the descent of a steep lane.

Distance: 18.5km/11.5miles. Ascent: 720m/2,350ft.
Walking time: 6 ½–7 hours.

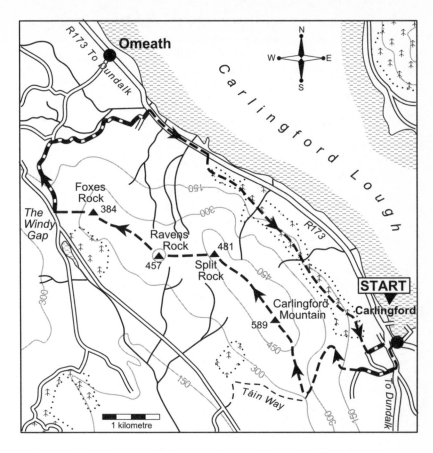

Reference Maps: OSNI Sheets 29; 36A; OS Sheet 36; Tain Way
Mapguide (all 1:50,000).

USEFUL ADDRESSES

Bord Fáilte Eireann (Irish Tourist Board)
Baggot Street Bridge, Dublin 2
Tel: 01–6765871. Fax: 01–6764764.

Northern Ireland Tourist Board
St Ann's Court, 59 North Street, Belfast BT1 19B
Tel: 028–902–31221. Fax: 028–902–40960.

Mountaineering Council of Ireland
House of Sport, Longmile Road, Dublin 12
Tel: 01–4507376. Fax: 01–4502805
E-mail: mci@eircom.net
Website: www.mountaineering.ie

National Waymarked Ways Advisory Committee
21 Fitzwilliam Square, Dublin 2
Tel: 01–2407000. Fax: 01–2407777
E-mail: info@irishsportscouncil.ie
Website: www.irishwaymarkedways.ie

An Oige (Irish Youth Hostel Association)
61 Mountjoy Street, Dublin 7
Tel: 01–8304555. Fax: 01–8305808.

YHANI (Youth Hostel Association of Northern Ireland)
56 Bradbury Place, Belfast BT7 1RU
Tel: 028–903–24733. Fax: 028–904–39699.

Bus Eireann Information Bureau
Travel Centre, Store Street, Dublin 1
Tel: 01–8366111.

Iarnrod Eireann
(rail passenger information) Tel: 01–8366222.

Ulsterbus
Milewater Road, Belfast BT3 9BG
Tel: 028–903–33000. Fax: 028–903–54090.

Independent Holiday Hostels of Ireland
22 Store Street, Dublin 1
Tel: 01–8364700 Fax: 01–8364710.

Ordnance Survey Office
Phoenix Park, Dublin 8
Tel: 01–8206100. Fax: 01–8204156.

Ordnance Survey of Northern Ireland
Colby Hse, Stranmillis Court, Belfast BT9 5BJ
Tel: 028–902–55755. Fax: 028–902–55700.

EastWest Mapping
Clonegal, Enniscorthy, Co. Wexford
Tel/Fax: 054–77835
E-mail: eastwest@eircom.net
Website: http://homepage.eircom.net/~eastwest

Folding Landscapes
Roundstone, Co. Galway
Tel: 095–35886
E-mail: tandmfl@iol.ie
Website: www.iol.ie/bizpark/t/tandmf

Harvey Maps
12–22 Main Street, Doune, Perthshire, Scotland
Tel: 00–44–1786–841202. Fax: 00–44–1786–841098
E-mail: sales@harveymaps.co.uk
Website: www.harveymaps.co.uk

Pat Healy
Cutbrush, The Curragh, Co. Kildare
Tel/Fax: 045–441625.

BIBLIOGRAPHY

General

Bardwell, S., et al., *Lonely Planet Walking in Ireland*, London 1999

Bellamy, Dr D., *The Wild Boglands*, Dublin 1986

Charlesworth, J. K., *The Geology of Ireland: An Introduction*, London 1966

Dempsey & O'Clery, *Complete Guide to Ireland's Birds*, Dublin 1993

Dillon, P., *The Irish Coast to Coast Walk*, Milnthorpe 1996

Dillon, P., *The Mountains of Ireland*, Milnthorpe 1992

Donaldson, F., *The Lusitanian Flora*, Dublin 1977

Evans, E. E., *The Personality of Ireland*, Cambridge 1973

Fairley, J., *An Irish Beast Book* (revised ed.), Belfast 1984

Fewer, M., *Irish Waterside Walks*, Dublin 1997

Fewer, M., *The Waymarked Trails of Ireland*, Dublin 1996

Flanagan, D.&L., *Irish Place Names*, Dublin 1994

Harbison, P., *Guide to the National Monuments of Ireland* (3rd ed.), Dublin 1992

Harbison, P. (ed.), *The Shell Guide to Ireland*, Dublin 1989

Hart, H. C., *Climbing in the British Isles, Ireland* reprint Holyhead 1981

Herman, D., *Hill Walkers Atlantic Ireland*, Dublin 1999

Holland, C. H. (ed.), *A Geology of Ireland*, Edinburgh 1981

Hutchinson, C., *Where to Watch Birds in Ireland*, Dublin 1994

Hutchinson, E. D., *Birds in Ireland*, Calton 1989

Joyce, P. W., *Irish Names of Places* (3 vols), London 1973

Lynam, J., *Irish Peaks*, London 1982

Mitchell, F., *The Way that I Followed*, Dublin 1990

Mulholland, H., *Guide to Ireland's 3000-foot Mountains*, Wirral 1988

Nolan, W. (ed.), *The Shaping of Ireland*, Cork 1986

O'Gorman, F. (ed.), *The Irish Wildlife Book*, Dublin 1979

Pochin Mould, D. D. C., *The Mountains of Ireland*, Dublin 1976

Praeger, R. L., *The Way that I Went*, Dublin 1969

Praeger, R. L., *The Botanist in Ireland*, Dublin 1934

Rohan, P. K., *The Climate of Ireland*, Dublin 1975

Webb, D. A., *An Irish Flora*, Dundalk 1977

Whittow, J. B., *Geology and Scenery in Ireland*, Harmondsworth 1974

Wilson & Gilbert, *Wild Walks*, London 1988

Wilson & Gilbert, *Classic Walks*, London 1982

Wilson & Gilbert, *The Big Walks*, London 1980

There are too many guidebooks to Long Distance Waymarked Ways to list here, but full information can be obtained from the National Waymarked Ways Advisory Committee.

Regional

East

Boydell, J. & McCarthy, M. J., *Walk Guide East of Ireland*,
    Dublin 1998
Boyle, K. & Burke, O., *The Wicklow Way, A Natural History*,
    Dublin 1990
Brunker, J. P., *The Flora of County Wicklow*, Dundalk 1950
Fewer, M., *The Wicklow Way*, Dublin 1988
Herman, D., *Hillwalkers Wicklow*, Dublin 2000
Herman, D., *Hill Strollers Wicklow*, Dublin 1994
Hutchinson, C., *Birds of Dublin and Wicklow*, Dublin 1975
Joyce, T. J., *Bladhma, Walks of Discovery in Slieve Bloom*,
    Rosenallis 1995
Joyce, W. St J., *The Neighbourhood of Dublin*, Dublin 1971
Lynam, J., *Easy Walks near Dublin*, Dublin 1999
Lynam, J., *Walking the Blackstairs*, Borris 1994
Malone, J. B., *The Complete Wicklow Way*, (revised ed.) Dublin
    1993
Warren, W. P., *Wicklow in the Ice Age*, Dublin 1993

South

Boydell, J. & McCarthy, M. J., *Walk Guide East of Ireland*,
    Dublin 1998
McGrath, D., *A Guide to the Comeragh Mountains*, Waterford 1995
Power, P. C., *Heritage Trails in South Tipperary*, Clonmel 1987

Southwest

Carruthers, T., *Kerry – A Natural History*, Cork 1998
Coleman, J. C., *The Mountains of Killarney*, Dundalk 1948
Corcoran, K., *Kerry Walks*, Dublin 1998
Corcoran, K., *West Cork Walks*, Dublin 1996
Cronin, J., *Rambles in Cork City and County*, Cork 2000
Cuppage, J., *Archaeological Survey of the Dingle Peninsula*,
    Ballyferriter 1986
Herman, D., *Hill Walkers South Kerry and West Cork*, Dublin 1999
Horne, R. R., *Geological Guide to the Dingle Peninsula*, Dublin 1976
Keane, B., *The Dingle Peninsula*, Cork 1998
Keane, B., *The Beara, Sheeps Head and Mizen Peninsulas*, Cork 1997
Keane, B., *The Iveragh Peninsula*, Cork 1997
Mersey, R., *The Hills of Cork & Kerry*, Gloucester 1987

Murray, J., *MacGillycuddy's Reeks*, Dublin 1990
O'Callaghan, T., *The Dingle Way Companion*, Blennerville 1998
Ó Súilleabháin, S., *Walk Guide Southwest of Ireland*, Dublin 2000
Sheehy, M., *The Dingle Peninsula – 15 Walks*, Dingle 1989
Sheehy, M., *The Dingle Way and The Saints Road*, Dingle 1989
Perrott, D. & Lynam, J., *Walk Cork & Kerry*, Edinburgh 1990

West

Archer, J. R. and Ryan, P. D., *The Caledonides of Western Ireland*,
     Dublin 1983
Corcoran, K. *West of Ireland Walks*, Dublin 1997
Herman, D., *Hill Walkers Connemara and Mayo*, Dublin 1996
Keane, B., *The Burren, Aran Islands and Co. Clare*, Cork 1999
Lynam, J., May, J. and Robinson, T. D., *The Mountains of
     Connemara — A Hillwalker's Guide*, Roundstone 1988
Nelson, C., *Wild Plants of the Burren and the Aran Islands*, Cork
     1999
O'Connell, J. W. & Korff, A. (eds), *The Book of the Burren*,
     Kinvara 1991
Robinson, T. D., *Connemara, Introduction, Gazetteer and Map*,
     Roundstone 1990
Tratman, E. K. (ed.), *The Caves of North West Clare, Ireland*,
     Newton Abbott n.d.
Whilde, T., *Birds of Galway*, Galway 1990
Whilde, T., *The Cliffs of Moher*, Belfast 1987
Whilde, T., *The Natural History of Connemara*, Galway 1994
Whilde, T. & Simms, P., *Walk Guide West of Ireland*, Dublin 1997

North

Dillon, P., *The Mourne Walks*, Dublin 2000
Dillon, P., *The Complete Ulster Way*, Dublin 1999
Hamill, J., *North Ulster Walks Guide*, Belfast 1987
Herman, D., *Hill Walkers Donegal*, Dublin 2000
Jones, G. H., *The Caves of Fermanagh and Cavan*, Enniskillen 1974
Lawson, L., *25 Walks in Down District*, Edinburgh 1998
National Trust, *Guides to Cushendun and Giant's Causeway*, Belfast
     n.d.
Rogers, R., *Ulster Walk Guide*, Dublin 1991
Warner, A., *Walking the Ulster Way*, Belfast 1989
Whilde, T. & Simms, P., *Walk Guide West of Ireland*, Dublin 1994

Glossary of the more common Irish words used in Place Names

Abha, abhainn (ow, owen) river
Achadh (agha, augh) field
Ail or *Faill* cliff
Alt height or side of glen
Ard height, promontory
Ath ford

Baile (bally) town, townland
Bán (bawn, baun) white
Barr top
Beag (beg) small
Bealach (ballagh) pass
Beann (ben) peak or pointed mountain
Bearna (barna) gap
Bignian little peak
Bó cow
Bothairin (bohereen) small (unsurfaced) road
Bóthar (boher) road
Breac (brack) speckled
Brí (bree, bray) hill
Buaile (booley) summer dairy pasture
Buí yellow
Bun foot of anything, river mouth

Carn pile of stones
Carraig (carrick) a rock
Cathair (caher) stone fort
Ceann (ken) head, headland
Ceapach plot of tillage ground
Ceathramhadh (carrow) quarter of land
Cill cell, church
Clár plain, board
Cloch stone
Clochóg stepping stones
Cluain (cloon) meadow
Cnoc (knock, crock) hill
Coill (kyle, kill) wood
Coire cauldron, corrie
Cor rounded hill
Corrán (carraun) sickle, serrated mountain
Cruach, cruachan steep hill (rick)

Cúm (coum) hollow, corrie

Dearg red
Doire (derry) oakgrove
Druim ridge
Dubh (duff, doo) black
Dún fort, castle

Eas (ass) waterfall
Eisc (esk) steep, rocky gully

Fionn (fin) white, clear
Fraoch (freagh) heath, heather

Gabhar (gower) goat
Gaoith (gwee) wind
Glais streamlet
Glas green
Gleann (glen) valley
Gort tilled field

Inbhear (inver) river mouth
Inis island

Lágh (law) hill
Leac flagstone
Leaca, leacan (lackan) side of a hill
Leacht huge heap of stones
Learg side of a hill
Leitir (letter) wet hillside
Liath (lea) grey
Loch (lough) lake or sea inlet
Lug, lag hollow

Machaire (maghera) plain
Mael, maol (mweel) bald, bare hill
Maigh plain
Mám, madhm (maum) pass
Más long, low hill
Mór (more) big
Muing long-grassed expanse
Mullach summit

Oilean island

Poll hole, pond

Riabhach grey
Rinn headland
Rua, ruadh red

Scairbh (scarriff) shallow ford
Scealp rocky cleft
Sceilig (skellig) rock
Sceir (sker, pl. skerry) rock, reef (Norse)
Sean old
Sescenn (seskin) marsh
Sidh (shee) fairy, fairy hill
Sliabh (slieve) mountain
Slidhe (slee) road, track
Spinc pointed pinnacle
Srón nose, noselike mountain feature
Sruth, sruthair, sruthán stream
Stuaic (stook) pointed pinnacle
Suí, suidhe (see) seat

Taobh, taebh (tave) side, hillside
Teach house
Teampull church
Tír (teer) land, territory
Tobar well
Tor tower-like rock
Torc wild boar
Tulach little hill